Lecture Notes in Computer Science   9090

Commenced Publication in 1973
Founding and Former Series Editors:
Gerhard Goos, Juris Hartmanis, and Jan van Leeuwen

More information about this series at http://www.springer.com/series/7409

Stefan Göbel · Minhua Ma· Jannicke Baalsrud Hauge
Manuel Fradinho Oliveira · Josef Wiemeyer
Viktor Wendel (Eds.)

Serious Games

First Joint International Conference, JCSG 2015
Huddersfield, UK, June 3–4, 2015
Proceedings

 Springer

Editors
Stefan Göbel
Technische Universität Darmstadt
Darmstadt
Germany

Minhua Ma
University of Huddersfield
Huddersfield
UK

Jannicke Baalsrud Hauge
University of Bremen
Bremen
Germany

Manuel Fradinho Oliveira
SINTEF Technology and Society
Trondheim
Norway

Josef Wiemeyer
Technische Universität Darmstadt
Darmstadt
Germany

Viktor Wendel
Technische Universität Darmstadt
Darmstadt
Germany

ISSN 0302-9743   ISSN 1611-3349   (electronic)
Lecture Notes in Computer Science
ISBN 978-3-319-19125-6   ISBN 978-3-319-19126-3   (eBook)
DOI 10.1007/978-3-319-19126-3

Library of Congress Control Number: 2015938750

LNCS Sublibrary: SL3 – Information Systems and Applications, incl. Internet/Web and HCI

Printed on acid-free paper

Springer International Publishing AG Switzerland is part of Springer Science+Business Media
(www.springer.com)

Preface

As games technologies have become more and more widely available, the ability of games to engage users effectively in specific, designed activities has been seized as an opportunity to use computer games for purposes beyond recreation. Since the term 'serious games' was comprehensively defined in 2002, they have been used as tools to give individuals a novel way to interact with games in order to promote physical activities, to learn skills and knowledge, to support social or emotional development, to treat different types of psychological and physical disorders, to generate awareness, and to advertise and promote in application areas such as engineering, education and training, competence development, healthcare, military, advertising, city planning, production, and crisis response to name just a few. Many recent studies have identified the benefits of using videogames for a variety of serious purposes. Serious gaming is a particularly timely subject as there has been recent re-emergence of serious games design and production; one 2010 market study indicated that the worldwide market for serious games was worth €1.5 billion. In the meanwhile, activities in development and research have exploded. For example, Google scholar research using the search item "Serious Games" evoked more than 18,000 hits.

In the academic field, numerous game-specific conferences have been established - among others the Game Developers Conference (GDC), International Conference on Entertainment Computing (ICEC), Foundations of Digital Games (FDG), Advances in Computer Entertainment (ACE) and International Conference of Interactive Digital Storytelling (ICIDS) as well as the specialized international conferences on EDUTAINMENT, European Conference on Game-based Learning (ECGBL), European Conference on Technology enhanced Learning (ECTEL), and Games for Health (G4H, G4H Europe) in the fields of education and health. Further, particular aspects of serious games are discussed at well-known, highly ranked academic conferences such as the ACM conferences on Computer Graphics (SIGGRAPH) or on Human Factors in Computing Systems (CHI), the Artificial Intelligence for Interactive Digital Entertainment Conference (AIIDE) or the International Conference on Computer-supported Cooperative Learning (CSCL).

The few conferences, which are directly and fully dedicated towards Serious Games, are the International Conference on Serious Games Development and Applications (SGDA), the International Conference on Games and Virtual Worlds for Serious Applications (VS-Games) and the GameDays – International Conference on Serious Games (GameDays, ICSG).

The International Conference on Serious Games Development and Applications (SGDA http://ddsgsa.net/sgda/) was founded by Prof. Minhua Ma (University of Huddersfield, UK) in 2010 with the First SGDA at Derby, UK in 2010 (its Proceedings were published in a Special Issue of the Elsevier journal *Entertainment Computing* Vol2:2); the Second SGDA conference was held at Lisbon, Portugal, in 2011 (Proceedings were published as Springer LNCS 6944), the Third SGDA conference at Bremen,

Germany, in 2012 (Springer LNCS 7528), the Fourth SGDA at Trondheim, Norway, in 2013 (Springer LNCS 8101), and the Fifth SGDA at Berlin, Germany, in 2014 (Springer LNCS 8778). The Conference was supported by ifip, the GALA Network of Excellence for Serious Games, University of Huddersfield, Glasgow School of Art, SINTEF Technology and Society, HTW (Hochschule für Technik und Wirtschaft) Berlin-University of Applied Sciences, NTNU-Trondheim (Norwegian University of Science and Technology), University of Bremen, BIBA, INESC-ID, Technical University of Lisbon, University of Derby, and a number of prestigious partners across the Europe.

The GameDays were established in 2005 by Dr. Stefan Göbel as "Science meets Business" event in the field of Serious Games, taking place on an annual basis in Darmstadt, Germany. The principal aim is to bring together academia and industry and to discuss the current trends, grand challenges and potentials of Serious Games for different application domains. Since 2010, the academic part has been emphasized resulting in a first Int'l Conference on Serious Games for Sports and Health with conference proceedings and a special edition with selected papers in the *Int'l Journal for Computer Science in Sport*. In 2011, the GameDays spectrum of topics was broadened and the different facets, methods, concepts, and effects of game-based learning and training were covered as well. In 2012 the GameDays were held in conjunction with the Edutainment 2012 (Springer LNCS 7516). In spring 2014, the fourth International Conference on Serious Games (Springer LNCS 8395) took place at Technische Universität Darmstadt as academic part of the GameDays (http://www.gamedays2014.de).

Due to the close relationship and overlap of the two conferences and corresponding communities, the organizers of SGDA and the GameDays conferences decided to bundle their activities resulting in a Joint Conference on Serious Games (JCSG), finally in order to strengthen the research activities fully dedicated to Serious Games.

The aim of JCSG is to disseminate and exchange knowledge on serious games technologies, game design and development; to provide practitioners and interdisciplinary communities with a peer-reviewed forum to discuss the state of the art in serious games research, their ideas and theories, and innovative applications of serious games; to explain cultural, social, and scientific phenomena by means of serious games; to concentrate on the interaction between theory and application; to share best practice and lessons learnt; to develop new methodologies in various application domains using games technologies; to explore perspectives of future developments and innovative applications relevant to serious games and related areas; and to establish and foster a cross-sector and cross-disciplinary network of researchers, game developers, practitioners, domain experts, and students interested in serious games.

The JCSG 2015 was hosted by University of Huddersfield in UK during June 3–4 2015. The conference appeared in the sequence of the successes of the previous SGDA conferences and GameDays.

Seventeen papers and one invited keynote covering a wide range of aspects of serious games design and use were presented at JCSG 2015. We received submission from authors from 12 countries throughout Europe and around the world, including UK, Germany, Australia, and US. Following the philosophy of previous conferences, all scientific papers were reviewed by four reviewers on average. The overall acceptance rate was ~40% (similar to 2014). The papers were published in the Springer LNCS 9090. The keynote speaker was Dr. Tim March from Griffith University, Australia.

We would like thank all the authors, speakers, and reviewers for their contributions to JCSG 2015 and welcome you to participate in our discussions at the conference. Special thanks go to Springer for publishing the proceedings of the first Joint International Conference on Serious Games in Springer LNCS, to Hessen-IT for supporting the GameDays since its early days in 2005, to the Forum for interdisciplinary research at Technische Universität Darmstadt for bundling and supporting the wide range of Serious Games research activities at the Technische Universität Darmstadt, and to KTX Software Development for sponsoring the Best Paper Award at JCSG 2015.

April 2015   Minhua Ma
                                                                     Stefan Göbel

Organization

JCSG 2015 was hosted by University of Huddersfield, UK, in cooperation with the Technische Universität Darmstadt, Multimedia Communications Lab; SINTEF Technology and Society, Norway; Bremen Institute for Production and Logistics (BIBA), Germany; and IFIP Technical Committee (TC14) Entertainment Computing - Working Group on Serious Games (WG 14.8).

Conference Chair

Minhua Ma   University of Huddersfield, UK

Organizers

Jannicke Baalsrud Hauge   Bremen Institute for Production and Logistics,
                                   Germany
Stefan Göbel   Technische Universität Darmstadt, Germany
Minhua Ma   University of Huddersfield, UK
Manuel Fradinho Oliveira   SINTEF Technology and Society, Norway
Josef Wiemeyer   Technische Universität Darmstadt, Germany

LNCS Volume Editors

Stefan Göbel   Technische Universität Darmstadt, Germany
Minhua Ma   University of Huddersfield, UK
Manuel Fradinho Oliveira   SINTEF Technology and Society, Norway
Jannicke Baalsrud Hauge   Bremen Institute for Production and Logistics,
                                   Germany
Josef Wiemeyer   Technische Universität Darmstadt, Germany
Viktor Wendel   Technische Universität Darmstadt, Germany

Program Chairs

Stefan Göbel   Technische Universität Darmstadt, Germany
Minhua Ma   University of Huddersfield, UK

Local Organizing Committee

Minhua Ma   University of Huddersfield, UK
Hannah Stephens   University of Huddersfield, UK
Hafsa Akram   University of Huddersfield, UK
Liz Jack   University of Huddersfield, UK

Program Committee

Aida Azadegan	University of the West of Scotland, UK
Jannicke Baalsrud Hauge	University of Bremen, Germany
Thomas Baranowski	Baylor College of Medicine, Houston, TX, USA
Gerald Bieber	Fraunhofer Institute for Computer Graphics, Rostock, Germany
Michael Brach	University of Münster, Germany
Marc Cavazza	Teesside University, UK
Stefano Cerri	Montpellier Laboratory of Informatics, Robotics and Microelectronics, France
Karin Coninx	Hasselt University, Belgium
Ahmed Dewan	University of North Carolina at Charlotte, NC
Ralf Dörner	RheinMain University of Applied Sciences, Wiesbaden, Germany
Tendai Dube	University of Derby, UK
Heiko Duin	Bremen Institute for Production and Logistics, Germany
Wolfgang Effelsberg	University of Mannheim, Germany
Abdulmotaleb El Saddik	University of Ottawa, Canada
Kai Erenli	University for Applied Sciences, Vienna, Austria
Baltasar Fernández-Manjón	Complutense University of Madrid, Spain
Mateus David Finco	Federal University of Rio Grande do Sul, Brazil
Stefan Göbel	Technische Universität Darmstadt, Germany
Abdelkader Gouaich	Montpellier Laboratory of Informatics, Robotics and Microelectronics, France
Helmut Hlavacs	University of Vienna, Austria
M. Shamim Hossain	King Saud University, Saudi Arabia
Jun Hu	Eindhoven University of Technology, The Netherlands
Ido Iurgel	Hochschule Rhein-Waal, Kamp-Lintfort, Germany
Fares Kayali	Universität für angewandte Kunst Wien, Austria
Michael Kickmeier-Rust	Technische Universität Graz, Austria
Christoph Klimmt	Hochschule für Musik, Theater und Medien Hannover, Germany
Martin Knöll	Technische Universität Darmstadt, Germany
Oliver Korn	University of Stuttgart, Germany
Peter Leong	Singapore Polytechnic, Singapore
Fotis Liarokapis	Coventry University, UK
Minhua Ma	University of Huddersfield, UK
Rainer Malaka	University of Bremen, Germany
Tim Marsh	Griffith University, Australia
Alke Martens	PH Schwäbisch Gmünd University of Education, Germany

Maic Masuch	University of Duisburg-Essen, Germany
Robin Mellecker	University of Hong Kong, Hong Kong
André Miede	Hochschule für Technik und Wirtschaft des Saarlandes, Germany
Wolfgang Müller	PH Weingarten, Germany
Jörg Müller-Lietzkow	University of Paderborn, Germany
Frank Nack	University of Amsterdam, The Netherlands
Andreas Oikonomou	Nottingham Trent University, UK
Manuel Fradinho Oliveira	SINTEF Technology and Society, Norway
João Pereira	Technical University of Lisbon, Portugal
Alenka Poplin	Iowa State University, USA
Johann Riedel	University of Nottingham, UK
Ulrike Spierling	Hochschule Rhein-Main, Wiesbaden, Germany
Daniel Steenstra	Cranfield University, UK
Roger Tavares	Universidade Federal do Rio Grande do Norte, Brazil
Erik van der Spek	Eindhoven University of Technology, The Netherlands
Steffen P. Walz	GEElab RMIT, Melbourne, Australia and GEElab Europe, Stuttgart, Germany
Viktor Wendel	Technische Universität Darmstadt, Germany
Josef Wiemeyer	Technische Universität Darmstadt, Germany
Kevin Wong	Murdoch University, Australia

Sponsors

University of Huddersfield
Technische Universität Darmstadt, Multimedia Communications Lab
Technische Universität Darmstadt, Forum für Interdisziplinäre Forschung
   (Forum for Interdisciplinary Research)
httc – Hessisches Telemedia Technologie Kompetenz-Center
KTX Software Development
SINTEF Technology and Society
Bremen Institute for Production and Logistics (BIBA)
University of Bremen

Partners

Hessen-IT
German Association of Computer Science
German Chapter of the ACM
IFIP Working Group 14.8 on Serious Games
G.A.M.E. (German Game Developers Association)
Glasgow School of Art

HTW (Hochschule für Technik und Wirtschaft) Berlin-University of Applied
   Sciences
NTNU-Trondheim (Norwegian University of Science and Technology)
INESC-ID
Technical University of Lisbon
University of Derby

Contents

Keynote

Designing for Positive and Serious Experience: Devices for Creativity, Engagement, Reflection and Learning

Tim Marsh[✉]

Griffith Film School, Queensland College of Art, Griffith University, Brisbane, Australia
t.marsh@griffith.edu.au

Abstract. Slow serious gameplay and interactions are slow movements intended to focus and sharpen attention/concentration, and provide openings and opportunities for reflection, contemplation, questioning and learning. Like devices used in film and theatre, this forms part of an emerging design repertoire of strategies and devices for creativity to articulate and manipulate time and space and narrative in interactions and games for the shaping of experience. To illustrate the idea of slow serious interactions this paper outlines devices and strategies for the design and development of a serious game that blends slow with fast interaction and gameplay to shape experience between positive and serious experience, to engage, stimulate thought and for reflection. The design strategies outlined herein can be used to inform design of other games, interactions and slow serious (art) games.

Keywords: Design · Experience · Devices · Analysis · Engagement · Serious experience · Reflection · Learning · Narrative · Film · Slow games · Serious art games

1   Introduction

Like devices used in film and theatre, there is an emerging design repertoire of strategies and devices for the manipulation of time and space, narrative, attention and reflection in interactions, games and serious games for the shaping of experience. For example, devices for the construction and articulation of off-screen space to suggest more than that seen and heard from within the confines of the display screen (Marsh and Wright 2001), to surprise, interrupt, provide emphasis, and shifts in focus of attention for contemplation (Marsh, Nitsche, Wei, Chung, Bolter, and Cheok 2008), to provide creative solutions to increase *both* fun and learning (Marsh, Zhiqiang, Klopfer, Chuang, Osterweil and Haas 2011), and an activity-based narrative approach to connect the process of design, development and analysis of learning objectives (Marsh, Yang and Shahabi 2006; Marsh 2010; Marsh and Nardi 2014). Adding to the repertoire of strategies for design, herein, the manipulation of interaction and gameplay speed and time is explored and in particular, slow movements in interactions and gameplay to encourage reflection are blended with fast gameplay to promote engagement.

© Springer International Publishing Switzerland 2015
S. Göbel et al. (Eds.): JCSG 2015, LNCS 9090, pp. 3–10, 2015.
DOI: 10.1007/978-3-319-19126-3_1

Modern technologies, digital media and games, are associated with a state of hyper attention, leading to expectations of faster and faster interactions and gameplay, increased impatience with waiting times and a preference for multi-tasking in order to keep non-active time to a minimum (Hayles 2007, 2012). Deep attention, in contrast to hyper attention, is associated with older traditions of human thinking and intense focus on a single task or theme for longer periods of time. Both modes of attention have their benefits but, as Hayles (2007) points out, hyper attention is perhaps more suited to most situations in the modern developed world. Deep attention might be becoming less common and possibly less appropriate, but this does not mean that it will disappear. Many see this as an opportunity to re-think not only the benefits of deep attention and reflection but also methods for attaining and maintaining it. Such deep attention, reflective, contemplative, and lingering experiences have a role to play within serious games and interactions with technology, particularly those that aim to enlighten, support learning and creativity, or present an argument, provide a message or an experience (Marsh 2011, Marsh and Costello 2013). Herein, slow serious games, interactions and play are described to provide a breathing space and to open opportunities for questioning, reflection and learning.

2   Background and Related Work: Slow Movement

While work in slow technology (Hallnas and Redstrom 2001) can be considered an antidote to faster interactions with modern technologies, our interest herein is more akin to performing interactions with digital media, interactive art, games and serious games in a leisurely and unhurried manner, at times requiring less effort and in a way similar to performing or *dancing with technology* – be it to allow participants to break away, clear one's mind, unwind, create a sense of calmness and open opportunities for reflection, contemplation, creativity and learning. Similar works are for example, Ernest Edmonds' The Shaping Form that is interactive but very very slow. People live with his works over a long time and notice the changes more on a day-to-day level rather than second-by-second e.g. through people walking-by and hand waving:

> *"...the work accumulates a history of audience activities and that history slowly changes the behaviour of the work, including colour saturation, timing and so on" "A month or two on display in a gallery, for example, can lead to clearly observable change." Edmonds and Francesca (2013) "...the general shift of colour is slow enough for the work to be quite different in the mid-afternoon to mid-morning...it is a changing exhibit" Ernest Edmonds (2000)*

Similarly, Bill Gavers' (2004) *The Drift Table* is also an artifact that people live with over a long period of time – functioning as coffee table and through a small round viewport in the top, people can observe the slow scroll across aerial photographs of landscapes. The slow movement is controlled by the positioning and the weight of objects on the coffee table and adding more weight causes the table both to accelerate and to descend towards the landscape below. But progress is always slow – travelling from one side of England to the other may take several days.

> *"...we started treating it more like a regular coffee table - you know, letting stuff pile up on it. That's how we wandered northwest into Wales and spotted a good place to go camping. After an evening out, we often bring people back for a bit of sightseeing. Sometimes though, when I'm on my own, I just end up daydreaming with it. I couldn't tell you where I go."*

The Drift Table captivates peoples' interest and curiosity in the changes of the artifact over time (as shown in the extract above) in response to users positioning and the weight of objects. There are shared design strategies in both The Shaping Form and The Drift Table in the form of slow interactions over long periods of time.

In game design, strategies for the manipulation of time and space have also been explored. In the game Vesper.5 Michael Brough takes an approach to slow interaction that is similar to the works of Edmonds and Gaver. The game is a navigable maze that only lets the player to take one step per day. With around one hundred possible steps it takes over three months to complete the game. The game's subversion of the usual three moves per minute speed of modern gaming completely changes the significance of each move. During gameplay, Vesper.5 replays all previous steps that have been made before pausing to wait for the player to take their daily step. This contrast between the fast speed of the replay that happens at the beginning of the game and the slow experience of each day's single move seems to give more weight to the step the player is about to take and leads to player reflection on the accumulation of actions that persist across time. *Ian Bogost's (2010) A Slow Year* is a collection of four games, one for each season, about the experience of observing things. Bogost's "art games" or "game poems" as he refers to them, were made for the now defunct Atari 2600, with primitive graphics and using past and passé slow technology by today's standards. So Bogost ingeniously blends games that are played in a continuous and real-time manner, through slow interactions and supported by slow technology. They are composed of "...neither action nor strategy: each of them requires a different kind of sedate observation and methodical input." The autumn game is a game about waiting for a leaf to fall off a tree and the challenge is catching it. In the winter game a cup of coffee cools near a window. The spring game's goal is to match thunder with lightning in a rainstorm. The summer game is the simple challenge to take a proper nap, this is a first-person game seen from behind drooping eyelids. The continuous and real time slowness of each game create openings for reflection.

These examples demonstrate that the manipulation of interaction and gameplay speed, with particular focus on slow interactions provides design strategies to create opportunities and openings for reflection and the shaping of experience. Informed from these examples, the next section describes on-going design and development of a serious game incorporating slow serious interactions with fast interactions to raise awareness on issues affecting ecosystems in Australia's Great Barrier Reef.

First mechanic / scene
- Slow gameplay
- Experiential / Exploration
- Experience: calm, tranquil

Second mechanic / scene
- Fast gameplay / complicit
- Experience: fun
- From Healthy to Unhealthy – dead fish, marine & plant life

Third mechanic / scene
- Slow gameplay
- Experiential / Exploration
- Serious experience: shocking
- Future Version: Restore Reef

Fig. 1. (top to bottom) Exploration / Beauty; Game / Management / Complicit; Exploration / Shocking (Restore)

3   Slow Serious Game Design and Development

Humans are taking more and more from Australia's Great Barrier Reef and are engaged in activities that directly and in-directly have negative impact on balanced and sensitive ecosystems. For some years I have been exploring ways to raise awareness on issues affecting the Reef, for example, in the creation of a virtual and simulation environment to bring issues to the attention of the player (Marsh, Thevalathom, Atkinson and Donaldson 2010), and looking to persuasive techniques in an attempt to make issues stick in the mind (Marsh and Nardi 2013) or to resonate and linger (Marsh and Costello 2013). While informing our research, it is argued that a more powerful design approach is needed in order to gain leverage with these approaches to create greater opportunities to stimulate thought and reflection. Towards this, at Griffith University I have been exploring design approaches for slow interactions and gameplay in environments conducive to slow movements and across a range of delivery platforms and interactions (point and click, touch, gestural, novel).

Described next are the design approaches similar to those outlined in the previous section for the manipulation of interaction and gameplay speed, and the corresponding changes / feedback, together with design strategies to create opportunities and openings for reflection and the shaping of experience between positive and serious experience (Marsh and Costello 2012) in a serious game to raise awareness on issues affecting ecosystems in Australia's Great Barrier Reef.

3.1   Game Description

The game is composed of slow serious interactions blended with traditional fast gameplay. The design strategy for varying the rhythm between slow and fast interactions was to open spaces for reflection and to captivate players' interest and attention. The game has three main levels or scenes as shown in figure 1. Each scene and transition between them is designed to provide an appropriate mood, feeling and experience, and together as a whole they encapsulate and convey messages and arguments and through reflection resonate with the participant/player during and following the game. The first and last scenes / mechanic only allow for slow interaction and exploration in the ocean to create opportunities for reflection. The deliberate and slow movement is intended to focus and sharpen concentration so players / participants experience and reflect on the beauty and tranquility (first mechanic) of the coral reef and marine life.

The second scene moves from slow to fast interaction initially incorporating fun gameplay, but after a time players become aware that they are complicit in the destruction of the reef. Gameplay is described in more detail in the next section. The last scene is again performed by slow interaction and exploration in the ocean in order for participants/players to reflect, but this time on the disruption and destruction from the affect of complicit gameplay in the second scene. The experience from the last scene is intended to be so intensely shocking and disturbing that it provokes thought and lingers, resonates or "bleeds" out from the game.

3.2   Gameplay: Fast and Slow Interaction

In this game, players engage with activities that increasingly escalate and in turn increasingly have a disruptive and destructive effect on the reef. The objective of the game is to "slow down" human activities in an attempt to keep the reef sustainable. But as human activities that are disruptive to the reef escalate, so gameplay becomes more frenetic in an attempt to "slow down" destruction. So there is a paradox of speeding-up to "slow down" - where increased gameplay represents the increase in effort and resources necessary to help protect and restore the reef. The idea in the game world of "slowing down" is a metaphor that extends to the rest of the world outside of the game.

The slow to fast gameplay (second mechanic) initially provides pleasurable gameplay. The objective for players is to counter the harmful human activities that are disruptive and threatening to the sustainability of the reef. These threats are from: mining, farming, tourism, watersports, and coastal developments. For example, the issues that arise from mining and that are implemented in the game are illustrated in figure 2. Using the analogy of the circus performance and manipulation art of spinning plates, the challenge for players is to appropriately "slow down" and balance each of these threats by selecting them in order to reduce their harmful affects and in an effort to balance the ecosystems of the reef towards being naturally sustainable.

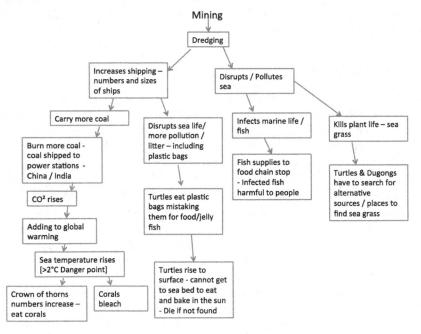

Fig. 2. Flow Diagrams / Tree Structures of Issues, Causes and Effects

However, as the destruction steadily increases, this means that gameplay inevitably becomes more frenetic in an attempt to balance or "slow down" destruction. And so after a time the player becomes aware that they can no longer manage to reduce the reef's destruction but have become part or complicit in the destruction of the reef.

3.3 Future Work

We are currently working on the next version to incorporate a fourth scene or level with gameplay for restoring or "rewilding" the reef back to a naturally sustainable ecosystem. In addition, future gameplay will allow expert players to eventually learn how to avoid disruption or cause minimal damage to the reef. Following this, a study will be carried out to assess players' experience and to see how effective the slow gameplay was in evoking thoughts and reflections on the topics and issues of purpose.

4 Conclusion

In this article I have described slow interactions and play with serious games, and refer to this as *slow serious (art) games*. While similar to, and sharing aspects with, the design philosophy of slow technology, the focus of our work is on deliberate and controlled slow movement, interactions and play intended to focus and sharpen attention/concentration, and provide openings and opportunities for reflection, contemplation, creativity and learning. Slow movement interactive art and games literature is reviewed to show that the manipulation of interaction and gameplay speed and the corresponding changes / feedback, provides design approaches to create opportunities and openings for reflection and the shaping of experience. To illustrate the idea of slow serious interactions we have described on-going design and development of a serious game to evoke slow movement from participants/players. This is blended with fast gameplay and together these design strategies engage players in positive and serious experience, and provide openings and opportunities for reflection on issues affecting ecosystems in Australia's Great Barrier Reef. Like devices used in film and theatre, slow serious games and interactions add to an emerging design repertoire of strategies and devices to articulate and manipulate time and space, narrative, attention and reflection in interactions and games for the shaping of experience.

Acknowledgements. This research was supported from Griffith University research award GFS2390/MARST. Thanks to the "Reef Game" development team, Lukas Halloran, Whitney Constantine and Elliot Miller. Thanks also to Brigid Costello for comments on an earlier draft.

References

1. Bogost, I.: A Slow Year: Game Poems, Open Texture (2010)
2. Brough, M.: Vesper.5 (video game). PC (2012). http://mightyvision.blogspot.co.uk/2012/08/vesper5.html
3. Edmonds, E.: Art practice augmented by digital agents. Digital Creativity 11(4), 193–204 (2000)
4. Edmonds, E., Franco, F.: From Communications Game to Cities Tango. International Journal of Creative Computing 1(1), 120–132 (2013)
5. Gaver, W. et al.: The drift table: designing for ludic engagement. In: CHI 2004 Extended Abstracts on Human Factors in Computing Systems. ACM (2004)

6. Hallnas, L., Redstrom, J.: Slow Technology: Designing for Reflection. Personal Ubiquitous Computer. **5**(3), 201–212 (2001)
7. Hayles, N.K.: Hyper and deep attention: the generational divide in cognitive modes. Profession, pp. 187-199 (2007)
8. Hayles, N.K.: Tech-TOC: Complex Temporalities in Living and Technical Beings. Electronic Book Review (2012)
9. Marsh, T.: Activity-Based Scenario Design, Development and Assessment in Serious Games. In: Van Eck, R. (ed.), Gaming and Cognition: Theories and Practice from the Learning Sciences, Chapter 10, pp. 214-227. IGI Global, Hershey, PA (2010)
10. Marsh, T.: Serious Games Continuum: Between Games for Purpose and Experiential Environments for Purpose. 2(2), 61-68 (2011)
11. Marsh, T., Wright, P.: Using cinematography conventions to inform guidelines for the design and evaluation of virtual off-screen space. In: AAAI 2000 Spring Symposium Series "Smart Graphics, pp. 123-127 (2000)
12. Marsh, T., Nitsche, M., Wei Liu, Chung, P., Bolter, J.D., Cheok, A.D.: Film Informing Design for Contemplative Gameplay, ACM SIGGRAPH, ACM Press (2008)
13. Marsh, T., Trevathan, J., Donaldson, R., Atkinson, I.: Exploring and Learning about Reef Data in Serious Games. Coast to Coast 2012, Brisbane, QLD, Australia (2012)
14. Marsh, T., Costello, B.: Experience in Serious Games: Between Positive and Serious Experience. In: Ma, M., Oliveira, M.F., Hauge, J.B., Duin, H., Thoben, K.-D. (eds.) SGDA 2012. LNCS, vol. 7528, pp. 255–267. Springer, Heidelberg (2012)
15. Marsh, T., Costello, B.: Lingering Serious Experience as Trigger to Raise Awareness, Encourage Reflection and Change Behavior. In: Berkovsky, S., Freyne, J. (eds.) PERSUASIVE 2013. LNCS, vol. 7822, pp. 116–124. Springer, Heidelberg (2013)
16. Marsh, T., Zhiqiang, L., Klopfer, E., Haas J., Chuang X, Osterweil, S., Haas, J.: Fun *and* Learning: Blending Design and Development Dimensions in Serious Games Through Narrative and Characters. In: Serious Games and Edutainment Applications. Springer (2011)
17. Marsh, T., Nardi, B.: Activity Theory-Based Approach for Design of Sticky Mechanics: Raising Awareness about Conserving The Great Barrier Reef, ICEC2013 Workshop on Mechanics, Mechanisms & Devices: to Inform. Reflect & Change Behaviour, São Paulo, Brazil (2013)
18. Marsh, T., Nardi, B.: Spheres and Lenses: Activity-Based Scenario / Narrative Approach for Design and Evaluation of Entertainment through Engagement. In: Pisan, Y., Sgouros, N.M., Marsh, T. (eds.) ICEC 2014. LNCS, vol. 8770, pp. 42–51. Springer, Heidelberg (2014)
19. Marsh, T., Yang, K., Shahabi, C.: Game development for experience through staying there. In: ACM SIGGRAPH Video Games Symposium, Boston, USA, ACM Press (2006)

Games for Health

Participatory Game Design
for the INTERACCT Serious Game for Health

Fares Kayali[1], Konrad Peters[2]([✉]), Jens Kuczwara[1], Andrea Reithofer[1],
Daniel Martinek[2], Rebecca Wölfle[2], Ruth Mateus-Berr[1], Zsuzsanna Lehner[3],
Marisa Silbernagl[4], Manuel Sprung[4], Anita Lawitschka[3], and Helmut Hlavacs[2]

[1] University of Applied Arts Vienna, Vienna, Austria
[2] Entertainment Computing, University of Vienna, Vienna, Austria
konrad.peters@univie.ac.at
[3] St. Anna Children's Hospital, Vienna, Austria
[4] Clinical Child Psychology, University of Vienna, Vienna, Austria

Abstract. In this paper we present results from our user-centered and participative design approach using methods from design thinking and explorative design with school children aged 8 - 14 in context with a game created for children after cancer treatment. After stem-cell transplantation, pediatric patients must remain in aftercare due to a high risk of suffering from a plethora of life threatening organic problems. In this phase, communication with the clinicians is key for an increased survival probability. The multidisciplinary INTERACCT aims at developing a child friendly communication tool based on gamification principles in order to foster this important communication and should stimulate physiotherapy exercises and treatment compliance. Finally, through analyzing gaming scores, INTERACCT should also act as a sensor for detecting problematic phases children are going through. Since the design of INTERACCT is key to its success, the results presented here act as important guidelines for designing the game world. The results of the evaluation are are game characters and story lines, which will provide starting points for creating the INTERACCT game world and which shall be subject to a future validation with sick children.

Keywords: Children · Game design · Serious games for health · User-centered design

1 Introduction

In this paper we present INTERACCT (Integrating Entertainment and Reaction Assessment into Child Cancer Therapy)[1], a multidisciplinary research project aiming at creating a communication tool for pediatric patients after cancer treatment with HSCT (hematopoietic stem cell transplantation) in after care. The communication platform should foster communication between patients and clinicians, but also increase motivation for treatment compliance by using appropriate

---

[1] http://www.interacct.at/

© Springer International Publishing Switzerland 2015
S. Göbel et al. (Eds.): JCSG 2015, LNCS 9090, pp. 13–25, 2015.
DOI: 10.1007/978-3-319-19126-3_2

designs and gamification elements. An important aspect of INTERACCT is the user centered research around entertaining and motivating schemes to reach this goal.

The results of the presented research are situated on two levels. Firstly we present detailed results from participatory design sessions with children and split these results by age and gender. Secondly we provide insights on the application of participatory design methods with children in the context of game design, and we provide a reflection of when, how and with which target audience such methods can be applied. We further discuss if and how the presented results can inspire the design of INTERACCT, a serious games platform for health, targeted at children after cancer treatment.

2   Related Work

Health related computer games have been intensively researched recently, covering all kinds of desired positive aspects including education for coping with health problems, keeping up motivation when going through difficult times, strengthening treatment compliance, up to supporting therapy through physical exercises [19]. An important subgroup in this field are children and adolescents with any form of cancer, and since 2008 more and more game and multimedia projects for this particular group have been developed.

Re-Mission and its successor Re-Mission 2² are computer games specifically tailored to be played by children during and after cancer therapy. In a large randomized study the positive effect of plying Re-Mission on motivation and compliance of pediatric patients has been proven [14]. The game principle is based on fighting cancer cells inside an infected body, using abstracted weapons like chemotherapy, antibiotics and the bodys natural defenses. The game's purpose is to strengthen positive emotion, increase self-efficacy, and shift attitudes toward chemotherapy.

Combat [7] is a game similar to Re-Mission, where children can fight against the cancer cells in their bodies. Here empowerment is reached via identification with a fighting hero.

In [4] the authors present the game Patient Empowerment (PE) Interactive exercise video game, designed to stimulate the self-efficacy of pediatric patients with cancer. The game tries to transform physical exercises into mental empowerment through metaphors involving cancer, hospital personnel etc.

The authors of [13] present a game-like multimedia entertainment system primarily for educating children and adolescents of various age groups to learn about their illness and the necessary treatments. The paper describes the user centered design process for different age groups and focuses on age dependent requirements.

In [1] the authors describe a system for supporting children during cancer treatment to keep up with the curriculum of their school classes. The system focuses on mobile platforms like smart phones or tablets.

---

² http://www.re-mission2.org/ (accessed May 21st 2014)

The Brazilian game called "Corrida da Saude" (Health Course) [8] aims at improving awareness about a healthy way of living in order to avoid developing cancer.

A different path is followed by the game "That Dragon Cancer" [11], which artistically reflects the fears and emotions of parents raising a young child with terminal cancer.

2.1 Research Through Design

The methodological approach of this research is informed by contemporary approaches in design research. We chose an approach where research is conducted through design. Such approaches have previously been framed as "design as research" (see [2] and [12]). They act as a means of knowledge construction and further result in reflective insights on the creative processes.

In arts Design Thinking is a well-established practice for conducting research through design. While the term Thinking refers to Aristoteles' episteme (intellectual knowledge) rather than making (poesis) and doing (praxis), Applied Design Thinking is the synthesis of thinking and doing, as Schön described in "The Reflective Practitioner" [21]. Knowledge embodied in art, which has been characterised as tacit, practical knowledge, is cognitive, though non-conceptual [3] and interconnects disciplines. Also basic and applied research is intertwined [5]. Their approach focuses on knowledge application as well as knowledge-based problem-solving. Design Thinking also embodies understanding and experimental application. It goes back to the design community and was shaped by design theorists and designers through their practical approach as "reflective practitioners" [21] [16]. Usually designers talk and reflect about the products they design, rather than the process, which led them to innovation. The aim of applied Design Thinking is to facilitate innovative solutions for complex problems through collaboration across multiple disciplines. According to Kristensen [15], many design problems arise because there is little integration of environment, people and technology. He recommends that physical space, virtual space and a visual working methodology need to be interconnected in order to enhance collaborative participation and performance for dispersed teams [17]. The process of Design Thinking iteratively passes through stages; the brainstorming process; time for ideation; prototyping; immediate testing. Between these iterative phases feedback has an essential part. Iterative phases of Applied Design Thinking can be compared to the Walt Disney Principles [10]: "Dreamer", "Critic" and "Realist": "The Dreamer enabled new ideas and goals to be formed. The Realist turns the dreamers ideas into reality. The Critic is the one who will filter out any ideas that are too ambitious or not believable" [24].

In computer science the term explorative design is used to describe an approach where design practices are utilized to facilitate research. The concept originated with John Deweys Theory of Inquiry [9], where he introduces the concept of "doing for the sake of knowing". Donald Schön built on the work of Dewey, when he observed that much of the knowledge needed and used in the design process is not known a priori, but acquired during the design process as a result of interacting with the object to be designed [21].

For game studies Stapleton defined the "RADDAR" method as an iterative loop where he reflexively defines research as design and design as research [20]. Regarding participatory game design approaches with children Moser found that creating low-fidelity prototypes in a workshop setting provides valuable insights for researchers while at the same time presenting a fun engagement for participating children [18]. It was also found that a user centered approach can help to further reception and acceptance of a game-based solution for children with cancer [13].

3   INTERACCT

This publication is made in a larger context with the project INTERACCT, which aims at investigating the enrichment of traditional E-Health platforms with entertainment elements, aimed at motivating young patients and fostering medical communication between young patients and their respective clinicians. We thus present the scope and goals of the INTERACCT project to provide context to the results presented here. Although our approach may be generalized to any child related chronic disease, due to the special area of expertise of our hospital partner Childrens Cancer Research Institute (CCRI) at the St. Anna Childrens Hospital, INTERACCT focuses on patients being taken care of in the outpatient clinic after stem cell transplantation.

3.1   Aims and Scope

We are currently developing an innovative, adaptive and entertaining/playful Web platform (INTERACCT) in a multidisciplinary approach at the interface of clinical research, design thinking and information and communication technology (ICT). Augmented clinician-patient communication may enable the clinician to early identify behavioral changes which precede manifest symptoms of diseases. Furthermore the tool should be adaptive to developing problems, e.g. enhanced "drinking games" if fluid intake is decreasing. An entertaining user interface specially designed for juvenile patients should foster interaction with the tool and improve long term treatment adherence. In the long run, the use of INTERACCT could lead to earlier diagnosis, and thus to a better quality of care after HSCT.

INTERACCT therefore should have the look and feel of modern entertainment platforms, including various elements of entertainment, challenges, games and social aspects, etc. (see Figure 1). Seen from the children's perspective, INTERACCT delivers mainly entertainment, and is a source of challenges, competitions, empowerment and fun. The E-Health aspects of fostering compliance, communication, and treatment should be visible, but not dominating.

INTERACCT does not require any newly created hardware devices. Unlike other E-Health projects, we do not aim at using special health sensor hardware that automatically detects and sends health data. Data collection will only

Fig. 1. Entry of medical data in the INTERACCT game

include information as requested in the patient handbook like eating and drinking behavior, bowel movement, observation of pain etc.). Any clinical examination will only take place in the hospital during the regular mandatory visits. Therefore, INTERACCT is a pure software solution, but will integrate state-of-the-art low-cost and off-the-shelf consumer equipment like web cams, smart phones or a Kinect sensor to increase the fun factor for children and adolescents. Also, we do aim at using the Kinect or Android based smartphones as input sensors for health data. The Kinect for instance can be used to guide treatment games fostering movement. Also, we aim at analyzing player performance data to help clinicians in detecting worsening of a patients condition.

3.2   Project Goals

The main project hypothesis is that the integration of specially designed playful elements into a Web based communication tool between clinicians and juvenile chronic patients fosters communication, compliance, and therapy.

– Continuous communication in such a volatile setting as given by HSCT is key to monitor the health status of the patients, and above all detect or even foresee upcoming crises as soon as possible. Since HSCT patients suffer from multi-factorial complications with varying organ manifestations, a disease progression can have many different causes. Early detection is a key factor for optimized therapy and the best clinical outcome. Our tool must be specially designed to allow clinicians to easily follow the status of all patients, and be alarmed in case deviations from normality (as characterized by the clinician for every patient) are detected.

– Enforcing compliance is a major factor in HSCT treatment, since patients must closely follow all treatments, and any deviation holds the potential of fatal consequences. Our tool will animate children to use it, as well as play-fully foster compliance by integrating therapy into a sequence of computer games.

– Our tool will also foster treatment since many computer games will be especially designed to cover certain treatment aspects. Examples include games for entering health data, drinking, movement, coordination etc. As an additional hypothesis we think that game related data such as scoring points per time unit are an indicator for the general well being of children and can also be used to detect upcoming clinical complications. Therefore the games themselves, being steered by Kinect, mouse or Android phone, may act as health sensor.

As main underlying hypothesize we think that INTERACCT is a tool that not only improves communication between clinician and juvenile patients, but also actively supports treatment through improved motivation of patients.

4   Experimental Results

The goal of INTERACCT is to develop a game world which appeals to a young target audience. Due to the nature of the primary disease, the target audience is highly heterogeneous. It includes children aged 8-14 with differing ethnic background and from different social classes. Children in the target audience are further separated by changes in health, well-being, psycho-motoric and psycho-social developmental status due to the HSCT treatment. The INTERACCT game shall be designed to provide high adaptability to accommodate changing circumstances in health, age and social context of patients.

We have so far conducted a review of relevant projects target at children and young adolescents, employed explorative design approaches within the project team, and conducted a quantitative survey (full results forthcoming in late 2014).

Fig. 2. A bright and happy version of the island players shall be able to explore in the INTERACCT game

Fig. 3. A dark and dangerous version of the same island

In the survey we compared groups of young gamers, school children and children after cancer treatment regarding their gaming habits and individual preferences. The results of the survey so far point towards environments which allow exploration and adventure. We further confirmed that there is a wide range of preferences regarding visual styles and that children prefer imaginative characters over realistic representations. We have thus settled on a fantasy island (see Figures 1 and 2 for possible representations of this island) as the environment for the game. The specific goal of the used participatory design approach is to find characters, stories and game mechanics within this given environment, which are interesting to young players.

5   Participatory Design Experiments

Following we present the results from qualitative design experiments conducted in two public schools in Vienna, Austria. The overall sample is comprised of 81 children aged 8 to 14. The qualitative evaluation was carried out in two schools, an elementary school and a secondary school. For the analysis of results in the following the sample is split into 4 groups; 17 female participants aged 8-10, 17 male participants aged 8-10, 29 female participants aged 12-14 and 18 male participants aged 12-14.

We visited classes in the two schools during drawing lectures which span two hours. There we briefly introduced the theme; children should draw comic strips of characters and their adventures on an island (see the preconditions defined beforehand). They were only given the context that these characters will be used in a video game and some hints about possible drawing techniques were given. They were handed two pictures of the island (see Figures 2 and 3) as inspiration and a blank comic strip with six panels for drawing their characters. They were encouraged to be imaginative and were told that everything is allowed to be drawn and that all ideas are welcome. The process of drawing was then supervised by members of our project team together with the classes' teachers.

For the evaluation we clustered the drawings and we present a summary of the findings and representative example pictures for the four groups separated by age and gender.

5.1   Female, Age 8-10

The girls developed three different character types, including (i) pure fantasy characters, (ii) fruit and plant characters, and (iii) special animals. Also, humans often appear in the stories. Drawings from the girls are usually colorful, with dominating colors being pink, yellow, red, blue and green (see Figure 4).

Colors are also often pastel, and girls seem to lay more emphasis on the background compared to boys, including floor, sun, clouds or trees, even if they are irrelevant for the story (see Figure 5). Characters are mostly friendly looking, having round and soft features. Most of them exhibit friendly human properties, often positive traits. Characters are active and like to do things, have heart-like

Fig. 4. Characters, female 8-10   **Fig. 5.** Background, female 8-10

shapes, hair is important, often growing. Animals include dogs, snails, turtles, ants, cats, butterflies and squids. Plant animals include mostly edible plants like bananas or cucumbers, but also clover leaves.

Interestingly, girls prefer complex story lines including fitting start and end. An important theme is finding friends, converting bad characters to do good, and saving the innocent. Stories are mainly driven by changing characters instead of weapons or tools.

5.2   Male, Age 8-10

Boys in this age group primarily focused on established fantasy characters like monsters, dragons, aliens and robots. Dragons appear frequently, since they can be used as positive, but also as dangerous characters. Some also described fantasy animals and plants, which had magical spells and other special abilities. The most used animals were birds, dogs, sharks, monkeys and snakes (see Figure 6).

Fig. 6. Fantasy and animal characters, male 8-10   **Fig. 7.** Fantasy and animal characters, male 8-10

Fantasy food as invented by the boys is dominated by sweets, ice cream or fast food. In comparison to the girls in the same age group real people had less presence in the stories (see Figure 7).

Recurring traits of the characters include multiple arms or heads, squared and triangular shapes, many teeth or spikes, and a generally evil or dangerous appearance. Boys tended to use less colors and preferred to use darker colors including shades of blue, black, green, brown and red (see Figure 8).

The characters often were equipped with tools and weapons, and they had special abilities like jumping very high, climbing, flying or shooting with weapons or spikes. Boys in this age group were less concerned with an overall story but rather focused on the appearance and abilities of many different characters each.

The main goal of the boys is to defeat enemies, fighting is the main storyline. Fights should be enhanced by special weapons, abilities and tools (see Figure 9).

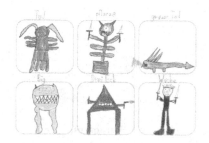   

Fig. 8. Abstract characters, male 8-10   **Fig. 9.** Tools and weapons, male 8-10

However, there are exceptions to the above described observations, boys using pastel colors, using a detailed, positive story line with detailed backgrounds, and friendship as main motive (see Figure 10), as well as girls drawing monsters or aliens without an embedding story (see Figure 11).

Fig. 10. A detailed story about friendship, male 8-10   **Fig. 11.** Monsters without story, female 8-10

5.3 Female, Age 12-14

Girls in this group primarily developed three different types of player characters: (i) fantasy beings, (ii) fruit characters and (iii) animal characters with special traits. Paintings in this group were very colorful with high use of the colors yellow, pink, red, blue and green.

The developed characters are mostly cute but often also have a dark and dangerous side (see Figure 12). This means that they should have the ability to change both visual appearance as well as abilities and character traits. Summarised many participants want an ambivalent character who can be good and bad depending on the situation. For example a cute rabbit was painted who could poison people with his carrots. The most used animal in this group are penguins followed by lions, giraffes, bears and rabbits. The fantasy being were mostly round and moved by rolling, flying or jumping (see Figure 13).

Fig. 12. Characters with detailed descriptions of particular strengths and weaknesses, female 12-14

Fig. 13. Round characters, female 12-14

For girls in this group, beating enemies was generally more important than interacting with fictitious friends. If they painted friend characters they were cute and benevolent. Enemy characters usually correspond to the story and player character. For example a cute lion battles a cute duck or a lemon fights a banana. Some participants also focused on collecting items including coins, food, hearts and stars. These collectible items can then be spent on abilities, weapons and cloth for the player character. The prevalent game idea in this group was to beat an enemy in order to free a friendly character.

5.4   Male, Age 12-14

The drawings of boys in this age group can be broadly structured into three groups, (i) fantasy beings, (ii) fictitious plants and (iii) fantasy animals. Most of the participants did not use colors but submitted black and white drawings. Similar to the characters designed by girls in this age groups, the characters drawn by boys can visually change between a good and an evil version. They grow with the player and can fully change their identity when need arises. The designed characters are rather militant and cool than cute and friendly like the girls' characters (see Figure 14).

The most common game goal of participants in this group is beating an enemy. Fighting usually is the core of the drawn story. Most game ideas also involve awarding points, which can be used to buy lives, energy and weapons. Two juxtaposed game concepts mentioned by this group are on the one hand saving the nature and plants on the island and on the other hand killing and wiping out all plant life (see Figure 15).

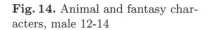

Fig. 14. Animal and fantasy characters, male 12-14

Fig. 15. Plant environments, male
12-14

6   Conclusions

In this paper we present the first results from the research INTERACCT, in
which we develop a gamified communication tool for children and adolescents
after HSCT. The biggest challenges are the fact that INTERACCT should work
for different age groups, genders, and cultural backgrounds.

The presented experimental results from design workshops with children of
different ages and sex show the influence of both variables. While for boys,
mainly fighting and weapons are of importance, here using often monocolors or
black and white, girls lay more focus on coherent story lines and relationships
with more colorful drawings. A common ground is the use of animal and plant
characters and the use of exaggeration and supernatural abilities.

The main different property between age groups is that older children design
more complex characters and story lines, characters become more adaptive and
versatile, gain depth and ambivalence. However, character types remain basically
the same. The preferences of the different age groups and genders will be taken
into account by offering a balanced selection of characters, including characters
explicitly designed to accommodate the taste of a specific group. Further the
game will be designed in a way that allows to play successfully with different
play styles (e.g. fighting versus exploration).

The participative approach proved insightful and will help shape the core
gameplay and visual style of the INTERACCT game. Differing drawing capabilities might have limited the scope of what children were able to depict and the
results are also limited insofar as there is no statistical evaluation yet. As such
they are no definitive measure to design the game but rather serve as means to
establish guidelines for the game's design. Further research will address this by
categorising the images according to art-psychological criteria.

The use of user-centered and participatory design methods is helpful in early
stages of a project, where it helps to find a general direction for the design. As
in the presented research a later stage of the project can even benefit more from
such an approach because more focused tasks can be given to children alongside
first materials for inspiration.

References

1. Barbosa, D.N.F., Bassani, P.B.S., Mossmann, J.B., Schneider, G.T., Reategui, E., Branco, M., Meyrer, L., Nunes, M.: Mobile learning and games: experiences with mobile games development for children and teenagers undergoing oncological treatment. In: Göbel, S., Wiemeyer, J. (eds.) GameDays 2014. LNCS, vol. 8395, pp. 153–164. Springer, Heidelberg (2014)
2. Burdick, A.: Design (as) Research. In: B. Laurel, ed., Design Research: Methods and Perspectives. MIT Press (2003)
3. Borgdorff, H.: The Conflict of the Faculties: Perspectives on Artistic Research and Academia. Leiden University Press (2012)
4. Caldwell, C., Bruggers, C., Altizer, R., Bulaj, G., D'Ambrosio, T., Kessler, R., Christiansen, B.: The intersection of video games and patient empowerment: case study of a real world application. In: Proceedings of The 9th Australasian Conference on Interactive Entertainment: Matters of Life and Death (IE 2013). Melbourne (2013)
5. Carayannis, E.G., Campbell, D.F.J.: Mode 3 Knowledge Production in Quadruple Helix Innovation Systems: 21st-Century Democracy, Innovation, and Entrepreneurship for Development. Springer (2011)
6. Clipper - an open source freeware library for clipping and offsetting lines and polygon. http://www.angusj.com/delphi/clipper.php
7. Combat. Playing can stimulate children with cancer to react against the disease. http://www.isaude.net/pt-BR/noticia/21458/ciencia-e-tecnologia/jogo-pode-estimular-criancas-com-cancer-a-reagir-contra-a-doenca
8. Corrida da saude (Health Course). http://www.accamargo.org.br/corrida-saude/
9. Dewey, J.: Logic: The Theory of Inquiry. Southern Illinois University Press, Carbondale (1938)
10. Dilts, R.: Strategies of a Genius, vol. 1. Meta Publications, California (1994)
11. That Dragon Cancer. http://thatdragoncancer.com/about
12. Ehn, P., Lwgren, J.: Design [x] research: Essays on interaction design as knowledge. Malm University, School of Arts and Communication (2004)
13. Gansohr, C., Emmerich, K., Masuch, M., Basu, O., Grigull, L.: Creating age-specific interactive environments about medical treatments for children and adolescent patients diagnosed with cancer. In: Göbel, S., Wiemeyer, J. (eds.) GameDays 2014. LNCS, vol. 8395, pp. 141–152. Springer, Heidelberg (2014)
14. Kato, P.M., Cole, S.W., Bradlyn, A.S., Pollock, B.H.: Video Game Improves Behavioral Outcomes in Adolescents and Young Adults With Cancer: A Randomized Trial. PEDIATRICS 122(2), 305–317 (2008)
15. Kristensen, T.: The Physical Context of Creativity. Creativity and Innovation Management 13(2), 89–96 (2004)
16. Lawson, B.: How designers think: the design process demystified. Elsevier (1980)
17. Mateus-Berr, R.: Applied Design Thinking LAB and Creative Empowering of Interdisciplinary Teams. In: Carayannis, E.G., Dubina, I.N., Seel, N., Campbell, D.F.J., Udiszuni, D. (eds.) Springer Encyclopedia on Creativity, Invention, Innovation and Entrepreneurship (CI2E). Springer, New York (2013)
18. Moser, C.: Children ideation workshop. In: Reidsma, D., Katayose, H., Nijholt, A. (eds.) ACE 2013. LNCS, vol. 8253, pp. 592–599. Springer, Heidelberg (2013)
19. Primack, B.A., Carroll, M.V., McNamara, M., Klem, M.L., King, B., Rich, M., Chan, C.W., Nayak, S.: Role of video games in improving health-related outcomes: a systematic review. Am. J. Prev. Med. 42(6) (2012)

20. Stapleton, A.J.: Research as Design-Design as Research. In: Proceedings of the DiGRA 2005 Conference - Changing Views: Worlds in Play (2005)
21. Schoen, D.A.: The Reflective Practitioner: How Professionals Think in Action. Basic Books (1983)
22. Triangle - A Two-Dimensional Quality Mesh Generator and Delaunay Triangulator. http://www.cs.cmu.edu/quake/triangle.html
23. Unity3D Multi-platform game engine. http://unity3d.com/unity
24. Wake, L. NLP. Principles in Practice. Human Resource Management International Digest, Ecademy Press: St. Albans 19, 6 (2010)
25. Logical Observation Identifiers and Names. http://loinc.org/
26. Health Level 7 Standard. http://www.hl7.org/

Design and Development of *Sur-Face:* An Interactive Mobile App for Educating Patients Regarding Corrective Surgery of Facial Deformities

Yeshwanth Pulijala[1(✉)], Minhua Ma[1], and Ashraf Ayoub[2]

[1] School of Art, Design and Architecture, University of Huddersfield, Huddersfield, UK
{U1475891,m.ma}@hud.ac.uk
[2] Glasgow Dental School, University of Glasgow, Glasgow, UK
a.ayoub@gla.ac.uk

Abstract. Corrective surgery of face, also known as orthognathic surgery, is a complex procedure performed to correct the underlying facial deformities. In case of elective surgeries like these, patients need to make voluntary decisions whether or not undergo the surgery. Hence, it is very important for them to understand the intricacy of the techniques and potential side effects of the surgery before they sign the consent form. Conventional methods of patient education using leaflet-based instructions were found to be ineffective in providing them the required information.

Sur-Face, named after **sur**gery of **face** is a healthcare app exploring a new dimension in patient education with the help of interactive 3D visualizations and serious gaming elements on a mobile platform. It demonstrates the surgical process and it's after effects using high quality 3D animations. The aim of this study is to evaluate the efficacy of Sur-Face by comparing two methods of delivery of instructions: a mobile app with interactive 3D animations and an audio file containing only verbal instructions. To evaluate these methods, participant's ability to understand and retain the instructions was analyzed using a questionnaire. The null hypothesis was that there would be no difference between the two methods of instructions. On analysis, participants of the 'app' group performed significantly better ($p<0.0034$) than the 'voice' group suggesting the role of interactive visualizations in improved understanding, intuitive knowledge transfer and communication. This paper describes the principles of design, development and potential advances of *Sur-Face*. Further it also explores the application of serious games in patient education and informed consent process.

Keywords: Mobile apps · 3D modeling · Visualization · mHealth · Facial deformities · Orthognathic surgery

1 Introduction

Face is one of the most visible and important organs of our body. Thus deformities of the face, which can be of skeletal or dental origin, distress the patients both physically and psychologically. Severe skeletal deformities can debilitate patients of their normal

© Springer International Publishing Switzerland 2015
S. Göbel et al. (Eds.): JCSG 2015, LNCS 9090, pp. 26–35, 2015.
DOI: 10.1007/978-3-319-19126-3_3

functions like breathing, eating and also disturb the overall aesthetics of the face. Orthognathic surgery or corrective jaw surgery is performed in these cases to re-establish proper functioning of the jaws and enhance facial aesthetics.

As patients voluntarily consent to undergo orthognathic surgery for correction of a prolonged functional deformity or an aesthetic requirement, informed decisions are to be made before undergoing the surgery (1). Having a good knowledge of the surgery helps patients to take responsibility of their health (2, 3) and give a well-comprehended informed consent. In addition to the actual surgery, knowledge about post-operative complications is imperative as any form of surgery has some potential-ly unpredictable outcomes. Given that orthognathic surgery is a prolonged procedure, which can last for more than a year (4), the consent process usually begins long be-fore the surgery. Hence, it is vital that the patients completely understand the surgical instructions and also remember the possible outcomes. However, this part of patient care has often been an underestimated factor (5) leading to poor post-operative satisfaction levels, and to litigation in some severe cases (6).

Research on the post-surgical satisfaction levels of the patients found that, the me-thod in which the information was delivered has an equally important role as that of the information itself (7). Conventionally, Surgeons use a verbal or leaflet-based method to communicate with the patients in their face-to-face meetings. But given the problems like complexity of medical terminology, cultural and educational gaps, it was found that these methods were not effective. When multimedia graphics were used for patient instructions, they gave better results (8, 9). However, in most of the existing resources information is in the form of static text with images stressing a need for better repre-sentation. These arguments were further supported when Azem et al., 2014 (10) have used 2D animations on a tablet device to deliver instructions regarding Le Fort I osteotomy. On evaluation of non-patient volunteers, this study showed that the partici-pants who were given 2D graphical illustrations could understand and retain the instructions better than those who were only given verbal instructions.

The application of animations in the explanation of medical procedures makes complex concepts easy to understand for the non-medical community. Though vari-ous companies (11, 12) have done a significant work in medical animation, they did not include 3D visualizations for patient education of surgical procedures. The recent rise in production and development of Internet using smart phones and mobile tablets has revolutionized their impact on patient behavior and decision-making. Health care apps are special category in mobile apps, which provide information regarding the issues concerning health. IMS Healthcare report, 2013 (13) has recently stated that there are over 43000 health apps on iTunes store and over 35,000 of them on Google Play store. Touch Surgery (14) is one of the first mobile apps that explain surgical procedures through pre rendered 3D animations. Essential Anatomy (15) is another popular mobile application, which demonstrates dental problems in a fully interactive 3D visualization format helping the patient to understand various treatment options. In case of orthognathic surgery, 3D animations by Dolphin imaging system's Aqua-rium (16) were commonly used. But most of the currently available visualizations over-simplify the treatment or complicate it leading to unrealistic expectations in patient's minds about the outcome of the surgery (17). Moreover, developments of apps, which misinterpret the healthcare guidelines, cause a lack of confidence on them by the physicians (18). Despite these studies clearly suggesting that patients are increasingly depending on Internet and mobile apps for healthcare decisions, a multimedia mobile app that can comprehensively explain about orthognathic surgery has not been found.

Sur-Face aims to fill this gap by explaining the surgery in a realistic and easily understandable format using 3D animations developed under the guidance of surgeons. This paper aims to provide an insight on development and impact of mobile apps in patient education by presenting the design and evaluation study. Further, it includes a note on role of gaming elements in mobile apps like *Sur-face*.

2   The Design of *Sur-Face*

2.1   3D Modeling

The entire application was built leveraging on realistic 3D modeling and interactive elements. Among the various available software packages, Autodesk Maya (19) was used as it allows creation of high quality animations and exports them to gaming platforms.

The content of Sur-face was strategically divided into pre surgical preparation, surgery and post-surgical complications for easy navigation and understanding of the entire procedure. Pre surgical preparation scenes explain the instructions to be followed by the patient before undergoing the surgery. 3D models of doctor, patient and a patient wearing hospital gown as shown in the Fig.1 and Fig. 2 were created from Zygote human body (20).

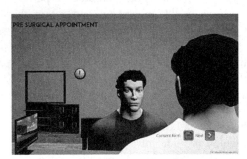
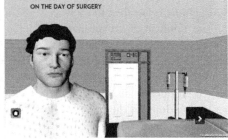

Fig. 1. Pre operative appointment   **Fig. 2.** Patient in hospital gown

In the design of surgical procedures, five surgeries namely, the upper jaw surgery, lower jaw surgery, double jaw surgery, chin surgery and bone graft from hip were represented. This section contains interactive 3D animations that demonstrate bone cuts, movements and final rigid fixation. Patients can also visualize the pre and post-surgical variations for each procedure with the help of a slider interactively as shown in the Fig.3.

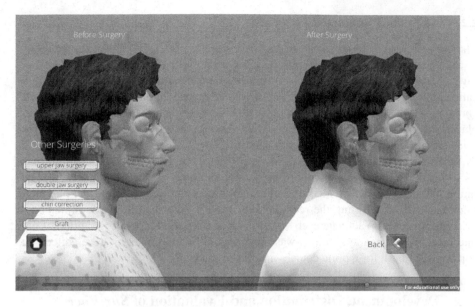

Fig. 3. Slider to show changes in face before and after surgery

Postsurgical complaints like numbness, pain and swelling as shown in fig. 4 were illustrated in a way that the patient is not scared of the procedure, but still gets the knowledge of complications that are involved. To further explain the surgery, verbal instructions without scientific jargon were recorded using Avid Pro tools (21) and Apple Garage Band.

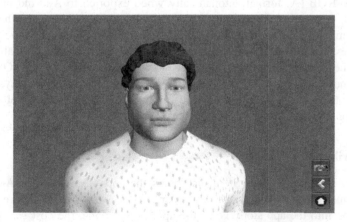

Fig. 4. Swelling after the surgery

2.2   Addition of Interactive Elements

There are various methods to add interactive user elements to 3D model. In the design of Sur-face, Unity 3D game engine was used as it can build mobile apps. It also allows creation of custom animations or import them from third party modeling applications like Maya or 3D Studio Max. In Unity 3D game engine, animation is a game component which can be of Legacy or Mechanim type. These animations can be played automatically or controlled based on a script. Most of the animations in *Sur-Face* are of Legacy type and are script controlled.

When an animation is imported into Unity3D from third party applications, care must be taken regarding the scale of the model and other import settings. Longer duration animations were divided into multiple smaller animations using the play back functionality and selecting the required key frames. After naming each animation, a c# script was used to activate each one of them at a separate instance. Addition of user interface with navigation buttons was done once all the animations were edited. The app was then built for mobile devices and distributed.

3   Development, Distribution and Evaluation of *Sur-Face*

3.1   Development of *Sur-Face*

Before the final Unity project is exported to a mobile platform, software development kit of Android was installed and target device is allocated. The Android developer portal (22) provides more guidance into how to install software development kit. Building the project for mobile devices on Unity 3D needs special attention towards textures, movie playback functionality and scripts (23). Unity 3D compresses all the textures into RGB (A) format automatically when exported to Android or iOS platforms. Also, the size of the texture files will be compressed to reduce the total file size. When movies are imported into Unity, it is possible for the system to apply movie files as textures to the selected game objects. However, this functionality is only limited to the Desktops. Because Sur-Face was built for Android and iOS devices, instead of movie playback, all the animations were either created in Maya or Unity 3D. Prior to the distribution of the app, it was built specifically for tablet devices as the resolution and details were well represented.

3.2   Distribution of *Sur-Face*

Google Play store and iTunes Store distributes the apps developed for Android and iOS platforms respectively (24). A developer account was created before exporting Sur-Face app into the app store. Once the upload was done, the cost was set to free and in 24 hours, it was made available for download. The app was downloaded 167 times till date with most number of downloads from Brazil followed by Russia and United Kingdom. Figure 5 shows the statistics of total installs by users in a month wise manner as represented in Android developer portal.

Fig. 5. Statistics showing total user installs of *Sur-Face* in a month wise manner. Source: Android developer portal (22)

3.3   Evaluation of *Sur-Face*

50 non-patient volunteers were recruited after giving brief overview about the purpose of this research and its scope, focusing on the need for prospective patients to properly understand the information before signing the consent form. Participants were randomly divided into two groups, namely "App" group and "voice" group based on the method used for delivering the instructions. Members of the app group were provided with *Sur-face* on a 10.1-inch Motorola zoom tablet, whereas voice group participants were provided with audio instructions on the same device along with a printed leaflet containing the same content. Instructions were given on navigating the app where and when required. After allowing the participants to use all the modules in the application and listen to all the instructions, they were given a questionnaire to complete. 13 questions were structured, 12 of which focus on the surgical process, side effects and post-operative complications of the surgery, as they are the most important aspect of consent process. One question on the signs of infection was asked to know the extent of knowledge about infection in general. Once the questionnaire was answered, results were analyzed using independent student t test on SPSS (25) to compare the statistical difference between the two groups. Null hypothesis states that, there would be no difference between the participants of app and voice groups. The total number of questions answered and the number of correct answers given by each group was analyzed to represent the understanding and retaining capacity of the participants. The results showed that the participants of the 'app' group have answered significantly ($p=0.0366$) more of number of questions than those in the 'voice' group. Out of 12 questions, the app group has answered an average of 11.12 questions whereas the voice group could answer an average of 9.56. Similarly, participants of the app group have given significantly higher ($p=0.0034$) number of correct answers than the voice group. Out of 12 questions, the app group has answered an average of 9.72 questions correct, where as the voice group has answered 7.64 of them. Hence, null hypothesis can be rejected and we can that interactive 3D visualizations are better than verbal instructions in improving patient understanding of complex surgical instructions. Also the 3D graphical visualizations support patients in remembering the details regarding the procedures.

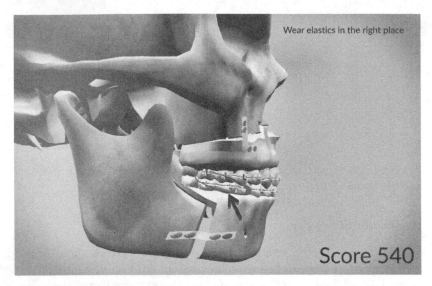

Fig. 6. Gaming elements to help patients wear elastics

4   Conclusion and Future Work

Innovations in technology when applied to healthcare provide a scope for development of novel interaction methods between patients and clinicians. Sur-Face was successful in providing the essential knowledge regarding orthognathic surgery in an interactive manner. 3D visualizations developed under the guidance of the surgeons were accurate in their representation. Additionally, easily understandable voice over instructions helped this app to comprehensively demonstrate the surgical process. Evaluation of the app clearly indicated the advantages of 3D visualizations over 2D graphics and verbal methods. All these findings further strengthen the need for redesigning the consent process. Inclusion of instructions through well-developed mobile apps helps patients to take responsible decisions on their health.

The main aim of the *Sur-Face* app is to provide knowledge regarding the basic surgical procedures and potential postoperative complications to help the patients give a well-understood informed consent. Based on the findings during the process of development, evaluation and user feedback, potential future developments to the current version of the app were charted for it to perform better.

Serious game elements:

Application of gaming elements can provide patients with motivation, control and game based learning. During pre-operative preparation, various steps to be taken by the patient can be represented in the form of buttons.

A right answer increases the score and denotes that the patient is well prepared for the surgery. Inclusion of features like these may reduce pre-operative anxiety in patients. Animations showing the surgical procedure can be made interactive by swipe functionality on touch devices. Similar to gaming, swiping at the right spot moves the bones in right direction. Features like these would help patients to get a deeper insight of the surgery they are about to undergo. As the questionnaire in evaluation of the study has proved that patient education through 3D graphics is significant, a real time quiz to assess patients' knowledge can be very useful. If a patient doesn't answer a question correctly, either because of lack of understanding or their inability to remember, feedback can be provided using audio or verbal aids along with scores. This will indicate their knowledge about the procedure and also reinforces the need for proper expectations about the outcome of the surgery. Image based questions allowing drag and drop features can be added regarding the side effects and complications of surgery. Because the patients will answer these questions interactively, they can remember the post-surgical complications for long. After the surgery, patients are advised to wear elastics in between the teeth to prevent movement of the bones. Post-operative instructions on how to wear elastics can be added using interactive drag feature as shown in the fig. 6. Addition of this feature may help patients to learn complex instructions in a simple and engaging manner.

Further developments:

Animations describing the nature of dentofacial deformity and postoperative instructions help the patient understand what needs to be done after the surgical process. This is very important as proper maintenance after surgery helps in a good recovery.

Leveraging on advances in mobile technology like camera, accelerometer and gyroscope can further enhance its usability. Currently apps like Colorimetrix (26) and Instant Heart Rate (27) use the phone's camera to perform various functions. In a similar way, if a camera on a mobile device could track the skeletal landmarks, it can be used to predict the outcome of the surgery and thereby help patients to get a realistic expectation.

Accessibility to the Internet is one of the key advantages of smart devices. By incorporating search functionality to help user find answers to their questions regarding the surgery makes the app more user friendly.

Access to other third party apps like Calendar, Evernote and Health-kit (28) helps the user to integrate the appointments of the doctor in the same app. These also play a key role to remind the patients about medications.

Evolution of mobile technology into health care has significantly changed the way people make their decisions regarding the treatment. At the pace at which the technology is advancing, there is an increasing need for creation of more apps like Sur-Face with interactive 3D graphics and gaming elements in them.

References

1. Hågensli, N., Stenvik, A., Espeland, L.: Patients offered orthognathic surgery: Why do many refrain from treatment? Journal of Cranio-Maxillofacial Surgery **42**(5), e296–e300 (2014). doi:10.1016/j.jcms.2013.10.009. ISSN 1010-5182
2. Kaplan, S.H., Greenfield, S., Gandek, B., Rogers, W.H., Ware Jr., J.E.: Characteristics of physicians with participatory decision-making styles. Annals of Internal Medicine **124**, 497–504 (1996)
3. Huber, J., Ihrig, A., Yass, M., Bruckner, T., Peters, T., Huber, C.G., Konyango, B., Lozankovski, N., Stredele, R., Moll, P., Schneider, M., Pahernik, S., Hohenfellner, M.: Multimedia support for improving pre-operative patient education: a randomized controlled trial using the example of radical prostatectomy. Annals of Surgical Oncology **20**, 15–23 (2012)
4. Robinson, R.C., Holm, R.L.: Orthognathic surgery for patients with Maxillofacial deformities. AORN J **92**, 28–49 (2010). doi:10.1016/j.aorn.2009.12.030. © AORN, Inc, 2010
5. Hussain, W.I.: How Apple's Health app and Health kit affects physicians (2014). http://www.imedicalapps.com/2014/06/apple-health-app-healthkit-physicians/ (accessed on June 7, 2014)
6. Krauser, H., Bremerich, A., Rustemeyer, J.: Reasons for patients' discontent and litigation. J. Cranio Maxillofac Surg. **29**, 181–183 (2001)
7. Wordford, L.M., Fields, R.T.: Maxillofacial Surgery, p. 1205. Churchill Livingstone, Philadelphia (1999)
8. Jones, J.M., Nyhof-young, J., Friedman, A., Catton, P.: More than just a pamphlet: development of an innovative computer-based education program for cancer patients. Patient Educ Couns **44**(3), 271–281 (2001). http://dx.doi.org/10.1016/S0738-3991(00)00204-4, 2001 Sep S0738399100002044
9. Muslow, J., Feeley, M., Tierney, S.: Beyond consent: improving understanding in surgical patients. Am J. Surg. **203**, 112–120 (2012)
10. Aseem, A.E., Benington, P.C.M., Khambay, B.S., Ayoub, A.F.: Evaluation of an interactive multi-media device for delivering information on Le Fort I osteotomy. Journal of CranioMaxilloFacial Surgery (2014). http://dx.doi.org/10.1016/j.jcms.2014.01.004
11. Nucleus Medical Media: Animations for patient education (2014). http://www.nucleusanimationlibrary.com (accessed on September 26, 2014)
12. 3D4 Medical: Essential Anatomy 5 (2014). http://applications.3d4medical.com/essential_anatomy_5/ (accessed on June 9, 2014)
13. IMS Healthcare Informatics: Patient Apps for Improved Healthcare: From Novelty to Mainstream. Report by the IMS Institute for Healthcare Informatics (2013)
14. Kinosis. Inc.: Touch Surgery (2015). https://www.touchsurgery.com (accessed on November 23, 2014)
15. 3D4 Medical: Dental Patient Education (2014). http://applications.3d4medical.com/downloads/press/Dental%20Patient%20Education%20-%20List%20of%20Animations.pdf (accessed on June 9, 2014)
16. Dolphin Imaging and Management solutions (2014). http://www.dolphinimaging.com/3d.html (accessed on June 3, 2014)
17. Alkharafi, L., Alhajery, D., Andersson, L.: Orthognathic Surgery: Pretreatment Information and Patient Satisfaction. Med. Princ. Pract. **23**(3), 218–224 (2014). doi:10.1159/000360735. Epub 2014 Apr 16

18. Hu, J., Yu, H., Shao, J., Li, Z., Wang, J., Wanga, Y.: An evaluation of the Dental 3D Multimedia System on dentist–patient inter- actions: a report from China. International Journal of Medical Informatics **77**, 670–678 (2008)
19. Autodesk Maya 2014. http://www.autodesk.co.uk/products/maya/overview (accessed on August 3, 2014)
20. Zygote media group: Polygonal 3D Models for Animators and Illustrators (2014). http://www.3dscience.com/3D_Models/Human_Anatomy/index.php (accessed on June 30, 2014)
21. Avid Pro tools: http://www.avid.com/UK/products/family/Pro-Tools (accessed on June 26, 2014)
22. Android development (2014). http://developer.android.com/index.html (accessed on August 3, 2014)
23. Unity 3D (2014). http://unity3d.com (accessed on June 26, 2014)
24. Google Play Store (2015). https://play.google.com/store?hl=en_GB (accessed on August 3, 2014)
25. IBM Inc.: SPSS software- Predictive analysis software solutions. http://www-01.ibm.com/software/uk/analytics/spss/ (accessed on May 23, 2015)
26. University of Cambridge: Pocket diagnosis: App turns any smartphone into a portable medical diagnostic device (2014). http://www.sciencedaily.com/releases/2014/03/140319103612.htm (accessed on August 13, 2014)
27. Instant Heart Rate (2014). http://www.azumio.com/apps/heart-rate/ (accessed on August 13, 2014)
28. Ryan Tate: Apple Health kit. Wired (2014). http://www.wired.com/2014/03/apple-healthbook-is-just-the-beginning/ (accessed on December 16, 2014)

ALFRED Back Trainer: Conceptualization of a Serious Game-Based Training System for Low Back Pain Rehabilitation Exercises

Sandro Hardy[1(✉)], Florian Feldwieser[2], Tim Dutz[1], Stefan Göbel[1],
Ralf Steinmetz[1], and Elisabeth Steinhagen-Thiessen[2]

[1] Multimedia Communications Lab – KOM,
Technische Universität Darmstadt, Darmstadt, Germany
{sandro.hardy,tim.dutz,stefan.goebel,
ralf.steinmetz}@KOM.tu-darmstadt.de
[2] Geriatrics Research Group, Department of Geriatric Medicine,
Charité - Universitätsmedizin Berlin, Berlin, Germany
{florian.feldwieser,elisabeth.steinhagen-thiessen}@charite.de

Abstract. Low back pain is common medical problem and often recurrent. Within the EU-funded project ALFRED, a serious game-based exercise regime focusing on the prevention and rehabilitation of lower back pain is currently being developed. This Serious Game tries to combine high player motivation with high training effects while using low cost technology and commercial game controllers. The exercise goals and assessment metrics of the Serious Game are elaborated by medical experts to allow scientifically based training while the training effects shall be increased by using state of the art technology for the personalization and adaptation of the training process. In this contribution we describe a prototypical approach which combines the use of widespread physiotherapeutic exercises (bridging exercises) in combination with biofeedback training. This approach aims to improve symmetrical function of the paraspinal muscles and improve overall muscle coordination which is important for optimal functioning of the lower back area.

Keywords: Serious games · Exercise · Biofeedback · Low back pain

1 Introduction

Lack of exercise is a well-known and worldwide phenomenon: Half of the ten most serious diseases are caused by a lack of exercise or can be alleviated by a sufficient amount of physical activity [2]. In the European Union, 60% of the inhabitants rarely or never participate in sports and this amount decreases uniformly with age. At the age of 70 and above only 22% of the population still do sufficient sporting activities according to the current recommended exercise guidelines [2, 8]. Possible reasons for this increasing inactivity are age-related limited mobility, gait impairments or other physical or mental limitations. Due to these facts and emphasized by the demographic

© Springer International Publishing Switzerland 2015
S. Göbel et al. (Eds.): JCSG 2015, LNCS 9090, pp. 36–47, 2015.
DOI: 10.1007/978-3-319-19126-3_4

developments - the need for appropriate training programs and technologies to preserve mobility and enhance physical health is obvious. Successful commercial movement and reaction games (exergames) such as Wii Fit – originally developed for pure entertainment – are promising motivational instruments also in movement therapy and rehabilitation, or as a training option in senior homes [10].

However, scientific studies show measurable training effects of exergames [1]. Based on these findings they could be a successful approach to improve peoples' health status. Further studies show that the effectiveness (e.g. in terms of short-term energy expenditure or long term training effects) of commercial entertainment games as training tool is lower than the impact of classic training [11]. A major drawback of commercial exergames is that they are not optimized for specific target user groups, purposes and corresponding training programs. Furthermore, they do not adequately consider personal characteristics or individual needs such as the vital state of the players or patients [4]. Domain experts such as medical doctors, therapists or scientists in sports and health underline the potential of game-based approaches (primarily for motivational reasons) on the one hand and simultaneously postulate the need for scientifically grounded, personalized training plans and programs for specific purposes and targeted user groups on the other hand. Therefore, appropriate tools and user interfaces enabling experts (e.g. therapists) to author and configure the programs 'on the fly' in daily practice would be extremely helpful.

Throughout society, low back pain (LBP) is a common medical problem and often recurrent. During their lifetime, 60-80% of the population will experience LBP at least once and up to 86% of these people will have another episode at some point. 90% of all LBP patients experience non-specific back pain and present no imaging results or other currently diagnosable diseases. The presence of clinical spinal instability is one possible cause for LBP. A decrease of the ability of the spinal muscles to stabilize the system of the spine due to pain or deconditioning can lead to damage of the spinal structures and therefore can be the cause for LBP. In turn, increased spinal stability can be achieved by training specific spinal muscles [3]. Exercise therapy is one of the most commonly used conservative treatments for LBP and has been proven to be effective at decreasing pain and improving function in chronic LBP patients and to a certain degree in sub-acute LBP patients [9]. With the help of a serious game-based biofeedback exercise system, activation and growth of the stabilizing spinal muscles could be achieved and thus lead to an overall reduction of LBP.

2   Methodology

The proposed exercise system is developed within the EU-funded project ALFRED[1] and tries to combine high motivation as well as high training effects while using low cost technology such as the Nintendo Wii balance board. The goal of the game is to control the center of pressure (COP) while performing a bridging exercise on two balance boards. This is achieved by controlling the body position accordingly to the

---

[1] www.alfred.eu

biofeedback provided by the game. The training goals and assessment metrics of the serious game are elaborated by medical experts from the Charité in Berlin, Germany, to allow medically founded training while the training effects shall be increased using state of the art technology for the personalization and adaptation of the training process.

Fig. 1. Bridging exercises for low back training, performed on two balance boards as they will be realized in the ALFRED Back Trainer assisted with game based visual feedback

Bridging exercises aim at strengthening the low back muscles, hip muscles, the gluteus and the hamstrings. Regularly, these exercises are performed on a flat ground. Many variations are possible depending on the focus of the training. In general, we can differentiate between static and dynamic exercises. Static exercises focus on keeping a specified position for a longer period of time while dynamic exercises require physical movement.

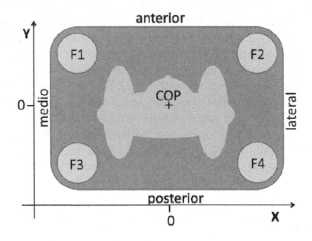

Fig. 2. Schematic drawing of a person standing on a balance board while performing balance training exercises. F_1- F_4: the forces measured by the four pressure sensors of the board.

For the assessment of the quality of movement during the exercises assessment metrics from the field of balance training will be considered and extended as needed. The center of pressure (COP) can be calculated as a position (x, y) from the weight distribution on a balance board (Figure 2) according to equation 1. While using two balance boards for the bridging exercise we can calculate the (COP) for the shoulders (COP_s) as well as for the feet (COP_f).

Center of Pressure (COP) (1)

$$COP = (x, y) = \left(\frac{(F_2 + F_4) - (F_1 + F_3)}{\sum F_i}, \frac{(F_1 + F_2) - (F_3 + F_4)}{\sum F_i} \right)$$

Anterior-Posterior Stability Index (APSI) (2)

$$APSI = \sqrt{\frac{\sum_{i=1}^{n} x_i^2}{n}}$$

Medio-Lateral Stability Index (MLSI) (3)

$$MLSI = \sqrt{\frac{\sum_{i=1}^{n} y_i^2}{n}}$$

Overall Stability Index (OSI) (4)

$$OSI = \sqrt{\frac{\sum_{i=1}^{n} x_i^2 + \sum_{i=1}^{n} y_i^2}{n}}$$

Area of Sway (5)

$$AS = (x_{max} - x_{min}) * (y_{max} - y_{min})$$

Sway Path (SP) (6)

$$SP = \sum_{i=1}^{n-1} \sqrt{(x_{i+1} - x_i)^2 + (y_{i+1} - y_i)^2}$$

Based on the COP, several parameters can be investigated to provide relevant hints about the physical performance of players. The Anterior-Posterior Stability Index (APSI, equation 2), Medio-Lateral Stability Index (MLSI, equation 3) and Overall Stability Index (OSI, equation 4) as a combination of APSI and MLSI provide metrics for the stability of the movement. The area of sway (equation 5) and the length of the sway path (SP, equation 6) might allow quantifying the error of movement, especially if taken into account in relation to the minimal/optimal way of movement. Therefore they will be considered as possible surrogate parameters to describe the skill and performance level of a player while exercising. Since all of these parameters are derived from regular balance training exercises, further research is needed to investigate the question of their applicability to the bridging exercises (Fig. 1) of the ALFRED Back Trainer, and furthermore, if the suggested separation between COP_f and COP_s allows adequate feedback in the developed games.

2.1   Technology and Framework

The Nintendo Wii balance boards used have four pressure sensors to measure the weight distribution of the player lying on the board. Based on the weight distribution, the center of pressure (COP) will be calculated which is used as input to control the game. The training system will involve two balance boards that need to be operated simultaneously. Contact points between the user and the board are the shoulders and feet, with the user lying on her back (Figure 1).

2.2   Adaptation and Personalization Approach

The scientific foundations from sport science show the demand to put focus on the question how exergames can motivate the user to interact in a way that this interaction complies with the identified training principles, since fulfilling the training principles is the first step to gain high training effects (as far as the underlying training principles are proven to be effective). The interaction therefore must meet the skill level of the individual user in order to provide adequate training stimuli. These training stimuli trigger the physical adaptation process of the player's body, e.g. increasing the strength and endurance of the low back muscles. Since the personal skill level differentiates between players, the interaction which is a substantial part of the gameplay needs to be individualized for every single player. The ALFRED Back Trainer follows the 3-Layer approach [7] for the adaptation of exergames shown in Figure 2. The used framework does not include concrete concepts or approaches for the adaptation and personalization process, but describes the context for the development of such approaches. The concrete instantiations of the adaptation and personalization algorithms will be developed in the project. This allows the further adaptation of basic models which focus on only one relevant domain. The Gameflow Concept [13], for example, is an approach that focuses only on Game Experience and different health recommendations [8] focus only on the health/sports domain. In this specific case, the ALFRED Back Trainer aims at motivating the player in a way which leads to optimal training effects. The Dual Flow Model [12] is a step to bring together both goals. As explained in [7], we expect that the used game controller (sensors, actuators and hardware) influence the user experience as well as the training while the training and the user experience influence each other (Figure 2, Layer "User Experience" and Layer "Training"). For the ALFRED Back Trainer e.g. different types of controllers or even a combination of different controller types could be used and evaluated. These might influence the user experience as well as the measurable parameters and therefore the interaction and by this also the performance of the players. For the selection of the controller hardware, different aspects play an important role. Beyond the measurement capabilities and data quality provided by the sensors of the game controller, also the cost and availability play an important role. For the ALFRED Back Trainer, the Wii balance boards act as mobile low cost force plates. The measurements capabilities seem to be sufficient and the price is low while the availability in different European countries is very good. Since the balance boards, in contrast to regular force plates, are not on floor level, a very thin foam plate will be put on the top of both boards to allow for a more comfortable position.

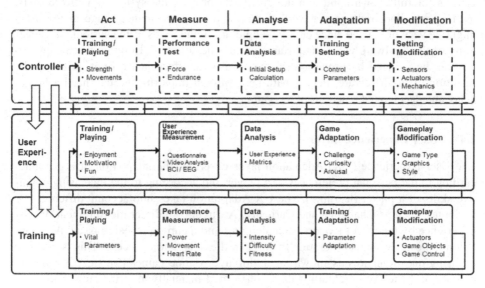

Fig. 3. Modified 3-Layer Approach for the adaptation and personalization of the ALFRED Back Trainer, based on the framework for personalized exergames [7]

In order to embed movement information in real-time in a game and in order to provide a precise movement control and feedback, the used sensors and the data processing chain need to work with high accuracy, low delay and sufficient sampling rates. Depending on the training goals, sensors applied in professional sports or amateur sports can be used or cheap alternatives, such as the used balance board, might be an alternative. The underlying model [7] for the use of sensors for the adaptation of exergames to a specific use (training goal) consists of the three layers Controller, User Experience Adaptation and Training Adaptation. These layers need to be considered separately, but they are interdependent. The term 'adaptation' describes if a system can be modified to fulfill a specified goal. The term 'personalization' is used if this adaptation takes into account individual attributes of multiple users. Figure 2 sketches the interdependencies among the different layers and the workflow within the layers.

2.3   Controller Layer

The layer 'Controller' describes the adaptation of the used game controller, more specifically the used mechanics, sensors, and actuators, as well as signal processing units according to the physical constitution of the player. In the general model this includes the stature, physical limitations and partly performance describing parameters such as maximum force. The goal of the constitutional adaptation is to adapt the whole hardware system to the physical preconditions of the player. The two balance boards used for the ALFRED Back Trainer allow a maximum weight of

150kg each and the distance between the two boards can be varied. This allows the application of the developed game for children and young adults (smaller people) as well as for full grown adults. In the ALFRED project, the system is targeted to be used by non-impaired users, nevertheless, since the performance range of the users might be very broad and since elderly people are in the focus of the system, the sensitivity of the hardware will be adjustable within the software. Limited visual capabilities can be covered by providing a suitable user interface and do not influence the selection of the hardware. People with perceptional impairments may need a higher delay and decelerated reactions of the game.

2.4   User Experience Layer

The User Experience (UX) Adaptation layer describes the adaptation of a game according to the personal preferences of a player and according to the increasing cognitive skills of a player (learning). The UX Adaptation takes into account different UX attributes, such as Challenge and Curiosity. A direct or indirect measurement of user experience by the use of sensors is challenging and a current research issue. An adaptation is possible by incorporating the user in the adaptation process. This is possible by using questionnaires as shown for multiplayer online games [9]. In ALFRED the process of difficulty adaptation will be performed manually at a first step. The Challenge of the games will be adjusted by changing the sensitivity and responsiveness of the balance boards. To address the Curiosity a set of games with increasing complexity will be provided. Based on this first approach methodologies of the automatic adaptation of the games will be investigated.

The first step in the UX adaptation process is the selection of an appropriate game from a set of games which meet the specified training goal. Within the ALFRED project, a component called "Game Manger" performs this step and this task is not an issue of the ALFRED Back Trainer.

A precise analysis and differentiation of the UX relevant attributes is suggested. To assess fun questionnaires will be used, for the UX aspect of challenge the gained points per time unit can be taken into account, but this is not necessarily corresponding to the experienced challenge or success level. Based on the measurements and on user ratings (perceived user experience) another game can be suggested or the game can be adapted. The methodologies for the adaptation and personalization of the games are planned to be developed within the ALFRED project.

2.5   Training Adaptation

The adaptation layer called "Training Adaptation" describes the adaptation of the game to the requirements posed by sport science. This layer consists of two adaptation loops, one short-term loop (real-time, during the runtime of a game) and one long-term loop (adaptation between two training sessions). While the requirements posed by sport science have been described in section 2, the technical issues of adaptation by using sensor-measured vital parameters are focused here. Sensors in exergames generally measure kinematics and kinetics of human limbs or the full body.

This data is sampled related to behaviors of virtual objects inside a game. The behavior of virtual objects in a game can be used to communicate different types of feedback (visual, auditory, haptic) about bodily movements to a player. The Training Adaptation can be done by the modification of parameter values, more specifically by changing the relations between game objects and therefore their behavior. These parameters are called Training Control parameters.

The ALFRED back trainer will provide the Training Control parameters, sensitivity and difficulty, similar as other prototypes based on the same technology do [5, 6]. Sensitivity (s) is the transformation factor between measured Force (F) and virtual movement (rotation, translation) of the game object. With a given Force, a higher sensitivity implies a greater reaction in the game. Depending on the sensitivity value more or less force and therefore strength is needed to move the object over a defined distance. Thus, the player has to move in a bigger (or smaller) area of sway. The difficulty is a parameter for the control skills (coordination, reaction) of the player.

Sensitivity s

$$M = s * F \qquad (7)$$

In order to respect the assumptions and models described in Sections 3.3 and 3.4 the developed serious game is based on a technical architecture called StoryTecRT which allows the adaptation during the games are played. This allows e.g. to exchange textures and therefore to modify the design of the game without changing the gameplay. By changing some texture and sound assets e.g. the two different versions A and B of the same game can be realized easily e.g. to compare two stimuli (such as positive user feedback in variant A through gain points, funny symbols, nice sounds and negative player feedback in variant B through loose points, dark symbols, bad sound) with exactly the same gameplay [5]. This provides the opportunity to evaluate the effects of different operationalizations of single psychological constructs which explain the mode of action of game experience.

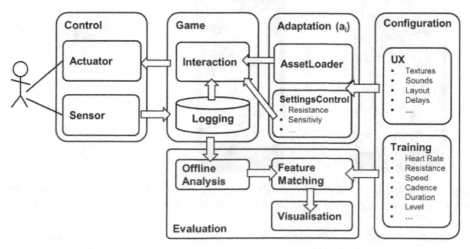

Fig. 4. StoryTecRT, Technology Framework for the Adaptation and Personalization of Exergames [5]

The adjustment of the training load is a challenging problem. The demand from the domain of sports science to adjust the training load in a wide range was concluded in Section 3.4, because the training load is directly correlated to the training effect (among other aspects). Otherwise a high training load can increase the difficulty level. This could lead to overcharging the player and therefore decrease the game experience, respectively result in lacking acceptance of the game at all. Therefore we decide to evaluate the acceptance and game experience of games, developed based on our approaches first. Afterwards we can use these findings as a baseline for future measurements with different concept and methodologies for the adaptation and personalization of the training load in these games.

3   First Prototypes

To keep the hardware costs low for the developed prototype, two regular Wii balance boards are used as game controllers. Both will be attached using an OTG-USB-Cable and a separate Bluetooth dongle since Android does not allow L2CAP connections with the regular Bluetooth stack since version 4.2. The games will be programmed with the Game Engine Unity3D since the used Framework StoryTecRT was developed for Unity3D. First experiments with simple visualizations (Fig. 5) show that the sensitivity of the pressure sensors integrated in the balance boards as well as the delay of the controllers seem to be sufficient to allow adequate feedback to the users. The integration of the different exercise routines seamlessly into a serious game seems to become a challenging task. We considered different possible gameplays. All of them have different shortcomings, therefore several minigames with different foci will be realized. The basic approach visualizes both measured COPs (Fig. 5, left).

Fig. 5. Visualization of the COP_s and COP_f (left), a possible visualization for static COP control (center) and a possible visualization for movements of multiple joints (right)

This allows very simple feedback which is needed to evaluate the measurability of the correctness during developing the specific exercises. Of course, this visualization by itself is just very simple feedback and not a game. Since all the exercises aim at controlling the COP, the game concept needs to stimulate the player to keep and to move both the centers of pressure of hip and shoulder in a defined way. For keeping the COP of in general the metaphor "balancing" seems to be intuitively understandable. Nevertheless, the visualization shown in Figure 5 (center), center allows to represent only one COP and only one stabilization axis. Combining two single but similar or equal visualizations, which both represent one single COP, results in a gameplay with two cognitively different tasks. The player would have to transfer two different visualizations into one motoric movement and therefore she would need to switch her focus between two different feedback items. This seems to be not optimal for high focus and high immersion. The extreme opposite is the visualization of the full skeleton of the player in example as puppet which should be controlled according to the gameplay. This visualization technically allows representing all joints of a human skeleton in all three axes, although probably not all joints will be part of the gameplay. The next step will be to identify optimal training exercises and to classify them according to the number of joints involved. We will then perform these exercises correctly and we will simulate major errors, while measuring the movements with the balance boards. The recorded data will be analyzed in order to provide us with sufficient information to find suitable visualizations.

4   Evaluation

A first prototype was implemented allowing to visualize the COP_s and COP_f (Fig 5. left). This prototype allows medical professionals to control visually the movements of the COP while first test users perform possible exercise on the balance boards. In this way real movements as well as the measured data can be observed synchronously. First qualitative test show that the sensitivity of the whole system seems to be sufficient to provide adequate feedback to the user. The different weights of individuals do not seem to be an influencing factor. At the moment, there are no adaptation and personalization algorithms integrated in the prototype. Therefore the visualization depends on the maximum performance of the users. First qualitative results show that normalization with the maximum performance, e.g. the maximum sway area (formula 5), might improve the feedback. The height of the bridging position cannot be controlled by using just the two balance boards. Further studies are planned to find out the impact of this problem. Quantitative evaluations are planned within the project but are not yet performed.

5   Summary and Outlook

In this paper we present a new application example, the ALFRED Back Trainer based on the previously published framework StoryTecRT for the development and use of personalized and adaptive game-based training programs in health sport. The approach allows the inclusion of experts from different domains. In contrast to existing approaches, the underlying framework StoryTecRT supports the creation and configuration of scientifically founded games for different training goals and the configuration of personalized training plans. More specifically, the framework allows the separation between three adaptation layers and identifies the corresponding adaptation parameters.

Altogether, the framework enables the creation and (adaptive) control of personal, game-based and technology-enhanced training programs for different training goals and user groups. In addition, further research will be conducted to develop models for the identification of relations and effects of single adaptation parameters within the concrete application scenario low back training. An additional goal is the integration of fine-grained concepts for the automatic adaptation and the measurement of their effects.

Acknowledgements. This research was partially financed by the European Commission under the FP7-ICT Project ALFRED (grant agreement no. 611218). We also owe our thanks to Polona Caserman, Constantin Franz, Kubra Kelly, Gerdi Panagiotopoulos and Alexander Schmitt for their support of this work.

References

1. Brumels, K.A., Blasius, T., Cortright, T., Oumedian, D., Solberg, B.: Comparison of efficacy between traditional and video game based balance programs. Clinical Kinesiology: Journal of the American Kinesiotherapy Association, **62**(4), (December 2008)
2. Etienne, C., Asamoa-Baah, A.: The World Health Report: Health System Financing: The Path to Universal Coverage. W.H.O. (2010)
3. Freeman, M.D., Woodham, M.A., Woodham, A.W.: The role of the lumbar multifidus in chronic low back pain: A review. PM&R **2**(2), 142–146 (2009)
4. Göbel, S., Hardy, S., Wendel, V., Mehm, F., Steinmetz, R.: Serious games for health: personalized exergames. In: Proceedings of the International Conference on Multimedia, MM 2010, New York, NY, USA, pp. 1663–1666. ACM (2010)
5. Hardy, S., Göbel, S., Steinmetz, R.: Adaptable and personalized game-based training system for fall prevention. In: Proceedings of the 21st ACM International Conference on Multimedia, MM 2013, New York, NY, USA, pp. 431–432. ACM (2013)
6. Hardy, S., Kern, A., Dutz, T., Weber, C., Göbel, S., Steinmetz, R.: What makes games challenging?: Considerations on how to determine the "challenge" posed by an exergame for balance training. In: Proceedings of the 2014 ACM International Workshop on Serious Games, SeriousGames 2014, New York, NY, USA, pp. 57–62. ACM (2014)
7. Hardy, S., Wiemeyer, J., Göbel, S., Steinmetz, R.: Framework for personalized and adaptive game-based training programs in health sport. Multimedia Tools and Applications (2013)
8. Haskell, W.L., Lee, I.-M., Pate, R.R., Powell, K.E., Blair, S.N., Franklin, B.A., Macera, C.A., Heath, G.W., Thompson, P.D., Bauman, A.: Physical activity and public health: Updated recommendation for adults from the american college of sports medicine and the american heart association. Physical Activity and Public Health **116**(9), 1081–1093 (2007)
9. Hoy, D., Brooks, P., Blyth, F., Buchbinder, R.: The epidemiology of low back pain. Best Practice & Reserach Clinical Rheumatology **24**, 769–781 (2010)

10. Jung, Y., Li, K.J., Janissa, N.S., Gladys, W.L.C., Lee, K.M.: Games for a better life: effects of playing wii games on the well-being of seniors in a long-term care facility. In: Proceedings of the Sixth Australasian Conference on Interactive Entertainment, IE 2009, New York, NY, USA, pp. 5:1–5:6. ACM (2009)
11. Kliem, A., Wiemeyer, J.: Comparison of a traditional and a video game based balance training program. International Journal of Computer Science in Sport **9**(Special Edition), 80–91 (2010)
12. Sinclair, J., Hingston, P., Masek, M.: Exergame development using the dual flow model. In: Proceedings of the Sixth Australasian Conference on Interactive Entertainment, IE 2009, New York, NY, USA, pp. 11:1–11:7. ACM (2009)
13. Sweetser, P., Wyeth, P.: Gameflow: A model for evaluating player enjoyment in games. Comput. Entertain. **3**(3), 3 (2005)

Games for Learning

From Game Characteristics to Effective Learning Games

Evaluation of a Component-Based Quiz Game

Philip Mildner[✉], Nicolas Stamer, and Wolfgang Effelsberg

University of Mannheim, Mannheim, Germany
{mildner,effelsberg}@informatik.uni-mannheim.de
nistamer@mail.uni-mannheim.de

Abstract. When developing learning games, emphasis should not only be put on a good integration of the learning content, but also on an engaging game design, in order to create learning tools that both train and motivate. In this paper, we examine the influence of specific game elements to both factors. Therefore, we first analyze models for the characterization of game elements. We then apply an adapted model to the design of a component-based learning game based on a quiz. Various game elements can be added to the game dynamically. This includes, among others, different forms of presentation, challenge, competition and constraints. Using this application we performed a user study to evaluate which game elements are most effective in delivering knowledge as well as in fostering motivation. Results show that a combination of game elements is suited best for influencing both factors positively.

1 Introduction

Digital learning games have become a common tool to deliver knowledge in a playful manner. One key aspect of them being created is the strong motivational factor that such games raise in players. Ideally, learning games foster the intrinsic motivation of players to learn and acquire more knowledge. However, while pure entertainment games evolved to a mass market attracting millions of players each day, learning games are still a niche market. This has several reasons. First, developing a learning game does not only involve the creation of an engaging gameplay. It also depends on a meaningful inclusion of the learning content. This content may be specialized or change frequently, making the game creation process costly. To overcome this, authoring tools have been developed that allow non-professional game creators such as teachers to create their own games in a convenient way. E.g., in previous work we presented game frameworks that allow for the integration of arbitrary learning content without the need of programming any game content [1,2]. However, there is another reason for learning games not being as successful as entertainment games. Due to limited budgets, the majority of games are developed with the primary focus on the integration of the learning content. This often leaves the fun parts of the game behind and thus does not cause that much motivation in players.

© Springer International Publishing Switzerland 2015
S. Göbel et al. (Eds.): JCSG 2015, LNCS 9090, pp. 51–62, 2015.
DOI: 10.1007/978-3-319-19126-3_5

When looking at specific game elements, not every element yields the same motivational aspects for all players. So when creating a learning game, designers have to decide on which elements to put emphasize, especially when dealing with limited development resources. Should much development effort be put into a visually pleasing graphical presentation of the game, or should the effort better be put into developing a multiplayer functionality? Is it better to have tight integration of learning and game parts, or will users be fine with having only some small motivational elements on top of a normal learning application? In this paper we examine this topic. After a look at related work in Section 2, we present a model for characterizing game elements in Section 3. We use the characteristics presented by Charsky [3] and extend them with the yet not considered element of *presentation*. Based on this model we then present a component-based learning game that is described in Section 4. It builds up on a simple quiz to that various game elements are added. Instead of evaluating a game as a whole, this modular game allows us to evaluate each game element on its own. By doing so, we can test which game elements have the highest influence on the perceived learning outcome and to the motivation of players. The evaluation of the conducted user study is presented in Section 5.

2   Related Work

Apart from Charsky's model of game characteristics [3] that is further explained in Section 2, similar models were introduced recently. Hunicke et al. presented the MDA framework which looks at game characteristics both from a designer and a consumer perspective [4]. Sweetser and Wyeth proposed a model for elements that create enjoyment in games called *GameFlow* [5]. It uses the flow theory [6] and distinguishes between eight elements: concentration, challenge, skills, control, clear goals, feedback, immersion and social interaction. Similar work is done by Cowley et al. who as well transfer the flow theory to video games [7]. These models deal with video games in general and thus do not take into account the learning aspect. Mitgutsch and Alvarado propose a *Serious Game Design Assessment Framework* to not only look at the content of serious games but also at their design [8]. Therefore, they work with six components: purpose, content, fiction/narrative, mechanics, aesthetics/graphics and framing. This categorization is used to evaluate existing games as a whole but not the isolated components. Other models concentrate on the distinction between *play* and *game*. Songer and Miyata argue to move away from using simple game elements often found in gamification approaches [9] and move to a "gameful" experience that fosters intrinsic motivation of players [10]. They propose a playful affordances model that builds around the elements contest, sensation, exploration and imagination. A similar approach is done by Lucero et al. in their *PLEX framework* [11]. It uses *experiences* taken from well-known entertainment video games and has the goal to not only use the restricted form of games found in gamification approaches but to use playfulness, non-restricted play that is spontaneous and not as much bound to rules.

Building up on the aforementioned models, several studies in the field of characterizing components in serious games have been conducted. Plass et al. evaluated an educational mathematics video game where both motivational aspects and learning performance are considered [12]. They used one game with different modes of player interaction, namely individual, competitive and collaborative gameplay. As a result, the competitive mode yields the highest learning performance, while collaborative gameplay helps to increase the long-term motivation of players. In another study Lomas et al. evaluated the connection of challenge to player engagement [13] using the "Inverted-U Hypothesis" [14]. Evaluating different levels of challenge in an online flash game on mathematics, they could not verify this thesis and instead stated that the easier the game is, the longer players continue to play it. As with the previous study they also enabled different game elements throughout the study, including time restrictions and a wider range of possible game actions. The elements of perceived challenge and performance are evaluated by Hardy et al., too [15]. Their study looks at influences of game elements to the perceived difficulty in an exergame. While these studies offer valuable results for specific aspects of game characterizations, still more work should be put into examining characteristics such as different presentation modes of learning games in order to get a deeper understanding how to optimize the effectiveness of learning games.

3   Game Characteristics

Enhancing the fun of a game leads to a higher motivation and therefore, the user is more engaged in playing. Malone even uses the terms "fun", "interesting" and "intrinsically motivating" synonymously [16]. Historically, he only established three categories of game characteristics in 1981: challenge, fantasy and curiosity. This categorization has been extended by Charsky, who considers five elements [3], or by Hunicke et al. whose MDA framework considers eight aesthetic components [4]. Compared to the model by Mitgutsch and Alvarado [8], *mechanics* would be the closest match of topics, but with their model there is no strict categorization of the actual game mechanics.

According to Charsky, the category of *competition and goals* is one of the most important, as almost every game incorporates elements of them [3]. Goals and competition are interrelated, as competition is established when there are rivals, both non-human ("player vs. computer") and human ("player vs. player") as well as "racing against the clock". *Rules* are another game characteristic that is used in almost every game. Setting up rules often makes a game unique, as rules give a "play" a structure [17]. As related to the aforementioned competition, rules are able to make a game fair for the whole game community, e.g., when participating in highscore rankings. The third characteristic is the characteristic of *choice*. It is similar to the term "control" that is used by other researchers as Malone [18]. Choice means to give the player the possibility to choose different options in order to accomplish a goal, so there is no single path that ensures a success but multiple paths. The characteristic of *challenge* describes a problem that demands the player's ability. The definition of games by Schell, calling a game a "problem-solving activity approached with a playful attitude", identifies challenges as a main element of games [19]. Challenge is closely related to the flow theory, as players have to have the right level of challenge to be in the flow channel [5–7]. *Fantasy* is the last game characteristic that Charsky lists. Fantasy elements try to motivate players, because they strengthen the aspect of identification with special characters of the game. They can also be an essential part that makes the difference of two or more games (e.g., fantasy vs. science-fiction setting). That makes players more involved in the game and also helps to create a playful/gameful experience [10,11]. Other frameworks such as the MDA framework look at the game experience more closely by distinguishing between social aspects, narrative elements and simple pastime components [4].

Apart from the previously presented game characteristics, we use another one related to the aesthetics/graphics component of Mitgutsch and Alvarado's model [8]. The aforementioned characteristics are intended to give play a structure, to raise motivation and to generate fun. But the first barrier of a game is the presentation. If the presentation of a game does not take a player's fancy, he or she will quickly lose interest in playing the game or will not even start playing it. This theory is also supported by Davis' Technology Acceptance Model [20]. The author investigates the motivation of the user to use technology, but not especially games. As games are a subset of technology, however, the implications are true for games as well. The "perceived ease of use" of a game is directly influenced by several design elements. If these are not satisfying, the player's "perceived usefulness" as well as the "attitude toward using" is lowered. As playing is generally associated with leisure, the usefulness of a game is assessed low by implication. That makes the factor of ease of use even more important. Therefore, providing a game with a clear design which is also intuitive, is an essential part of increasing the motivation of a (potential) user. Beside graphics, appearance and usability, presentation also considers the sound of the game and the type of input device a player can control, because they are able to enhance the feeling of immersion which means that a player gets deeply involved in a game.

4   Implementation of a Component-Based Serious Game

In order to test different game characteristics, we implemented a quiz game called *Quiz+* that incorporates various game elements. The game is implemented on the Android platform to provide players with a well-known usability pattern compared to similar games. The basis is a quiz that consists of one question and four answers of which one is correct. Questions can be entered by instructors in a web-based tool. Users then can download new question sets and store them in a local database for offline usage. Furthermore, a tutorial is implemented that describes the different game mode to new users.

The game is built out of different components that can be enabled or disabled during runtime. By providing different game characteristics which can be set individually, the short-term and long-term motivation of a player can be increased. It also serves as an evaluation platform as all mixes of game elements can be considered individually without having to alter the actual implementation.

4.1 Components

As described in Section 3, there are various characteristics that should be considered in game design. In the following, all components that are built into the game and that can be switched on or off during the game are presented.

Presentation. Since the basic game mechanics of a quiz are given, the first element focuses on the representation of the game. To provide the user with different possibilities to answer a question, there are two presentation modes implemented: *Text* and *Three in a Row*.

In the *Text* mode, the appearance is very straightforward. The player can see the question and four answers in boxes (see Figure 1a). To give an answer, he or she simply has to click on one box.

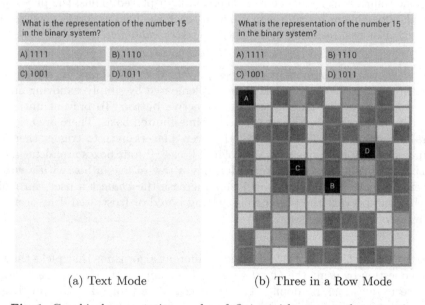

(a) Text Mode   (b) Three in a Row Mode

Fig. 1. Graphical presentation modes of *Quiz+* with an exemplary question

The *Three in a Row* mode inherits the element of the text mode, so the questions and the four answers are presented at the top of the screen. Furthermore, there is a table of 100 boxes forming a board for the Three in a Row game (see Figure 1b). Every rectangle has a colour and four of them are labelled with the letters from A to D standing for the respective answer. To give an answer, the player has to bring the rectangle that represents the answer to the bottom. This can be done by swapping a rectangle with one of its neighbors, forming rows of at least three boxes of the same color making these boxes vanish. If a rectangle which represents an answer is at the bottom, the game recognizes the respective letter of the box as an answer. A wrong answer will make the specific rectangle as well as the wrong answer at the top vanish. If the right answer is at the bottom, the user will see a success message and the next question will be asked. Every time a new question is asked, the table of rectangles is shuffled.

The aforementioned mode has parts of several game characteristics that are mentioned in Section 3. Giving the right answer to the quiz is a clear *goal* that has to be achieved by following the *rules* of the Three in a Row game. Here the player has the *choice* which boxes to move and how to come up with a solution. Thereby he or she faces two *challenges*: knowing the correct answer and moving the boxes in a as good as possible way.

Move Constraint. In contrast to the basic gameplay where players cannot lose, a *Move Constraint* component is available for the Three in a Row mode. When enabled, the user has a random number of moves (15-24) to give an answer by bringing the respective rectangle to the bottom. If he or she fails to do so, the game round is lost and the next question is displayed. Thus, the player has to think about his or her moves in order to reach the goal without overshooting the limit of moves, resulting in a higher degree of *challenge*.

Joker. The *Joker* component provides players with assistance in solving the game. In the Text mode, two jokers are implemented by simply removing one or two wrong answers by clicking on the respective button. To prevent misuse of this function, it can only be activated on a time-limited basis. There are also two jokers in the Three in a Row mode. However, players have to trigger them by forming special formations with the colored boxes. If four boxes are aligned, the lowest row vanishes instantly. When forming a row of five, a box with a wrong answer is removed. Both forms of jokers increase the *choices* a user can make and they can prevent the player from getting bored or frustrated if he or she is not aware of the right answer.

Question Selection. A user can choose different algorithms that picks the following question by using the *Question Selection* component. The basic algorithm just selects questions randomly. The advanced algorithm takes the previously given answers of the user into consideration. A prerequisite is that all questions are classified from 0 (easy) to 9 (hard). By saving all answers a player gives, the algorithm then can adapt the difficulty level. E.g., if a user manages to answer at least 60% questions correctly in one difficulty level and if he or she answered at least three times, the level is incremented by one. This mechanism falls into the *challenge* characteristic as it helps players to have just the right amount of challenge and thus to get into the flow state [6].

Highscore. While Plass et al. explicitly examined multiplayer characteristics [12], our game itself has no direct multiplayer functionality. Instead, a ranking system is built into the game so that players can compare their results after matches. There are two highscores, one for the Text mode and one for the Three in a Row mode. Players score points for answering questions correctly and lose points for not knowing an answer in both lists. Additionally, in the Three in a Row list players can score points for building rows of boxes. The highscore ranking is presented to a player showing the name of the user, number of questions that were answered, the score and an average ratio of the points per question. Thus, it creates *competition* among players.

5   Evaluation

The evaluation is set up in order to be able to answer two research questions:

(a) Does the implementation of game characteristics in a learning tool help improving the user's motivation and his or her learning success?
(b) Which game characteristics are especially qualified for the improvement?

The first question investigates whether the integration of game characteristics really is beneficial for the learning outcome. The idea of the game was to add game elements that motivate the player. As the game elements can also distract the user from the learning content, the learning outcome could decrease, as well. The second question analyses the different game elements and their individual benefits for learning outcome. There may be game elements described in Section 4.1 that are very well suited for improving motivation or learning success. In contrast, there can also be components that even worsen the learning outcome.

The implemented quiz game provides just a basic example for a learning game. While there could be more game elements and a deeper integration of the learning content, it still depicts a realistic scenario, as quiz games can be well used to train previously acquired knowledge.

5.1   Framework

The evaluation for the serious game *Quiz+* is directly embedded in the game, so the user can click on a button in the main menu and will be directly led to the evaluation mode. It consists of two main parts that are repeated several times: Playing the game under certain conditions and then filling in a questionnaire. First, an easy quiz without any game elements is tested. After that, the *Three in a Row* mode is enabled, followed by four scenarios that alternately include another game element. Finally, a scenario with all components enabled concludes (see Table 1). Therefore, it is possible to compare the pure learning tool and the full-fledged game.

During the evaluation, each user played each scenario consecutively, starting with scenario 0. After three minutes, the game was automatically interrupted

Table 1. Scenarios of the Evaluation

#	Presentation	Move Constraint	Question Selection	Joker	Highscore
0	Text	No	Random	No	No
1	Three in a Row	No	Random	No	No
2	Three in a Row	Yes	Random	No	No
3	Three in a Row	No	Adjusted	No	No
4	Three in a Row	No	Random	Yes	No
5	Three in a Row	No	Random	No	Yes
6	Three in a Row	Yes	Adjusted	Yes	Yes

and the user was asked to fill in a questionnaire. The first survey also contained questions about sociodemographic data as well as general data about the familiarity with cell phones and games. The questions about the scenarios were the same in every scenario, so they are comparable. After the seventh questionnaire, the user finished the evaluation in about 30 minutes.

5.2   Results and Discussion

15 people (7 male, 8 female) with ages between 17 and 53 (average 28.4) participated in the evaluation and every participant tested all seven scenarios, resulting in a data basis of 105 entries. They had to agree or disagree several statements on a scale of 0 (totally disagree) to 4 (fully agree). The same question catalog was used for all participants. It consisted of a set of general knowledge question categorized in 10 difficulty levels.

The first part of the results focuses on the achievement of the objective of the game which was to enhance motivation as well as learning success. While the statement "I had fun playing the game" has an average degree of agreement of 1.2 for scenario 0, this degree rises to 3.8 when all game components are enabled in scenario 6. Similar results are achieved for the statement "I would recommend the game". This outcome indicates that fun as well as short-term and long-term motivation are increased by the presence of game characteristics.

The learning success was assessed with different statements in order to have a well-founded result. For the statement "I learned a lot", the degree of agreement rises from 1.7 to 2.7 comparing the scenarios 0 and 6. This increase is not as high as for the fun statements, but it shows that the perceived learning success is better by playing the full-fledged game. As the average number of answered questions are substantially higher in the *Text* mode (23) compared to the *Three in a Row* mode (4), participants may have rated the quality of learning success over quantity of content. However, more in-depth studies may be needed here.

In Figure 2, the distribution of the degrees of agreement can be seen. It shows that the results of the assessment of fun get clearer in scenario 6, so it is not just that the average increases, but the standard deviation falls from 0.8 to 0.4. For the assessment of learning success, a decrease of standard deviation cannot be observed as it remains on a relatively high value of 0.9. As a consequence,

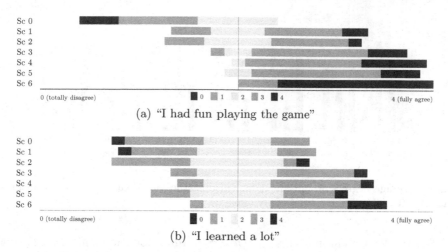

(a) "I had fun playing the game"

(b) "I learned a lot"

Fig. 2. Distribution of degrees of agreement for two statements on a scale of 0 (totally disagree) to 4 (fully agree)

while fun increases for everybody, the learning success does not automatically increase for everybody.

Additionally, a significant correlation of 0.6 between the assessment of fun and learning shows that a game that is motivating through fun automatically increases the perceived learning success. This is an exceptional relationship, since fun and learning are basically seen as two independent variables. On the contrary, this regarded fact supports Dewey's theory which does not see a general difference in work and play [21].

In sum, the first research question that investigates the improvement of the motivation and the learning success of the user can be generally affirmed. However, the implementation of game characteristics does help improving both fun and learning. Nevertheless, it is important to be aware of the fact that the learning success rests on the individual evaluation of the user rather than on an objective assessment. Furthermore, the number of question that are answered in the same time essentially differs depending on the presentation mode.

The second part of the results focuses on the assessment of the various game characteristics that were implemented. An overview of the results is presented in Figure 3.

For scenario 1 which only implements the *Three in a Row* mode, there is a doubling of the degree of agreement for the statement "I had fun playing the game" from 1.2 to 2.5. This is a very high increase, but it can be explained by the various game characteristics this element contains. Similar results are given by the statement "I would play the game again" as well as the statement "The game was boring". This proves the effectiveness for motivation when the presentation is extended. In the assessment of the learning success, there is no improvement from scenario 0 to scenario 1. Thus, this presentation brought an increase in motivation but no achievement for learning.

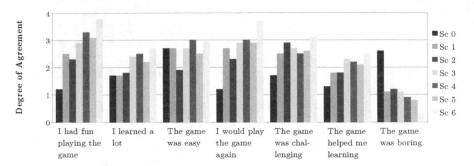

Fig. 3. Average degrees of agreement for various statements and seven scenarios on a scale of 0 (totally disagree) to 4 (fully agree)

Scenario 2 which implements the *Three in a Row* mode and a move constraint is slightly lower assessed concerning fun compared to scenario 1. This is due to the more challenging game, so the game is significantly valued more difficult, as also described in the "Inverted-U Hypothesis" [14]. Furthermore, the degree of agreement for playing the game again falls from 2.7 to 2.3. Thus, the move constraint on its own does not have a positive impact for both fun and learning.

The next scenario shows improvements in fun and learning success. While the assessment of fun increases by 16 per cent, the perceived learning success increases by 41 per cent compared to scenario 1. Since this scenario implements the algorithm for selecting appropriate questions that fit to the user's abilities, the player can be moved to the flow state. This observation verifies Csikszentmihalyi's theory [6]. The effectiveness of the implemented algorithm is proved by the assessment of the difficulty of the question, since 87 per cent of the users rate the difficulty in scenario 3 "exactly right". In scenario 6 where the algorithm is enabled, too, everybody rates similarly.

Scenario 4 is similarly successful, as the fun increases by 32 per cent and the learning success rises by 47 per cent. This game elements makes the game easier, since it enables the users to use jokers, so they have a bigger scope to act. In this evaluation, the availability of jokers is the most promising single game element. This may also due to the fact that the user is able to manage difficult arrangements of rectangles that are described in Subsection 4.1. Thus, the user does not get stuck in problematic situations and therefore preventing him or her from getting frustrated. Surprisingly, this scenario improves the learning significantly. This may·be because the user is able to answer more questions.

The highscore ranking which is enabled in scenario 5 is also successful in both fun and learning success, but the improvement is not as much as for scenario 4. The highscore challenges the user and creates competition. The user can see his or her position in the ranking after every correctly answered question, so he or she feels encouraged in going up in the ranking.

The last scenario incorporates all game elements and shows the best results concerning fun and learning success. For example, the ratio for boredom decreases from 2.6 to 0.3 compared to scenario 0 where all game elements are disabled.

Furthermore, the standard deviation falls when more game elements are enabled. Additionally, the degree of agreement for the statement "I would play the game again" is extremely high, so the game offers good expectations in the long run. As this scenario always beats every other scenario, the combination of multiple game elements depicts the best way to transform a learning tool into a serious game that is motivating as well as educational.

6 Conclusion

In order to examine the connection of fun and learning outcome in learning games we analyzed models for game characteristics. Using an adapted model by Charsky [3], we implemented a component-based quiz game that incorporates various game elements. A user study assessed the achievement of the aforementioned objectives. In general, the game is able to improve motivation as well as learning success significantly. The analysis of every single game characteristic returned different results. While a move constraint, which challenges the user more, does not have a positive impact on fun and learning success, the implementation of an algorithm that selects the question a user has to answer regarding to his or her abilities leads to an improvement in both fun and learning success. As these two game elements can be linked to the game characteristic of challenge, the theory of flow can be verified. A highscore ranking is able to enhance the examined variables, as well. The best result for learning outcome is provided by the implementation of jokers, which simplify the game and enlarge the actions a user can take, while the addition of presentation modes only increases motivation. In future work, more game characteristics should be examined, especially more forms of presentation and the not yet considered characteristic of fantasy. This could be combined with using a more complex game setup which comprises these characteristics.

All in all, the approach of adding game elements to a learning tool has proven to be a successful way to enhance motivation and learning success. Although there are elements that are able to improve results more than others, the combination of multiple game elements returns the best result for creating learning games that are intrinsically entertaining as well as valuable learning tools.

References

1. Mildner, P., Campbell, C., Effelsberg, W.: Word domination: bringing together fun and education in an authoring-based 3D shooter game. In: Göbel, S., Wiemeyer, J. (eds.) GameDays 2014. LNCS, vol. 8395, pp. 59–70. Springer, Heidelberg (2014)
2. Mildner, P., John, B., Moch, A., Effelsberg, W.: Creation of custom-made serious games with user-generated learning content. In: NetGames 2014: Proceedings of the Annual Workshop on Network and Systems Support for Games (2014)
3. Charsky, D.: From edutainment to serious games: A change in the use of game characteristics. Games and Culture 5(2), 177–198 (2010)
4. Hunicke, R., LeBlanc, M., Zubek, R.: MDA: a formal approach to game design and game research. In: Workshop on Challenges in Game AI (2004)

5. Sweetser, P., Wyeth, P.: GameFlow: A Model for Evaluating Player Enjoyment in Games. Computers in Entertainment **3**(3), July 2005
6. Csikszentmihalyi, M.: Flow: the psychology of optimal experience, vol.1, p. 991. Harper Collins (1990)
7. Cowley, B., Charles, D., Black, M., Hickey, R.: Toward an understanding of flow in video games. Computers in Entertainment **6**(2), 20:1–20:27 (2008)
8. Mitgutsch, K., Alvarado, N.: Purposeful by design? a serious game design assessment framework. In: Proceedings of the International Conference on the Foundations of Digital Games - FDG 2012, pp. 121–128. ACM Press (2012)
9. Deterding, S., Dixon, D., Khaled, R., Nacke, L.: From game design elements to gamefulness: defining "gamification." In: Proceedings of the 15th International Academic MindTrek Conference: Envisioning Future Media Environments, pp. 9–15. ACM (2011)
10. Songer, R.W., Miyata, K.: A playful affordances model for gameful learning. In: Proceedings of the Second International Conference on Technological Ecosystems for Enhancing Multiculturality - TEEM 2014, pp. 205–213. ACM Press (2014)
11. Lucero, A., Karapanos, E., Arrasvuori, J., Korhonen, H.: Playful or Gameful?: Creating Delightful User Experiences. Interactions **21**(3), 34–39 (2014)
12. Plass, J.L., O'Keefe, P.A., Homer, B.D., Case, J., Hayward, E.O., Stein, M., Perlin, K.: The Impact of Individual, Competitive, and Collaborative Mathematics Game Play on Learning, Performance, and Motivation. Journal of Educational Psychology **105**(4), 1050–1066 (2013)
13. Lomas, D., Patel, K., Forlizzi, J.L., Koedinger, K.R.: Optimizing challenge in an educational game using large-scale design experiments. In: Proceedings of the SIGCHI Conference on Human Factors in Computing Systems - CHI 2013, pp. 89–98. ACM Press (2013)
14. Abuhamdeh, S., Csikszentmihalyi, M.: The Importance of Challenge for the Enjoyment of Intrinsically Motivated, Goal-Directed Activities. Personality & Social Psychology Bulletin **38**(3), 317–330 (2012)
15. Hardy, S., Kern, A., Dutz, T., Weber, C., Göbel, S., Steinmetz, R.: What makes games challenging? - considerations on how to determine the "challenge" posed by an exergame for balance training. In: Proc. of the 2014 ACM International Workshop on Serious Games - SeriousGames 2014, pp. 57–62. ACM Press (2014)
16. Malone, T.W.: Toward a theory of intrinsically motivating instruction. Cognitive Science **5**(4), 333–369 (1981)
17. Prensky, M.: Digital Game-Based Learning. McGraw Hill Book Co (2007)
18. Malone, T.W., Lepper, M.R.: Making learning fun: A taxonomy of intrinsic motivations for learning. Aptitude, Learning, and Instruction **3**, 223–253 (1987)
19. Schell, J.: The Art of Game Design: A book of lenses. Taylor & Francis US (2008)
20. Davis, F.: A technology acceptance model for empirically testing new end-user information systems: Theory and results. PhD thesis, Massachusetts Institute of Technology (1986)
21. Dewey, J.: Democracy and education. Courier Dover Publications (2004)

Educational Opportunities of a Social Network Game

A Review of Possible Learning Outcomes

Heinrich Söbke[(✉)] and Jörg Londong

Bauhaus-Institute for Infrastructure Solutions (b.is),
Bauhaus-Universität Weimar, Weimar, Germany
{heinrich.soebke,joerg.londong}@uni-weimar.de

Abstract. Social network games (SNG) constitute a game genre with both easy accessibility and low development costs. However, their educational usage is impacted by their reputation as effortless, click-and-reward games. In this case study we apply a taxonomy of learning outcomes in serious games to an elementary SNG (Fliplife). The work is based on long-term gameplay experiences and two online surveys. Each taxonomy component can be mapped successfully to examples from Fliplife. Therefore we argue that SNGs in general, notwithstanding their limited game appeal, can have educational potential. They can be a cost-efficient tool in the context of game-based learning.

Keywords: Social network games · Game-based learning · Taxonomy · Learning objectives · Game design · Case study

1   Introduction

Social network games (SNGs) constitute a genre of browser-based games which has emerged over the last few years. Its appearance has brought new facets to gaming: SNGs generally require less effort to implement. They cater to a different demography of players than that of traditional video games and thus reach an extended audience. They are highly accessible both in terms of technical and economic hurdles: anyone who is able to operate a web browser can access such a game. Initially there is no need to complete a payment, and SNGs don't require all players to be present at the same time but mainly allow for asynchronous gaming [1]. These characteristics seem to be an appropriate foundation for exploiting this game genre in educational contexts. On the other hand, SNGs generally have the reputation of being stupid and repetitive [2, 3]. "Hardcore" gamers in particular tend to consider them as non-games. These attitudes may be partly justified by negative game mechanic spin-offs driven purely by profit. Other reasons may lie in differences with regard to game culture and players' preferred game types. SNGs have been described as "employ[ing] Skinner-like techniques" [4]. Although this relates to the complexity of possible interactions and doesn't rule out educational outcomes per se, such a declaration may overshadow other more positive aspects. There is evidence that SNGs can serve as educational tools: we found examples of collaborative knowledge building [5], SNGs being used

© Springer International Publishing Switzerland 2015
S. Göbel et al. (Eds.): JCSG 2015, LNCS 9090, pp. 63–76, 2015.
DOI: 10.1007/978-3-319-19126-3_6

as frames for player-definable complex problems [6], and their use as an assessment tool to help companies identify potential employees [7].

This article describes a case study of the SNG 'Fliplife' [8] in the context of learning: Fliplife is an HTML5-based SNG combining the characteristics of low development effort, very simple game mechanics and yet an apparently high level of player engagement. Such a combination is especially valuable in educational contexts, given that development resources are normally restricted and considering the vital role of player engagement in digital game-based learning. This work provides a review of potential educational opportunities provided in such a game. We use a taxonomy of learning objectives in serious games to systematically evaluate the potential learning outcomes from Fliplife.

1.1   Method and Structure

The foundation of our work is a gameplay experiment we pursued over 3 years from May 2011 to September 2014 (when Fliplife was discontinued). Based on these gaming experiences we conducted two online surveys in 2012 and 2014. The first questionnaire focused on eliciting the potential of Fliplife as a storytelling instrument; it was put online from 14th to 25th April 2012 and was completed by 127 respondents. Having experienced a lot of social interactions in Fliplife, we conducted the second survey mainly to investigate third place characteristics of this game. It was open from 12th December 2013 to 7th January 2014 and attracted a total of 313 participants, 255 of whom completed it. In order to acquire participants, the surveys were announced in Fliplife-related forums. However, most were recruited via personal messages in Fliplife. The Fliplife level was a criterion for selecting players as candidates: players of all levels of experience contributed to the survey.

The results give further pointers - and to some extent evidence - for various learning outcomes. We use a taxonomy of learning outcomes for characterization. This allows for a systematic and comprehensive review of all probable types of learning outcomes in the game.

In the next two sub-sections we introduce the game 'Fliplife' and the taxonomy used for learning outcomes. Guided by the elements of the taxonomy we then examine the potential learning outcomes from Fliplife, documenting them with examples. We continue with a discussion of these findings, their prerequisites and their limitations.

1.2   Fliplife

Core Game Mechanics. Fliplife, which was launched in 2010, is denoted by its developer as a simulation of life [9]. The player defines their avatar and lets it take part in different areas of life. These include work, education, shopping and leisure activities. The main game metaphor is a *Project*, which is an element of work simulation: A player registers for a project and has to collect a reward after a project-specific period. The reward will expire after a defined interval which is also specific to the project, and the project then will be flagged as failed. Fliplife is a multiplayer game. This is mirrored in the *Project* metaphor, which has a fixed number of 1 to 8 participants (The screenshot in Figure 1 shows a project for 2 co-workers). If just one participant fails to collect the project reward, none will receive a bonus. This rule generates a large proportion of the game's dynamics: it causes conflicts between players, it demands that players choose their co-workers carefully (and indirectly it leads to the formation of groups based on the members' mutual trust in the reliability of their co-members). Another consequence of the rule is the emergent gameplay feature called *Bonus Projects*: the reward of each project includes a piece of *Material*. This is a kind of resource which can be used in a project to increase the bonus reward. Bonus projects accumulate a vast amount of targeted material and lead to a far greater reward for all participants. Such a bonus reward allows players to level up faster.

Each player must choose a *Career* they want to pursue. Such a career is typically offered by a company and consists of a set of typical projects. By means of such a career a company is able to present itself and utilize the storytelling function of Fliplife. A career is completed when career-specific projects have been mastered. Besides real-life careers, several fantasy careers are also offered, e.g. *Style Icon* and *Gangster*.

Energy is another relevant game element. Participation in a project requires energy. Energy is recovered automatically at a constant rate and instantly via leisure activities such as parties and sports. A *Party* is an example of a multi-player activity that implies synchronous collaboration. There is a party host who invites other players who must then accept the invitation. During the party, players have to buy virtual rounds; the amount of virtual money spent is a measurement of the energy gained. If however too many rounds are bought at the same time, the party fails and no energy is issued to the players.

Interactions Between Players. Players interact with their fellow players in common activities such as *Projects*, *Parties* and sport events. As already described in the previous section, these interactions consist of elementary activities such as registering for a *Project* or buying a round at a *Party*. Each result is accomplishable by a single mouse click. A chat tool, which is integrated in the *Project* and *Party* page and various other locations in the game, allows more meaningful communication. It especially allows the purposeful coordination of elementary interactions. Controlling a *Party* and organizing a *Bonus Project* are enabled by textual communication.

Technical and Economic Aspects. From a technical point of view, Fliplife is a collection of interconnected, dynamic websites with only a few graphics and almost no sound effects (SFX). Commercially it is used as a storytelling platform for companies. This meant that real-life companies such as Bayer, Daimler and Ernst & Young were among the career-providing paying customers of Fliplife. Besides storytelling, Fliplife was said to be used partly for assessing potential employees [7]. Another source of income for the developer is the possibility of in-game purchases of the hard currency (*Flips*) [10].

Player Demography and Profiles. We asked players how long they had already been registered in Fliplife. 58% of survey participants (n=270) had been playing Fliplife for at least one year. More than half (54%) the participants spent more than one hour a day in Fliplife. We consider these figures to be proof of the high engagement observed. Two thirds (68%) of the players were female. The average age of participants was 32 years (min=12, max=63). 51% of respondents were in work; another 30% in education. 43% had achieved at least a higher education entrance qualification.

Fig. 1. Project registration page (Screenshot [8], Nov. 22. 2011)

1.3   Taxonomy of Learning Outcomes

Initially we observed that Fliplife serves multiple types of learning outcomes. This led to the demand for a systematic classification of the latter. Bloom created a well-known taxonomy of learning objectives which uses three main domains: *cognitive*, *affective* and *psychomotor* [11]. Bloom's taxonomy has been reworked: Anderson et al. supplemented it with a Knowledge Dimension [12]. Kraiger et al. suggested another taxonomy of learning outcomes influenced by Bloom's taxonomy [13].

Whereas previous taxonomies refer to learning outcomes in general, research has also been done on learning outcomes in the context of computer games. O'Neil et al. [14] build their classification on two theoretical models for rating not learning outcomes, but the process of learning itself: Kirkpatrick's four levels of evaluation [15] focus on the classification of training outcome assessment. The CRESST model of learning [16] is based on five "families of cognitive demands": Content Understanding, Problem Solving, Self-Regulation, Communication and Collaboration/ Teamwork. O'Neil et al. suggest augmenting this framework with an affective component. Wouters et al. [17] limit their analysis of games and how they impact on learning to cognitive and motivational influences, for which they refer to their comprehensive taxonomy of learning outcomes. This contains in addition a communicative domain and a motor skills domain (cf. Figure 2) [18]. It comprises virtually all the other classifications and was created in the context of video games. Furthermore it appears to be applicable to our observations in Fliplife, which is why we chose it to frame the findings.

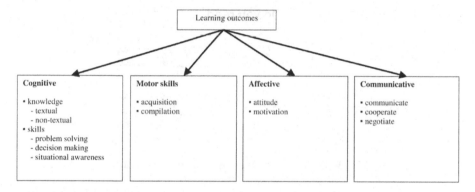

Fig. 2. Taxonomy of learning outcomes [18]

2   Learning Outcomes in Fliplife

This chapter is structured according to our chosen taxonomy for learning outcomes. For each (sub-)category we present examples found in Fliplife. The examples are discussed regarding their (assumed) learning outcomes and - if applicable – backed up by questionnaire data.

2.1   Cognition

Traditional education often focuses on learning objectives in the cognitive domain. Bloom defined 6 levels for this domain. In a revised version, a *Knowledge Dimension* has been added and leads to a fine-grained domain model [12]. Wouters et al. distinguish here between knowledge and cognitive skills.

Knowledge. The *Career* metaphor is used to present knowledge in Fliplife. A career is company-specific and consists of different career steps. For each step, players must accomplish projects representing typical tasks that go with a professional career in this company. A project is described by means of a name and a written description. Non-textual knowledge is included in the form of project-specific graphics and symbols.

Another way to transfer knowledge is via multiple choice questions (MCQs) in *Fliplife-University*. This is a more direct approach, as the intended learning outcome is obvious. As in real-life education, cheat sheets are provided by players. Fliplife-University is connected to the core game mechanic: the rewards can be used to receive improved project gains. Besides Fliplife-University, some careers require the gamer to master MCQs.

Players were asked if they care about project names and descriptions. 56% of respondents indicated that they regularly read project names. Project descriptions are read by 30% of players (cf. Figure 3).

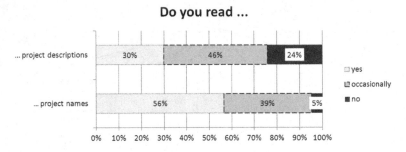

Fig. 3. Reading of information about projects (n=124)

We wanted to know if players had memorized project names. We presented a number of project names and asked interviewees if they could identify projects names as Fliplife projects. The answers provide evidence that players were able to recognize existing projects. However, modified project names were not identified as such. Imaginary project names were partly filtered out (see Figure 4). We interpret these results in general as learning effects.

Cognitive Skills. Running a bonus project requires *problem-solving* skills: Reliable co-workers have to be acquired. The most efficient *Tools* (a type of special material) have to be collected in order to further increase the project gain. A time schedule, which all co-workers must agree upon, has to be planned. Finally, a reward collection strategy has to be used. In all of these steps players have to solve problems.

An example for *decision making* is skill training: Player's abilities are determined by a *Skill* set. Skills determine for example a proportional project bonus, or the number of projects which can be processed in parallel. Each of these skills can be improved by time-based training. The number of skills which can be trained at the same time is limited. Thus the player has to decide on an order of training in alignment with their goals.

Joining a project is an opportunity to train *situational awareness*. Co-workers with a low success rate (i.e. low percentage of projects collected in time) increase the likelihood of a project failing. For this reason, players often check the success quotas of the other participants in the project and decide if they want to take the risk or not.

Which projects can you identify as part of the following careers?

Career	Project name	Yes	Unsure	No	Remark
Engineer	Teste den Klang	31	7	4	
(n=47)	Ermögliche Cabriofahren im Regen	29	5	9	modified name
	Poliere die Felgen	42	2	0	
Scientist	Bei Bayer-Leverkusen mitspielen	19	9	11	modified name
(n=47)	Floh-Scann-App entwickeln	36	5	1	
	Überwache den IT-Rollout in Mexiko	37	2	3	
Physician	Entferne deinen Blinddarm	45	3	0	
(n=51)	Zähne putzen	6	6	30	does not exist
	Unlesbare Handschrift üben	45	2	1	
Journalist	Kaffee aufsetzen	27	5	4	modified name
(n=39)	Interview mit einem Vampir	36	1	1	
	Im Fernsehen weinen	28	5	2	
Style Icon	Gesangsunterricht nehmen	20	5	1	
(n=29)	Boss verführen	9	3	12	does not exist
	Kameraposen üben	22	1	2	
Gangster	Atombomben-Sprengkopf stehlen	27	4	0	
(n=33)	Geld waschen	26	4	0	
	Safe knacken	14	6	10	does not exist
Cook	Kartoffeln schälen	48	2	0	
(n=52)	Pflaume im Speckmantel zubereiten	8	8	31	does not exist
	Honig-Senf-Sauce abschmecken	39	6	4	

Fig. 4. Test of project name memorization

2.2   Motor Skills

The domain motor skills include the ability to carry out defined spatial movements. It corresponds to the *Psychomotor* domain in Bloom's taxonomy. Wouters et al. [18] differentiate between acquisition and compilation of these skills. Fliplife doesn't provide a 3D virtual world. Nor can it be considered a 2D virtual world, as most of its web pages look like documents. These are not ideal prerequisites for exercising motor skills. However, there are some facets of playing this game that we would consider a challenge in terms of hand-eye coordination. One example is the setup of a *Party*, a synchronous, collaborative leisure event to generate energy (cf. Sec. 1.2). Players have found different strategies for succeeding. One well-known strategy requires the help of at least 15 players. Known players are preferred, so the host has to browse a list of players who are currently online. Each player has to be invited individually by a click. Players who fail to respond or who turn down an invitation must be removed from the guest list, which often requires use of the scroll bars. Besides this, the host has to monitor the party chat and answer questions. All these actions have to be accomplished by using the mouse (and probably the keyboard). There is always time pressure, because participating players are waiting for the party to begin. Players may leave the party before it has started so that the host has to acquire other participants, which is even more time-consuming. Once the party gets underway, players have to buy rounds via rhythmic mouse clicks. If they click too fast, the "mood" spills over and the party fails.

Fliplife-University is another game mechanics feature which can challenge motor skills: Fliplife-University enforces a time limit for each question. Some players reported that succeeding in these tests depends on their ability to engage in "high-speed googling": when a question is presented the player has to decide if they know the answer. If not, they have to switch to another tab or window and google for the right answer. After reviewing the result, the player has to switch back to the Fliplife window and press a button.

2.3   Affective

Attitude. Fliplife is positioned as a storytelling platform for companies, which makes it a kind of advergame. It thus aims at creating or maintaining a positive attitude towards each participating company. We therefore wanted to know to what extent Fliplife is able to accomplish this goal. We asked for players' opinions about the linkage between virtual and real-world companies. Half the players (49%) gave a positive response, 6% gave a negative response and almost one third (32%) didn't care (13% didn't answer). Furthermore, half (47%) of the participants said they clicked a link to a company website in Fliplife at least once. In another question we wanted to know their reason for choosing the current career. Almost half the participants (46%) said the reason was simply to play the game: they just wanted to master another career in Fliplife. However, 15% were able to identify with this career, and another quarter (24%) were interested in this career and the respective company (cf. Figure 5).

Another question referred to the content: Half the players (53%) answered that they liked the project names. The question as to whether MCQs were found interesting was answered by more than half (51%) affirmatively; only 22% responded in the negative; the remaining 27% had no opinion.

Motivation. We interpret a bonus project with more than ten thousand pieces of material (an equivalent of multiple months of regular game play) as an indicator for motivation. Such a steady gameplay pattern can also be seen as "compulsion" [3]. So we asked about respondents' reasons for returning regularly to the game: Two thirds of players (68%) return because they want to progress in the game. For 34%, communication with fellow players is a reason to return to the game (see Figure 6).

The phenomenon of bonus projects and the required magnitude of work are especially interesting in the context of reward deferral. SNG players are not generally credited with being able to defer rewards. This is reflected in the Freemium business model which also allows purchase of game progress. With a bonus project however a player works and waits a few months for their reward.

In the context of Fliplife-University, MCQs are elements of the game. Most players answered the question as to whether the MCQs were an advantage for them with "sometimes" (58%). The answer "always" was given with approximately the same frequency as "never" (9% vs. 12%). 21% of participants replied with "often". Players therefore seem to acknowledge that the quiz mechanic is useful for them. This assumption is supported by answers to the question as to whether the player would be interested in career-specific questions in order to receive more insights into the profession. 51% answered "yes" and 14% "no". This impression is supported by the question as to whether players would like to participate in other educational mini-games which reveal more information about career and company: 60% responded affirmatively and 5% negatively.

Why have you chosen your current Fliplife career?

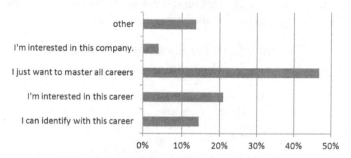

Fig. 5. Career selection reason (n=124, single choice)

Reasons for returning regularly to the game

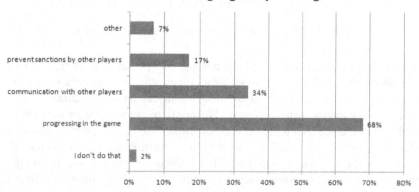

Fig. 6. Re-login motivation (n= 277, multiple selections allowed)

2.4   Communicative

Communicative learning outcomes are not explicitly mentioned in Bloom's taxonomy. They are however part of the so-called 21st Century Skills [19]. Video games in particular are known to foster communication and social interactions [20, 21]. Fliplife provides a wide variety of examples. In the following we give examples of activities for each communicative subcategory mentioned in Figure 2. Given that they are required in order to succeed in the game, we suggest they be considered as educational outcomes of Fliplife.

Communicate. One of the main activities in Fliplife is textual communication via chat. Figure 7 shows a distribution of topics as indicated by players. The majority of players communicate about Fliplife-related issues. However, a considerable amount of communication effort is spent on players' real-life issues. The question implied that all players communicate via chat. This turned out not to be true. In fact most answers in the "other" category indicated that the chat tool is not used.

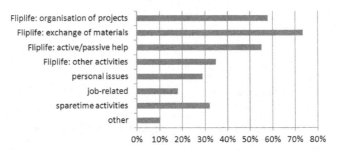

Fig. 7. Chat topics (n=256, multiple selections allowed)

Negotiate. Bonus projects require a huge amount of a predetermined type of material. In addition the piece of material issued as a co-reward for each successful project is arbitrary. In order to maximize game success players have to exchange materials, which means negotiating with each other. Negotiation issues might include the type of material to be accepted as a trade-off and sometimes the exchange ratio. Structures of "wholesale dealers" and "retail users" have also been observed, i.e. single players specialized in the trading of materials. These gamers made a point of asking other players for material. Conversely, their reputation as a trading hub led to them being offered materials when fellow players were in need of something in particular.

The demand for materials causes players to use opportunities creatively: players will make public requests while waiting for a party to begin. Another habit is browsing the stores of other players for the desired material and, if they find what they are looking for, approaching them with an offer.

Cooperate. The *Project* metaphor is an example of cooperation between players in Fliplife, as players can only succeed if all players fulfill their tasks. Bonus projects represent the most sophisticated form of cooperation in Fliplife. Players collect and barter materials over months: projects with 20,000 pieces of material have been observed. So in bonus projects a great deal of work is at stake. This requires reliable co-players who adhere to strict organizational rules. Figure 8 shows a message where players can register for participation in such a project with defined rules regarding time and number of materials. A player registers by putting their name on this list and sending this copied message to all users on the message list.

Großprojekt Sonntag 18.11.2012 um ca. 20.00 Uhr

Fig. 8. Coordination of a Bonus Project through messages

A further example of cooperation is emergent gameplay in a sports event: *Tennis* is one such mini-game with the aim of restoring energy. It is a rock-paper-scissors competition between two players. If one player communicates their choice to the other player beforehand, the latter automatically wins within a minimum delay. If the roles of loser and winner are then swapped, both players acquire energy in the shortest possible time, as matches do not continue to 9:8, for instance, but 9:0.

3   Discussion

Fliplife is certainly not a universally applicable learning tool. However, we have found a surprisingly broad range of potential learning outcomes. As shown in Table 1, we have been able to identify examples for skills required to succeed in the game for each category of the taxonomy used. The wide spectrum of these skills is a remarkable result given that Fliplife is a simple game with plain game mechanics. Thus, the main finding is that successful game-based learning doesn't necessarily require complex technologies and concepts but may also be possible with less effort. Besides the integrated learning opportunities, we attribute this to the community-building characteristics of Fliplife: its game mechanics create a latent pressure to return to the game, which in turn provides possibilities to communicate at virtually every turn. Players spend time in the game and form a community while solving problems, which is an almost perfect foundation for learning.

However, there are important restrictions when it comes to the details. First, the majority of the examples given represent only learning "opportunities": in most cases we do not deliver proof of learning. As an example: while we argue that there are attitudes, we do not prove any changes in attitudes which could actually be considered as learning. More importantly, in striving for a purposeful game design it would be helpful to provide a recipe for constructing a serious game, taking defined learning objectives as the starting point. Our work does not deliver such a recipe. It does however provide examples of game mechanics which are appropriate for learning. The *Project* metaphor as a designed conflict which fosters communication is one such example. At this point there is an obvious link between game play and learning: communication is required during the course of a successful project. To apply this game mechanic to other technical content, it could be supplemented by roles and sub-tasks to provide more detailed opportunities to learn. Another example of a transferrable game mechanic is the use of quizzes.

Table 1. Categories of potential learning outcomes: Examples found in Fliplife

Category	Subcategory	Examples
Cognition	Knowledge	— Career path
		— MCQs at Fliplife-University
	Cognitive Skills	— Running bonus projects
		— Strategy making in training of virtual skills
Motor skills		— Optimized organization of a Party
		— Answering MCQs and researching answers in parallel
Affective	Attitude	— Advergame function
		— Attitude towards companies
		— Career
	Motivation	— Bonus projects
		— Daily login
		— Communication with fellow players as motivation to login
		— Quizzes
		— Deferral of rewards
Communicative	Communicate	— Game-wide textual communication about game coordination and personal issues
	Negotiate	— Bartering of material
		— Acting as trading hub
		— Staffing the department
	Cooperate	— Organization of Bonus Projects
		— Emergent gameplay in Sports Events

Of course the learning outcomes identified here are not evenly distributed in the taxonomy categories. Some categories are supported rather rudimentarily. When it comes to motor skills, for example, Fliplife is far less demanding than a genre such as 3D ego shooter. And then there is the general challenge of transfer [22]: Are learning outcomes of the game applied in real life? Moreover, the attractiveness of a game depends on the player type. It is therefore probable that Fliplife will not appeal to all players. In this context the results of our online surveys are impacted by a selection bias: only those persons participated who are at least partially attracted by the game. This fact especially may have influenced the findings on attitudes. A positive attitude towards the game, its contents and context could be considered as a prerequisite to play the game.

The demography of our last survey [23] may have been influenced by the game's already declining popularity. The game had lost players and there were rumors of closing it. Thus the group of passionate players with a high binding to the game may have been overrepresented.

4 Conclusions

Fliplife is a webpage-based SNG with moderate graphics, almost no SFX, and a manageable amount of straightforward game mechanics. Nevertheless, it has proven its attractiveness for an established group of players. In this article we argue that this game – despite its simplicity – serves all types of learning objectives at least partially. Therefore the game architecture and its design can be seen as an appropriate foundation for educational games requiring low development effort. A similar approach has been described by Clark Aldrich: "Marketing mini-games might be the insects of the educational simulations ecosystem. Ubiquitous, inventive, quick to mutate, quickly replicating success, this unassuming vehicle might be the vector that most quickly spreads the simulation message" [24]. In general these results should encourage further evaluations of commercially successful games for potential learning outcomes. This could deliver both games usable in educational contexts and game mechanics eliciting specific learning outcomes. The chosen taxonomy provides an appropriate frame for this task.

Acknowledgements. We thank F. Brüß, K. Brunner, J. Hünemörder, S. Kühn, and K. Meisgeier [23] and N. Müller [25] who pursued the online surveys with great commitment. Moreover, we thank the anonymous reviewers of this contribution for their valuable comments.

References

1. Stuart, K.: 10 ways Facebook changed gaming for ever. http://www.theguardian.com/technology/2014/feb/04/10-ways-facebook-changed-gaming-for-ever
2. Anderson, S.: Just One More Game ..., http://www.nytimes.com/2012/04/08/magazine/angry-birds-farmville-and-other-hyperaddictive-stupid-games.html?_r=2
3. Bogost, I.: Cow Clicker - The Making of Obsession. http://www.bogost.com/blog/cow_clicker_1.shtml
4. Jackson, B.: Hard Fun - The Zynga abyss. Distance **1** (2012)

5. Söbke, H., Corredor, J.A., Kornadt, O.: Learning, reasoning and modeling in social gaming. In: Pan, Z., Cheok, A.D., Müller, W., Iurgel, I., Petta, P., Urban, B. (eds.) Transactions on Edutainment X. LNCS, vol. 7775, pp. 243–258. Springer, Heidelberg (2013)
6. Söbke, H., Bröker, T., Kornadt, O.: Social gaming – just click and reward? In: Felicia, P. (ed.) Proceedings of the 6th European Conference on Games Based Learning, pp. 478–486. Academic Publishing Limited (2012)
7. Söbke, H., Hadlich, C., Müller, N., Hesse, T., Hennig, C., Schneider, S., Aubel, M., Kornadt, O.: Social game fliplife: digging for talent – an analysis. In: Felicia, P. (ed.) Proceedings of the 6th European Conference on Games Based Learning, pp. 487–494. Academic Publishing Limited (2012)
8. Fliplife: Fliplife. http://fliplife.com/
9. Crunchbase: Fliplife. http://www.crunchbase.com/organization/fliplife
10. Kelly, T.: CityVille explained, part 2. http://gamasutra.com/view/feature/134616/cityville_explained_part_2.php?print=1
11. Bloom, B.S.: Taxonomy of Educational Objectives. Longman, London (1956)
12. Anderson, L.W., Krathwohl, D.R., Airasian, P.W., Cruikshank, K.A., Mayer, R.E., Pintrich, P.R., Raths, J., Wittrock, M.C.: A Taxonomy for Learning, Teaching, and Assessing: A Revision of Bloom's Taxonomy of Educational Objectives, Abridged Edition. Allyn & Bacon (2000)
13. Kraiger, K., Ford, J., Salas, E.: Application of cognitive, skill-based, and affective theories of learning outcomes to new methods of training evaluation. J. Appl. Psychol. **78**, 311 (1993)
14. O'Neil, H.F., Wainess, R., Baker, E.L.: Classification of learning outcomes: evidence from the computer games literature. Curric. J. **16**, 455–474 (2005)
15. Kirkpatrick, D.L., Kirkpatrick, J.D.: Evaluating training programs: The four levels. Mcgraw-Hill Publ. Comp. (2006)
16. Baker, E.L., Mayer, R.E.: Computer-based assessment of problem solving. Comput. Human Behav. **15**, 269–282 (1999)
17. Wouters, P., van Nimwegen, C., van Oostendorp, H., van der Spek, E.D.: A Meta-Analysis of the Cognitive and Motivational Effects of Serious Games. J. Educ. Psychol. (2013)
18. Wouters, P., van der Spek, E.D., van Oostendorp, H.: Current practices in serious game research: a review from a learning outcomes perspective. In: Connolly, T., Stansfield, M., and Boyle, L. (eds.) Games-Based Learning Advancements for Multi-Sensory Human Computer Interfaces. IGI Global (2009)
19. PARTNERSHIP FOR 21ST CENTURY SKILLS: 21st CENTURY STUDENT OUTCOMES. http://www.p21.org/documents/P21_Framework_Definitions.pdf
20. Steinkuehler, C.A., Williams, D.: Where Everybody Knows Your (Screen) Name: Online Games as "Third Places". J. Comput. Commun. **11**, 885–909 (2006)
21. Ducheneaut, N., Moore, R.: More than just "XP": learning social skills in massively multiplayer online games. Interact. Technol. Smart Educ. **2**, 89–100 (2005)
22. De Corte, E.: Transfer as the productive use of acquired knowledge, skills, and motivations. Curr. Dir. Psychol. Sci. **142**, 142–146 (2003)
23. Brüß, F., Brunner, K., Hünemörder, J., Kühn, S., Meisgeier, K.: Fliplife als virtueller Third Place (2014)
24. Aldrich, C.: Learning by doing: A comprehensive guide to simulations, computer games, and pedagogy in e-learning and other educational experiences. John Wiley & Sons, Inc. (2005)
25. Müller, N.: Erweiterung von Fliplife mit bauphysikalischen Inhalten (2012)

Blitzmerker: Learning Idioms with a Mobile Game

Laila Shoukry[(⊠)], Polona Caserman, Stefan Göbel, and Ralf Steinmetz

TU Darmstadt, Rundeturmstrasse 10, 64283 Darmstadt, Germany
{laila.shoukry,polona.caserman,stefan.gobel,
ralf.steinmetz}@kom.tu-darmstadt.de

Abstract. In this paper, we present a mobile learning game for helping children understand idiomatic expressions. This is particularly helpful for Autistic children as they have problems understanding abstract concepts which can hinder their natural interaction. The game is also suitable for children from a foreign background who often encounter such expressions in their everyday communication and also usually misinterpret them into their verbal meaning. The game has the option of learning either the English or the German Idioms and can be easily extended to include other languages. The game was created for Android phones and tablets and evaluated with 12 autistic children. Participants indicated that they enjoyed playing the game and that it helped them learn many idioms.

Keywords: Game-based learning · Serious games · Child computer interaction

1   Introduction

Autism is the third most common cognitive disability with a prevalence rate of about 1 in 88 children worldwide and mainly affects social skills, communication skills and interests [1]. Children with Autism Spectrum Disorder (ASC) usually lack the knowledge of how to properly interact with their peers and thus lack the motivation to engage in social interaction [2]. One factor contributing to this problem is their inability to understand abstract concepts during conversations: In situations where people use metaphors and idioms, it gets more difficult for autistic individuals to respond [3]. Fortunately, studies have shown improvements in social skills of people with ASD in response to exposure and training [4]. However, failure in social interaction decreases motivation to get involved in such situations in the future increasing the social gap [5]. In addition, early intervention in childhood can be crucial, as the more children grow up, the more they become aware of their problem and thus the more their social anxiety can increase [6]. This can also hold true for non-native speaking children who find difficulties in interaction with their peers during first-time exposure to foreign language idioms and thus may become introvert or show negative social behavior [7]. Using simulations and games to support training social skills in non-real world situations can provide encouraging environments for learning which have reduced risk and thus do not induce as much fear of failure [8,9]. Another advantage of such environments is that children with autism are usually inherently interested in computer games, partly because they are more predictable and consistent than real-life social

© Springer International Publishing Switzerland 2015
S. Göbel et al. (Eds.): JCSG 2015, LNCS 9090, pp. 77–88, 2015.
DOI: 10.1007/978-3-319-19126-3_7

interaction [10]. In general, serious games are considered to have positive effects on learner engagement and thus are used to indirectly benefit players while they are enjoying their playing experience [11]. For these reasons we have developed a game for helping children to learn idioms through conversation simulation in a personalizable, playful mobile environment. The game was evaluated with 12 autistic children and showed promising results.

2   Related Work

A conventional behavioral therapy method which has shown significant effectiveness for enhancing social skills of children with ASD is Applied Behavior Analysis (ABA) [12]. In intervention programs based on ABA principles, children practice social communication skills in different situations with these skills being broken down into small steps gradually increasing in difficulty and achievements being rewarded through positive reinforcement techniques. As these therapies are often too expensive because of the significant amount of time needed by a therapist to prepare appropriate materials, several applications have been developed based on ABA approaches to automate some intervention practices and thus make them more accessible for a wider audience [13]. TeachTown5 [14] is one example of a computer-assisted curriculum based on ABA principles for practicing social and cognitive skills which has shown to be effective for children with developmental disorders. In general, the use of multimedia to simulate real-life situations for children with autism to teach them social communication has shown positive effects in several studies [13]. Here, it was found that using motivating visual and auditory stimuli was a common element used for engaging players in these successful applications as many individuals with ASD are visual learners [13,15, 16]. Another success factor was found to be the ability of the software to adapt to progress and individualize interactions for different users [17,18]. As children with autism frequently suffer from sensory defensiveness, they may have an adverse reaction to ordinary sensory stimuli including sounds and images. This has to be considered when designing multimedia elements for autistic children and the best solution is to have different configuration options to make the applications suitable for use by different children [18,19]. Parents and caregivers can then configure them according to their child's individual needs. These design guidelines, among others, were considered in the development of our game Blitzmerker with the aim of providing a motivating learning experience for helping autistic children understand idioms used in everyday conversations.

3   Game Design

Blitzmerker is a learning game for children with ASD in which the player indulges in a virtual conversation with a character which constantly uses different German/English proverbs. Each phrase is followed by a quiz for the player to choose the correct meaning of the phrase and consequently choose a suitable response. If the player makes a mistake, s/he is presented with concrete cues and hints which lead to the correct answer. Different responses to the same question or phrase can be correct and thus allow for different paths in the game story. This feature increases the replayability of the game making it possible to repeat the game several times and learning new idioms. After finishing one iteration of the game, the player can compare his score to other players' scores and if a number of points is reached, a new level is unlocked. If not, the level can be repeated to improve the score. There is a total of three different levels. In the first level, the player is talking to a classmate and

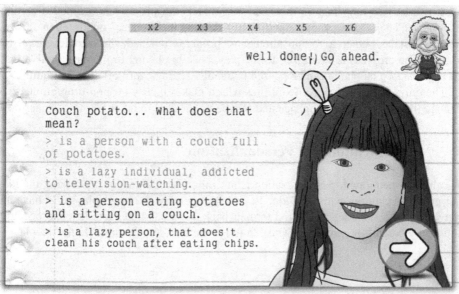

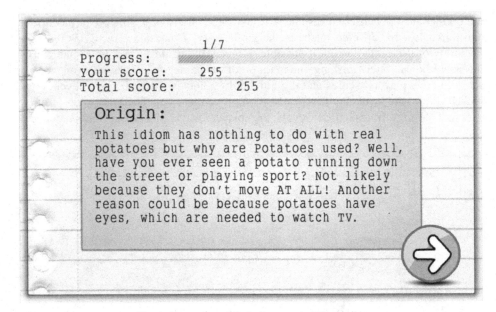

Fig. 1. Examples of Quiz Screens in Blitzmerker

learns common idiomatic expressions which are used more often in daily conversations. In the second level, more complex proverbs are presented in conversations with an adult character. Finally, in the third level the character leading the conversation is a grandparent using more difficult, old proverbs which still occur in everyday life often enough to play a role in social interactions. At the time of writing this paper, only the first level has been implemented.

The scoring system is based on the Experience Points (XP) scoring system: This system uses weighing factors to make sure that if the player has reached a certain experience level, s/he cannot significantly deteriorate in later rounds even if s/he makes mistakes. Once a certain number of points is reached, the next level can be loaded. The progress is visualized to the player while playing to increase motivation. At any instance the game can be paused to change settings, turn off sound or quit.

The quizzes are loaded from xml files which makes it easy for non-programmers to change the content or the language and maybe even adapt to other learning scenarios.

4   Configuration and Personalization

As already mentioned, personalization is an important feature for addressing the target group of children with ASD due to its heterogeneity. It allows players to have an individual play experience tailored to their background and characteristics, especially if used by parents or caregivers who can judge the best settings suitable for the player.

In Blitzmerker, the settings view can be used to change the language, the active user, the background image and music, the color of text and buttons. From interviews with parents, caregivers and therapists, it was found that many children with ASD have problems with certain sounds or sound levels and colors and this is why this feature was especially important. Personal pictures and music can be chosen from the device to personalize the experience. The player can choose between female and male characters and choose to turn off the reading aloud of the conversation. The camera can be used to take a photo of the player which is then also integrated in the game instead of the predefined characters. Some settings are meant only for the parents and can only be accessed using a password. For example, parents can set the maximum playing time per day. In addition, the log-in process includes a short questionnaire to be filled in by the player to determine his/her preferences. It consists of three questions which can be answered by yes or no. According to the answers it is decided where the player's score, the timer and/ or the bonus will get displayed during play. The player's selected options are then stored in an XML file to display the correct player preferences when reloading the game. Since this questionnaire is displayed only for newly registered players, there is afterwards the possibility to change these preferences in the settings menu.

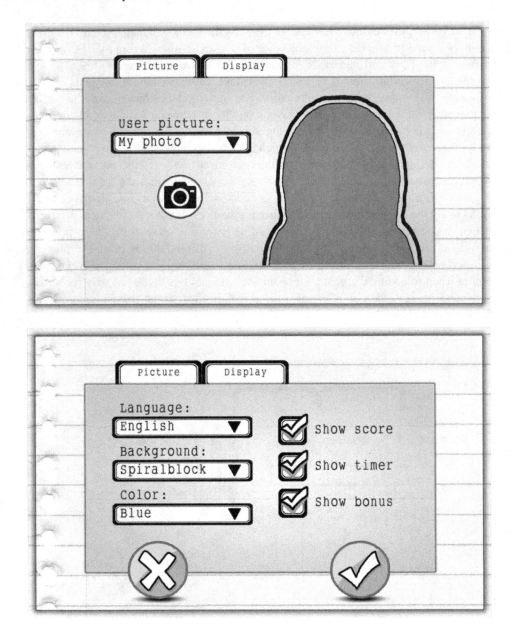

Fig. 2. Some Personalization Options

5   Logging

In this game different data is recorded about players' interactions to provide insights for both game design and player progress evaluation. The path which the player took from start to end is saved, all tapped points in all scenes are stored as

XY-Coordinates, the time required for individual sections as well as the total time played are recorded. In addition, attempts of the players to select the right answer and how long they needed for each answer are recorded as well as interruptions of game play by quitting. This data not only provide important information to improve the game but also provide progress reports for parents and caregivers to track the improvement of the child.

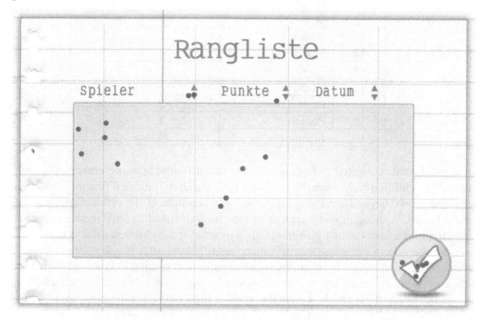

Fig. 3. Logging of Tapping Coordinates

6   Evaluation

6.1   Evaluation with Children

The game was evaluated by twelve male children with ASD aged from eight to sixteen divided into three sessions in two different locations in Germany. They came with their parents and two teachers. The children played the game using Android tablets and filled out evaluation forms before and after the sessions. Table 1 shows information about the participants and the number of times they played the game, with an average of 2.5 iterations. It was observed that children motivated each other, compared their achievements and discussed the stories they played. It was also observed that all children had experiences with mobile devices and therefore had no difficulty to interact with the devices. Only while typing their username, some children did not know how to close the touch keyboard.

Table 1. Participants in the Evaluation Stud

Age	Name	Game Iterations
8	Dino	1
10	Anthony	2
10	Erik	2
12	Franz	3
12	Mop	2
12	Tobias	1
13	Tim	8
13	Lars	1
13	Leon	1
13	Pauli	5
15	Philipp	1
16	Johannes	3

From the data collected through questionnaires, differences in preferences and abilities of the children were found. Even though all children indicated that they spend at least one to two hours a week playing game, only one third of the children play educational games. Although more than half of the children stated to have medium or a lot of difficulties understanding proverbs, only a quarter of the children tried to memorize proverbs before. In the questionnaire which was filled out after playing the game, four of the children showed a strong interest in the game and wanted to continue playing it at home. Table 2 summarizes the ratings given by the children for different aspects in the game. Most of the children gave the game a high rating for the idea, audio, comprehensibility and ease of use. Content, Graphics and controls were rated good to very good. Fun was rated good and the overall game was rated good to very good.

Table 2. Ratings for Different Aspects of the Game

Criteria	Average Rating (1 is best, 3 is worst)
Idea	1.4
Content	1.5
Graphics	1.8
Fun	2.1
Control	1.5
Audio	1.3
Comprehensibility	1.3
User friendliness	1.4

As for the effectiveness of learning the idiomatic phrases, the following were the results obtained from the questionnaires: Almost all of the children stated that they already knew at least one of the proverbs except for one child who didn't know any. Three participants (8, 13 and 15 years old) indicated that they learned one to two new idioms using the game (two of them had played the game once and one had played it eight times), one participant (13 years old) who played five iterations of the game indicated that he learned three to four idioms using the game and that the hints were helpful for him. Four kids (two 12 and one 16 years old) indicated that they have learned more than seven idioms using the game. The other four (one 9, one 12 and 2 13 years old) felt they didn't learn any new proverbs using the game. Three of these four children had played the game only once and could answer all questions correctly from the first time. The fourth kid has played it twice and showed improvement in correctness in the second time.

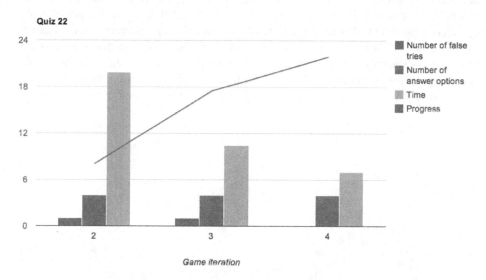

Fig. 4. Progress in Performance in Different Iterations of the same Quiz

6.2   Evaluation by Experts

The game was also evaluated by two experts, both working as special education teachers in a priority school for children with autism in Germany and know all partic016ipants of the evaluation study, one of them also mother of an autistic child herself. They tried out the game, watched children play, filled out questionnaires and answered interview questions. They liked the fact that proverbs were explained in the game, that the order of answers was varied and that the game can be adapted to the player. They have criticized the monotonous praise and the lack of enough action in the game. They find the learning game appropriate for children with ASD as there are not many elements which can distract them from their tasks and hinder their interactions. They confirmed that autistic children are usually attracted to computer game and thus the game can teach them in an indirect way.

6.3   Logging Statistics

More evaluation results, especially concerning game settings, tapped points, story paths and learning progress could be extracted from the Logging data and visualized using Google Charts. The option of personalizing the game by taking a photo of oneself using the camera was very popular and used by all children. This is consistent with the observation in the evaluation studies were children were very happy while using this feature. One child has also changed the color of the buttons in the game and one child turned the audio off as he found the voice to be very disturbing. Nine of the children took a look at the leaderboard to compare their score. The tapping points showed that three children sorted the list by score, two sorted it by date and two by name (see Figure 3). Figure 5 shows that a lot of children tried interacting with the character by clicking on it. This might have distracted them from focusing on the questions and might also have frustrated them because the character didn't react to touch. For most children, a rising performance was observed from the logging statistics Figure 4 shows an example of a player's performance improvement in one of the quizzes in different iterations. Although in the 2nd and 3rd iteration the player made one mistrial, on the fourth time he answered correctly from the first time.

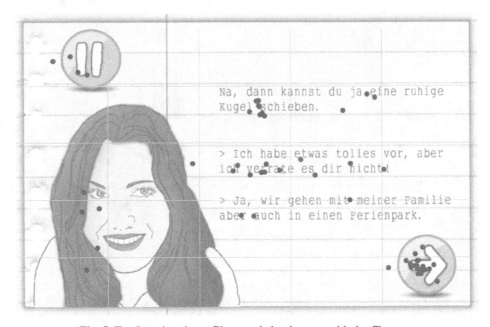

Fig. 5. Tap Logging shows Players tried to interact with the Character

7   Conclusion

In this paper we have presented an Android learning game primarily targeting autistic children who have problems understanding proverbs by engaging them into conversations with virtual characters and explaining the real meaning behind these abstract phrases. The game was designed after interviewing autistic children as well as parents and teachers of children with ASD and evaluated with twelve autistic children, their parents and teachers. The game is available on Google Play for free download. The game evaluation shows promising results and suggests that games like this have the potential to help autistic children improve their social skills. More animations and interactions were desired to make the game more fun, but personalization features were found to be an important factor for engagement.

References

1. Division of Birth Defects, National Center on Birth Defects and Developmental Disabilities, Centers for Disease Control and Prevention
2. Welton, E., Vakil, S., Carasea, C.: Strategies for increasing positive social interactions in children with autism: A case study. Teaching Exceptional Children **37**(1), 40–46 (2004)
3. Le Sourn-Bissaoui, S., Caillies, S., Gierski, F., Motte, J.: Ambiguity detection in adolescents with Asperger syndrome: Is central coherence or theory of mind impaired? Research in Autism Spectrum Disorders **5**(1), 648–656 (2011)
4. Adolphs, R., Sears, L., Piven, J.: Abnormal processing of social information from faces in autism. Journal of Cognitive Neuroscience **13**(2), 232–240 (2001)
5. Kasari, C., Chamberlain, B., Bauminger, N.: Social emotions and social relationships: can children with autism compensate? (2001)
6. Tantam, D.: The challenge of adolescents and adults with Asperger syndrome. Child and Adolescent Psychiatric Clinics of North America **12**(1), 143–163 (2003)
7. von Grünigen, R., Kochenderfer-Ladd, B., Perren, S., Alsaker, F.D.: Links between local language competence and peer relations among Swiss and immigrant children: The mediating role of social behavior. Journal of School Psychology **50**(2), 195–213 (2012)
8. Mitchell, P., Parsons, S., Leonard, A.: Using virtual environments for teaching social understanding to 6 adolescents with autistic spectrum disorders. Journal of Autism and Developmental Disorders **37**(3), 589–600 (2007)
9. Kandalaft, M.R., Didehbani, N., Krawczyk, D.C., Allen, T.T., Chapman, S.B.: Virtual reality social cognition training for young adults with high-functioning autism. Journal of Autism and Developmental Disorders **43**(1), 34–44 (2013)
10. Boelte, S.: The ICF and its meaning for child and adolescent psychiatry. Zeitschrift fur Kinder-und Jugendpsychiatrie und Psychotherapie **37**(6), 495–497 (2009)
11. Connolly, T.M., Boyle, E.A., MacArthur, E., Hainey, T., Boyle, J.M.: A systematic literature review of empirical evidence on computer games and serious games. Computers & Education **59**(2), 661–686 (2012)
12. Fernandes, F.D.M., Amato, C.A.D.L.H.: Applied behavior analysis and autism spectrum disorders: literature review. In: CoDAS, vol. 25, no. 3, pp. 289–296. Sociedade Brasileira de Fonoaudiologia (2013)
13. Wainer, A.L., Ingersoll, B.R.: The use of innovative computer technology for teaching social communication to individuals with autism spectrum disorders. Research in Autism Spectrum Disorders **5**(1), 96–107 (2011)
14. Whalen, C., Liden, L., Ingersoll, B., Dallaire, E., Liden, S.: Behavioral improvements associated with computer-assisted instruction for children with developmental disabilities. The Journal of Speech and Language Pathology-Applied Behavior Analysis **1**(1), 11 (2006)

15. Rayner, C., Denholm, C., Sigafoos, J.: Video-based intervention for individuals with autism: Key questions that remain unanswered. Research in Autism Spectrum Disorders **3**(2), 291–303 (2009)
16. Burckley, E., Tincani, M., Guld Fisher, A.: An iPad™-based picture and video activity schedule increases community shopping skills of a young adult with autism spectrum disorder and intellectual disability. Developmental Neurorehabilitation, 1–6 (2014)
17. Shane, H.C., Albert, P.D.: Electronic screen media for persons with autism spectrum disorders: Results of a survey. Journal of Autism and Developmental Disorders **38**(8), 1499–1508 (2008)
18. Sehaba, K., Estraillier, P., Lambert, D.: Interactive educational games for autistic children with agent-based system. In: Kishino, F., Kitamura, Y., Kato, H., Nagata, N. (eds.) ICEC 2005. LNCS, vol. 3711, pp. 422–432. Springer, Heidelberg (2005). ISBN 978-3-540-29034-6
19. Paron-Wildes, A.J.: Sensory stimulation and autistic children. In: Implications: A Newsletter by Informedesign, vol. 06(04) (2007)

Games for Other Purposes

Bringing Biome Exploration into the Classroom Through Interactive Tablet Experiences

Michael G. Christel[✉], Jessica Trybus, Siddhant D. Shah, Bo Hsuan Chang,
Roma Dave, Adarshkumar Pavani, Ojas D. Sawant, Jimin Song, James Inglis,
Sai Shashank Kairamkonda, Christian Karrs, Xuyan Ke, Eric Kron, and Xinghu Lu

Entertainment Technology Center, Carnegie Mellon University, Pittsburgh, PA, USA
christel@cmu.edu, jtrybus@andrew.cmu.edu

Abstract. Through advances in game engines and tablet technology, experiences that formerly required a field trip can now be brought into the classroom. Two interactive experiences, "Hello Ocean" and "Arctic Stars: The Far North", were developed to bring a swim-through exploration of a Caribbean reef and a walk-through experience of an Alaskan tundra to an elementary school located far from an ocean and far from Alaska. The experiences were tested for their appeal and whether they encouraged children ages 8-11 to learn more about the respective biomes. The paper reports on various formative playtests with children and documents how the experiences evolved over time as a result of those playtests, as well as the unique attributes of the two biomes which led to different interaction styles for the two experiences. The reef was navigated well using the gyroscope in tablets to change the virtual world camera view by manipulating the tablet position in physical space. The tundra used a virtual joystick to see the activity in a sparser landscape with less need for up/down movement. High navigational freedom was important to both experiences.

Keywords: Virtual field trip · Playtesting · Iterative game development · Visual realism · Navigational freedom · Virtual reality game · Educational game

1 Introduction

Computer and entertainment technologies today offer amazing capabilities that can be brought into the classroom to deliver experiential learning. Piaget noted that children develop cognitive structure through action and spontaneous activity [1]. Piaget's constructivism is rooted in stimulating interest, initiative, experimentation, discovery, play, and imagination as fundamental to the development of a child's capacity to learn. Decades later (in 2004), Roussou surveyed uses of virtual reality (VR) to immerse child learners in three-dimensional multisensory, immersive, interactive environments [2]. She noted the importance of interactivity: of letting children drive the experience. Today, technologies like Kinect for motion control, tablets for handheld delivery and Oculus Rift for head-mounted responsive immersion have let users drive and appreciate experiences with greater fidelity than ever before. A learner's senses can be brought in more completely. Rather than read about an experience, or watch

© Springer International Publishing Switzerland 2015
S. Göbel et al. (Eds.): JCSG 2015, LNCS 9090, pp. 91–102, 2015.
DOI: 10.1007/978-3-319-19126-3_8

one passively captured earlier, one can actually have the experience. Children can construct their learning in line with Piaget's theories as they make use of technologies to discover new worlds.

With technology advances, schools can offer virtual field trips opening up the world to students [3]. Companies like EducateVia360, Inc. [3] and Kolor [4] offer image stitching and virtual tours with 360 degree views. They often fold in new techniques like using the gyroscope in tablets to navigate through the imagery space by manipulating the tablet position in physical space. These techniques work well for historic settings and provide a strong sense of place. What may be lacking is a sense of life, e.g., of discovering animal behavior that is dynamic, not always in the same place at the same time. Modeling animals in natural ways is the subject of Omasa, a Unity3D game where learners observe and interact with animal agents to learn predator/prey roles [5]. Real life captured through webcams, e.g., activity at a bald eagle nest in Pennsylvania [6], can be followed with very rich real-world fidelity but low interactivity: the viewer cannot modify the situation or schedule events such as hatching or feeding. Similarly, very high resolution imagery through Gigapan technology could be explored to offer extreme visual fidelity [7], but here too the user changes the view, but not the world under study.

A study with Czech high school students found that higher visual fidelity was considered more authentic, more attractive, and a better source of information in an educational simulation [8]. Two design parameters, visual fidelity and navigational freedom, were studied carefully by Maria Harrington using a Virtual Trillium Trail experience through a forest populated with featured plants and animals [9]. Working with 8-11 year olds, Harrington found that high visual fidelity was significantly better than low visual fidelity with respect to learning activity. There was a positive interaction with navigation freedom: high visual fidelity and high navigational freedom produced the greatest impact on a knowledge-gained measure. This study concludes that the combination of realistic worlds and free navigation features improves learning [9].

This paper discusses the development of two experiences for mobile tablets that can be played by children to explore different nature biomes. The experiences were each developed using the Unity game engine supporting export to both iOS and Android tablets and phones. All reported playtesting was done with Android tablets. The first two authors are faculty instructors for the two semester-long projects developing these experiences. The paper opens with the design and development of *Hello Ocean*, for an underwater biome, produced by the authors listed third through eighth. It then discusses the design and development of *Arctic Stars: The Far North* which was delivered to the same school (produced by the six authors at the end). Both are available for free download on Google Play for use on current Android devices.

2   *Hello Ocean* Design and Development

A graduate student team of six students produced *Hello Ocean*, with two faculty instructors advising the project-based course during its 15-week semester. Weekly meetings to review decisions and progress were held with teachers and administrators at a West Virginia elementary school (students in grades K through 5, ages 4-11), who served as clients for the project. At this particular school, there is a broad range of backgrounds, from students who have never seen an ocean to the well-traveled, from different ethnicities and various income levels. The six students took on the various roles of producer, user experience designer, 2D/3D artist, animator, interaction programmer, and technology programmer.

The first weeks of the semester were devoted to exploring the use of various classroom technologies, with early pilot tests narrowing the candidate technology to the use of tablets. Tablets were attractive for their potential to be used for other classroom exercises, and based on their appeal to deliver an immersive first-person experience to the person holding the tablet. We began the semester with a visit to the client elementary school, meeting with students, teachers, and administrators to get a better sense of what was hoped for with the experience to be developed. The context data from the early investigative work led us to make the following choices:

1. The experience should open the children's awareness to other nature biomes not seen in the West Virginia Appalachian Mountains.
2. The experience should be very easy to use.
3. The experience should offer the opportunity to explore a rich environment, with "rich" playing off of visually rich with audio optionally turned off in classrooms.
4. The experience should be simple. Do something small well in the semester development timeframe, rather than do a vertical slice of a broader activity that might never get filled in due to time, staff, and budget constraints.
5. The experience should start a conversation. It does not need to provide the lesson: teachers can use it as motivation to delve deeper into topic areas in science and other subject areas. If the experience gets child players to want to learn more about the topic area, e.g., to check out relevant library books or be more attentive in follow-up work directed by the teacher, then it will be deemed a success.

With an emphasis on visuals, the team settled on Caribbean Sea coral reefs for their beauty, diversity of life within a small area, appeal to children, and positive reception by teachers at the school. The team integrated a marine biologist expert into development to improve on the experience fidelity. We focused on sea animals, as their movement in the world would attract the eye and interest of child users.

As for technology, the use of the tablet gyroscope to generate a dynamic view into the underwater world was received well by game design faculty in our school. We watched them operate a tablet where moving the tablet angled upward would look toward the surface of the water, downward to the sea floor, left and right in those directions, with a press on the tablet to propel forward. This interaction is an Oculus Rift-like view into a world controlled by the player, but using a tablet rather than a device worn over the eyes. Over time, the swim-through interaction was enhanced with multi-touch support to propel forward more quickly.

As you navigate anywhere through the space, with very high navigational freedom supporting discovery learning [2, 9], you can interact with the sea creatures. To keep interactions simple, we looked to games like Pokémon Snap where the player snaps pictures of the virtual world. In our world, the player snaps pictures of the shown view, dynamically manipulated by the player's tablet positioning, via a tap on the camera icon. This simple picture-taking is natural for children, and allows the world to be discussed further via the collected picture gallery after the interactive swim-through is completed. We also wanted the sea creatures to react to player touches.

Two artists worked to populate our underwater biome with a series of tools. One artist collected real-world imagery to aid in generating photo-realistic textures of the sea creatures. He continued to model the creatures and texture them using ZBrush, converting them to low-poly meshes in 3ds Max. A second artist then added rigging skeletons to the models in the Maya tool. She authored 3D animations using Maya, so that the creatures would move in natural ways, based on their model and rig. Programming comes into play in managing fish behavior in the world. Some creatures rarely move (starfish), some stay very close to seaweed (seahorses), some swim together in a dense pattern (boga fish) requiring a schooling behavior. Over time, the unique types grew from a set of three to five, then eight, ten, and finally fourteen different species; a few are seen in Fig. 1.

Fig. 1. Hello *Ocean* view with final artwork for terrain, coral, fish, and shader renderings

The terrain was modeled from actual terrain maps of Caribbean reef areas. We wanted the experience to have high visual fidelity, in agreement with prior work that such fidelity can result in more motivated users and enhanced learning opportunities [8, 9]. We carefully modeled reefs, rocks, and seaweed textures as background art so that the world would be rich and attractive. We made use of shaders with the Unity game engine for lighting and underwater effects.

The work was reviewed by the marine biologist and approved to be natural for this environment, with one notable exception. Throughout all playtests, the leading cause of frustration was straying from hot zones of activity for too long and being lost in the sands of the terrain with nothing to discover. We raised the terrain edges into sand walls that surrounded the experience, to bind the player in. When players are up against the sand wall they naturally turn around and go back to neighborhoods of activity. We did not reduce the navigation freedom beyond what we knew was necessary. We could not offer an endless sea swim in all directions: we did not have enough time to generate the art assets and dynamically populate such a world. We did, however, have the time to craft a rich reef biome, deep enough in the sea to not be repeatedly clouded by tidal effects, shallow enough to support pockets of plant and animal life. We kept the child player focused on our developed territory by bounding it with sand walls, with teachers happy that the children are much more likely to en-counter sea creatures when using the tablets for bursts of minutes at a time.

We sought early feedback for the tablet gyroscope mechanic driving the expe-rience, the snapshot feature, and the "touch to trigger reactions." For our first proto-type, we deployed an interaction where the tapped fish would approach the player and indicate its species. We pilot-tested with six girls ages 12-14 using direct observation followed by interviews. Two playtesters were at first uncomfortable with the gyros-cope effect as it was new for them and they were familiar with the traditional swipe mechanism, while four thought it was an excellent feature. We noted the value of a tutorial as needed future work, to introduce the navigation mechanism. All playte-sters loved the snapshot feature and could easily take pictures in the world. All playtesters wanted more to discover in the world: it initially had only three types of fish, all finned. The testers suggested we add more variety and make the world more colorful.

Tapping added a text label to the fish identifying it, a label scaled within the 3D space. In this initial prototype, second and third touches would trigger additional animations in the fish and different avoid/seek behavior. The playtesters never dis-covered third touches, so we dropped third tap interactions completely. Second tap reactions were a surprising reward to players, so we kept that interaction, but varied it according to the type of sea creature and modified its timing to be a double tap.

After this first pilot test, we redesigned the terrain and added a variety of plants, weeds, rocks, corals to make it look more natural. Programmers improved the collid-ers in the world for more comfortable swim-throughs by players, and improved the fish artificial intelligence (AI, primarily path-tracking) for more natural fish move-ment. The next playtest offered 5 sharks, 3 eagle rays, 15 blue tangs, 15 angelfish and 2 jellyfish with a variety of environmental assets. It was conducted in the client ele-mentary school with tens of children in kindergarten through fifth grade. Again, data collection was through direct observation of students using the tablet individually and in groups of two, with some follow-up interviews of randomly chosen children based on availability. The response was overwhelming: 90% of the students loved our world and navigating through it. They were shown how to navigate, as the tutorial was not yet in place. The remaining 10% were the kindergarten and 1st graders who were rather confused and found the technology very intimidating. Students in grades K-1 would tire quickly and rest the tablet on a flat surface rather than hold it and move it to drive navigation. Based on this playtest, we refined our target demograph-ic to be students from third to fifth grades, i.e., ages 8-11. Comments from these stu-dents included "I want to live in this world", "Am I a Mermaid?", "Wow shark!" and other exclamations of curiosity and interest. The children ages 8-11 wanted more: they were eager to play longer, and asked us if they can download this application and play it at home. The children were also willing, active collaborators when paired with a single tablet. One child would drive, the other converse and suggest directions with the first. They would swap roles after a brief time. This collaboration surprised us, but was received well by teachers at the school. It could become an interesting future study: virtual field trips conducted in pairs with one tablet rather than individual usage.

The teachers and some school staff also played our game and were very happy with our progress. They did suggest some changes like adding more information about the fish and the environment. As a result, we developed a teacher resource with complete details on the virtual environment and operational instructions for the experience. We also incorporated "fun facts" about encountered sea creatures into the next prototype. We made the snapshot feature smoother and tweaked the fish AI to make it look more realistic. There were teacher concerns about focusing the exploration and discovery. To solve this, the team decided to work on a new feature: quests. The player will be directed to complete a stated quest through free-form exploration of the world.

For the next playtest, a single quest was presented to the user via a text directive in the tablet experience: find 5 different fish and take snapshots of them. A gallery icon would pop up upon quest completion and users could browse their collected picture set. When the user touches any fish, a name shows on top of the fish in the 3D space, along with a "fun fact" dialog box at the bottom of the screen in a 2D graphic overlay.

We tested with 30 people (22 female) in a broader age set of 8 to 16, using direct observation. One developer would watch the tablet interaction, and then ask a small set of questions afterward to the participant. We found that the given quest was interesting, but was shifting the focus completely away from free exploring to just solving the quest. Playtesters were ignoring the names of the sea creatures and their fun fact text overlays completely. They were navigating only to find something new to add to their set of five, i.e., taking pictures only to achieve the quest. When done with the quest, the playtesters were returning the tablet rather than free-form exploring on their own. The major design lesson from this playtest was that a "gamified" quest can diminish desire for navigational freedom and exploration. Also, a quest independent of information delivered through text resulted in the text being completely ignored.

Quests were hence redesigned in a number of ways. First, they could be turned on or off; if off, players were always in free-form exploration. Second, (if on) quests did not start immediately, but rather the player was free to explore for a few minutes before the first quest triggered and was shown. Third, if a quest went on for longer than two minutes, a dialog would ask the user if they wanted to continue the quest. Fourth, the current quest, if forgotten, could be shown again as a text block by tapping on a small "Quest" icon. The interface was minimized to only this icon and the camera icon to photograph the scene, to keep the virtual world emphasized in the view. Fifth, quests were tied to the sea creatures and fun facts about them presented as text overlays, drawing interest back to the text.

The user interface was also changed with respect to the names of the tapped sea creatures. Showing text within the water scene in 3D scaled to the creature could produce text that was difficult to read, and it made the underwater world less realistic. We moved the name of the creature into the 2D overlay, as shown in Fig. 2.

Taps on a creature produces the name and fun fact display. Double taps trigger movement toward the player if the creature is aggressive. If it is a community fish, it will move about. If it is a special animal like a puffer fish, it will puff up or otherwise play its special animation. In this way, we retained the surprises of double taps on discovered sea creatures. Providing player surprise, especially for experiences for children, is one of the lenses of good game design presented by Schell [10]. Notes on the fun facts, visuals on the sea creatures, and actions that are taken on taps are all documented for the teachers in their special teacher resources packet. Sea creature actions were all approved by the marine biologist for real-world fidelity.

Fig. 2. Fun fact text shown when player taps a blue tang (at middle right of Fig. 1)

We tested the revised prototype with 12 children (8 female) ages 8-14. As expected, the new quest system provided for more exploration in the game. The fun facts were read and successfully recalled in a follow-up questionnaire to the experience, showing that a quest can lead to increased attention on the fun facts. More importantly, quests were no longer central to the experience. Players explored, did quests when they came up, but continued exploring during and after quests.

The tested prototype was also the first by the team to present an in-game tutorial to learn how to have the Oculus-like VR experience through tablet movement. The children appreciated the tutorial and understood it, but the tested tutorial at this time was a screen-shot based sequence. Children instead expected an interactive tutorial: move tablet left and see the ocean world scroll accordingly, move up and see the water surface, and so on. As a result, the tutorial was revised in the final iteration to be an interactive experience where the player must succeed with a tablet orientation instruction in order to proceed. In less than a minute in the tutorial, the child player is now comfortable using the tablet to navigate the ocean reef. We saw the children enjoying the improved colliders. We revised the final terrain to include some swim pathways through tunnels and past rocks and coral. The settings button was revised based on both the past few playtests, and communication with teachers. Quests could be turned on or off in the settings as well.

An optimization of the entire project included baking of lights after multiple attempts to reach the best level of frame rate improvements with consideration for visual appeal. Occlusion culling was performed so that only a neighborhood of the VR world assets were rendered based on camera position, with a fog effect in place to hide the drop-off in the distance to absolute nothingness. These steps were taken to retain a high frame rate in playback on the tablets with the fully populated world.

The final playtest was conducted in classrooms for each grade from third through fifth in the presence of one teacher per class, one class at a time. Four teachers also went through the experience. The intention was to simulate the environment in which this app will be used in future.

83 students ages 8 to 11 tested the experience: 33 female, 42 male, and 8 not reporting a gender. We made use of direct observation as before, but in a crowded classroom environment rather than one-to-one. Given the volume of children playing, we also used a paper-based questionnaire to survey the 83 participants. We vetted the questionnaire with children during earlier tests, including iconography and a range of words, e.g., "bad – good" along with "frustrating – satisfying." Children played either alone or in pairs on each of 16 identical Android tablets. As noted earlier, further study into paired use of the experience is warranted as we did not focus on this issue.

Overall, the students were thrilled to see all the new species of fish and the enriched terrain. The interactive tutorial was rated as easy or very easy to understand on a 5-point scale by 82% of the children; another 13% had no opinion. Asked afterward whether *Hello Ocean* helped them to know about the ocean and about sea creatures, the children were very positive, as shown in Fig. 3. 88% agreed or strongly agreed about learning more about the ocean environment, and 95% of those tested agreed or strongly agreed about knowing more about fish after the experience. The graph for response to the quests was not as positive. A significant fraction of the children self-reported quests as frustrating. There was a strong correlation between the age of the child and their frustration with quests. Three frustrated third graders also gave the lowest ratings to the other survey questions.

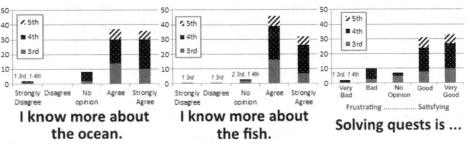

Fig. 3. Responses (N=83) to 3 survey questions by children in grades 3, 4, 5 (ages 8-11)

The Settings menu was noted as a means by which quests could be turned on or off. As teachers of 8-year olds wanted simpler quests than teachers of 11-year olds, in agreement with the data of Fig. 3, we produced two tiers of quests: simple and advanced. The simple quests play off a sea creature's name or strong visual characteristics, e.g., "take a picture of a sea creature that has 8 arms." The advanced quests make use of fun facts details. The teachers also encouraged the development of a "teacher resource page" where they could find additional information about the reef biome. The final deliverable to the West Virginia school included the revised experience supporting no quests, simple quests, or advanced quests along with the teacher resource page. In the final deployed version of *Hello Ocean*, there are 246 sea creatures created from the 14 types. The population counts for any creature range from two (for whales) to sixty (for boga fish divided into two schools).

3   *Arctic Stars* Design and Development

A graduate student team of six students produced *Arctic Stars*, with two faculty instructors advising the project-based course during its 15-week semester, the semester after the one producing *Hello Ocean*. The same West Virginia elementary school served as clients for the project, with this tundra biome running on the same Android tablets in the school. The six students took on the various art, design, programming, and production roles needed for the work. The goal was to bring a biome into the classroom that is not likely to be witnessed first-hand due to cost and distance: the Alaskan tundra. The student developers worked with the same 5 guidelines framing the *Hello Ocean* work (enumerated in Section 2), i.e., a simple small experience that promotes a conversation between students and teachers. The developers sought to emphasize the vastness of the arctic tundra, acknowledge its emptiness and extremes, while promoting a feeling of discovery. An Alaskan field researcher was recruited to review materials produced by the team for accuracy.

The tundra looks vastly different at day or night, and encourages a walkthrough exploration rather than a "go in any direction" as in *Hello Ocean*. We cycle through day/night to provide variety to the students' tundra exploration, with night shown in Fig. 4. The virtual joystick shown at lower left with compass points moves the player, with slow "sneak" navigation when the joystick remains in the inner circle.

Fig. 4. At left, *Arctic Stars* view during night cycle, showing ice, mountains, and snow; at right, *Arctic Stars* toolbar icons for binoculars, scientist logbook, "thermal view" and map

The user interface arrow at the right of the screen expands out into a four-icon pane as shown in the right portion of Fig. 4. A series of playtests were conducted to iterate on the utility of the virtual joystick for navigation, the vastness of the terrain, and the complexity of the integrated logbook.

The first test one-third into development was done with Grade 3-5 students at the West Virginia client school, using observation, a post-test survey, and game logs. Our main goals were learning if players perceived objectives that aligned with what we intended, understood our mechanics, and retained information from the game. In a pre-test asking about arctic animals from 57 users, only 8 students mentioned wolves and 2 students mentioned caribou before playing. However, after playing, 46 students mentioned wolves and 25 students mentioned caribou, indicating that our format had some success for content retention immediately after playing. Player log data showed issues needing work: long periods with no player response or discovery, and confusion over visual "hints" in the scene such as antlers and scat. We changed the visual cueing from disruptive particle effects and glows to simple markers, such as the "i" to show information about the polar bear shown in the binoculars view of Fig. 5.

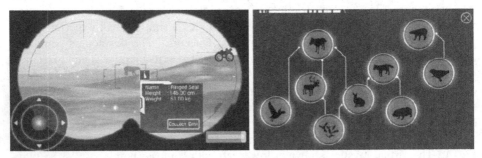

Fig. 5. Two *Arctic Stars* views: binoculars (to see far-away animals) and logbook (with food web; as animals are encountered, silhouettes are replaced with colored images and data)

Arctic Stars uses text "hints" as *Hello Ocean* uses "quests" but only to get the player introduced to filling out the food web in their scientist log (Fig. 5 right). After that, we hoped the player would take up the open-ended exploration and associated learning as found by Harrington [9]. In this first playtest, 55% of children noted the explicit goals we directly communicated to the player in-game, such as finding animals, with 48% noting implicit goals we hoped the player would take up, such as collecting data and investigating. The early test confirmed that players responded to provided objectives, understood tap interactions and the virtual joystick, and highlighted the excitement of children encountering animals. The terrain was too sparse or too vast, a separate button to trigger a "sneak up to animal to place tracker on them" did not work, and some expected interactions like pinching to zoom the binoculars view did not work. These lessons were folded into subsequent development.

Three significant playtests occurred in the final half of the semester: 14 children ages 8-11 outside of school, 71 students in 4 classrooms at the client school (2 classes who saw the earlier version and 2 fresh classes), and 20 students at the school who saw an earlier version for their commentary on the final release. Direct observation was used for the first two playtests, with surveys used for all three.

The playtests showed that visual appeal mattered: snow effects, the day/night cycle, water, and, most of all, the animals themselves rigged to move naturally and textured to look realistic were noted as high points of the experience by playtesters. As the interface was refined to that shown in Figs. 4 and 5, players had less failure in sneaking up on animals to track them, and greater success in filling out their logs with animals and information on various animals. The final experience features caribou, polar bears, king eider ducks, lemmings, ringed seals, arctic wolves and foxes, and arctic hares. The terrain itself was first expanded four-fold, but then users reported annoyance at the difficulty in finding anything of interest. As with *Hello Ocean*, the terrain was tweaked repeatedly to reduce sparse zones. It was shrunk back to original size but with ravines and water's edges providing well-marked activity areas while also giving visual interest as seen in Fig. 4. Child players needing help can turn on animal area overlays in their in-game map, and teachers can promote exploration routes by noting behavioral points, e.g., that polar bears are often on ice seeking seal breathing holes in a hunt for food. The final terrain was well-received by players, appearing to be both more vast and more interesting. The interest was fed by additional animations such as the polar bear breaking the ice to get to the seal, or the wolf pursuing a fleeing caribou. Surprise points such as animal vocalization in the logbook, 3D rotating of scat, and the richly colored thermal view increased player enthusiasm. Direct observation, teacher input, and surveys showed the students eagerly engaging with their game and with classmates ("Look what I found! It's over by…"), with natural pauses in the tundra exploration giving children the opportunity to share discoveries. As with *Hello Ocean*, there was much shared play seen with children using the tablets in a class at the same time, a usage context worth further study.

4   Discussion and Conclusion

The presented experiences *Hello Ocean* and *Arctic Stars* each grew from an iterative development process over 15 weeks, iteration as recommended in developing free-form experiences for children [11], centered on a series of playtests. Tutorials were added to provide practice with each experience's unique navigation through the virtual world, and to introduce more novel and playful elements. Teachers' abilities to turn on or off quests and quest complexity for *Hello Ocean*, and to give more or less context regarding food web and animal habitat for *Arctic Stars*, let both biomes be used for open-ended exploration across a grade range. For *Hello Ocean*, elements of gamification, i.e., being purely quest-driven, was found to stifle player exploration, much like too many rules stifles child open-ended play [11]. For *Arctic Stars*, animals were not surrounding you in 360 degrees as they were in the reef. A virtual joystick worked better for a walk-through experience in the tundra, while the gyroscope-based tablet motion to change the ocean view worked well for the reef. The logbook filled in shadowed slots as animals were encountered; using collection to entice students to continue their exploration. For both, clever terrain manipulation and visual clues in the biome are used to drive students toward appealing animal activity and keep them actively engaged.

Prior work showed the value of free-form navigation and visually rich worlds [2, 8, 9]. *Hello Ocean* and *Arctic Stars* were designed to allow such navigation throughout the respective biomes, discovering creatures that were vetted by experts to have realistic look and behavior, with children commenting positively on the visual appeal. We did not test the educational effectiveness of the experiences, only their appeal to child users and elementary school teachers who plan to use the experience in different ways. Follow-up pedagogical studies looking at particular usage cases are planned. One other shortcoming was in not using exclusively children ages 8-11 in iterative testing, as for some iterations we had easy access to broader groups. We confirmed choices made with such iterations by following up with tests with 8-11 year olds. In an ideal work flow, unique testers in the target demographic would be constantly available to run through every iteration of the open-ended play design process [11].

These biome experiences are not expected to stand in isolation with respect to resources for teachers in the classroom regarding coral reefs, tundra, or other biomes. Teachers can conduct a very rich and lively experience using multiple sources. For example, ultra high resolution stitched imagery such as a GigaPan coral reef [7] could be shown. Nature cams like [6] could be shared. 360 degree visits to aquariums or museums like a Smithsonian Institution Ocean Hall virtual visit are possible [3, 4]. All could be used by a teacher to "bring" the biome to a classroom. *Hello Ocean* fills the spot of a high fidelity very highly interactive swim-through experience in which children can tap the sea creatures and trigger additional reactions in the world. *Arctic Stars* presents a high fidelity very highly interactive tundra walk-through experience including day-night cycle and an emphasis on the arctic food web. Both were received well by children, and improved iteratively through a series of playtests. Next steps include working with teachers to determine whether these biome experiences meet goals of facilitating constructivist learning [1] in teacher-moderated classroom settings. The first stage has been completed: teachers now have released apps which bring the reef and the tundra into the classroom.

References

1. Piaget, R.: To Understand is to Invent: The Future of Education. Grossman, New York (1973)
2. Roussou, M.: Learning by Doing and Learning Through Play: An Exploration of Interactivity in Virtual Environments for Children. ACM Computers in Entertainment **2**, article 1 (2004)
3. Howard, W.: The Virtual Field Trip. SouthEast Education Network (2013). http://www.seenmagazine.us/articles/article-detail/articleid/3281/the-virtual-field-trip.aspx
4. Kolor, Image-Stitching & Virtual Tour Solutions. http://www.kolor.com
5. Price, S., Jewitt, C.: A multimodal approach to examining 'embodiment' in tangible learning environments. In: Proc. TEI, Barcelona, pp. 43–50. ACM Press (February 2013)
6. National Aviary, www.aviary.org (links to various bird nest nature cameras, e.g., Hays Bald Eagle Nest webcam for 2015 season at http://www.pixcontroller.com/eagles/)
7. Buchheim, J.: GigaPan. Fiji Reef Top Panorama. www.gigapan.com/gigapans/148116
8. Selmbacherova, T., Sisler V., Brom, C.: The impact of visual realism on the authenticity of educational simulation: a comparative study. In: Proc. ECGBL 2014, pp. 520-528 (2014)
9. Harrington, M.C.R.: The Virtual Trillium Trail and the empirical effects of Freedom and Fidelity on discovery-based learning. Virtual Reality **16**(2), 105–120 (2012)
10. Schell, J.: The Art of Game Design: A Book of Lenses, 2nd edn. CRC Press, Boca Raton (2015)
11. de Valk, L., Bekker, T., Eggen, B.: Leaving room for improvisation: towards a design approach for open-ended play. In: Proc. IDC, New York, pp. 92-101. ACM Press (2013)

A Hypothesis of Brain-to-Brain Coupling in Interactive New Media Art and Games Using Brain-Computer Interfaces

Polina Zioga[1](✉), Paul Chapman[1], Minhua Ma[2], and Frank Pollick[3]

[1] Digital Design Studio, Glasgow School of Art, Glasgow, UK
{P.Zioga,P.Chapman}@gsa.ac.uk
[2] School of Art, Design and Architecture, University of Huddersfield, Huddersfield, UK
M.Ma@hud.ac.uk
[3] School of Psychology, University of Glasgow, Glasgow, UK
Frank.Pollick@glasgow.ac.uk

Abstract. Interactive new media art and games belong to distinctive fields, but nevertheless share common grounds, tools, methodologies, challenges, and goals, such as the use of applications and devices for engaging multiple participants and players, and more recently electroencephalography (EEG)-based brain-computer interfaces (BCIs). At the same time, an increasing number of new neuroscientific studies explore the phenomenon of brain-to-brain coupling, the dynamics and processes of the interaction and synchronisation between multiple subjects and their brain activity. In this context, we discuss interactive works of new media art, computer and serious games that involve the interaction of the brain-activity, and hypothetically brain-to-brain coupling, between multiple performer/s, spectator/s, or participants/players. We also present *Enheduanna – A Manifesto of Falling* (2015), a new live brain-computer cinema performance, with the use of an experimental passive multi-brain BCI system under development. The aim is to explore brain-to-brain coupling between performer/s and spectator/s as means of controlling the audio-visual creative outputs.

Keywords: Brain-to-brain coupling · Brain-Computer Interface (BCI) · Human-Computer Interaction (HCI) · Electroencephalography (EEG) · New media art · Computer games · Serious games · Performer · Audience · Spectator · Participant · Player

1 Introduction

Although interactive works of new media art, computer and serious games belong to distinctive fields, they also share common grounds, tools, methodologies, challenges, and goals. Their development and implementation is based on the use of computer software, like programmes for audio-video creation and 3d animation. They seek to communicate a message to the spectators/participants/players, help them achieve a level of understanding of an idea/concept and motivate them to reflect upon notions.

© Springer International Publishing Switzerland 2015
S. Göbel et al. (Eds.): JCSG 2015, LNCS 9090, pp. 103–113, 2015.
DOI: 10.1007/978-3-319-19126-3_9

They search for optimum ways to inspire them, in order to pursue specific tasks during a performance, inside an environment (physical, digital or virtual) or during a game, interact with the work/game and each other and through this interaction to achieve a meaningful engagement. The result of this engagement might be a new perception and/or exercise of a new attitude, that in the case of serious games could also have an educational or health benefit.

Nowadays, in both fields the use of different applications and devices for engaging multiple participants and players is highly disseminated and rapidly increasing, from the use of mobile applications, to human-computer interaction devices and after 2007, electroencephalography (EEG)-based brain-computer interfaces (BCIs). The development of new low-cost wireless devices has radically changed the use of BCIs in the arts, which originates in the 1960s [1], and alongside the research on applications for populations suffering from neurological deficiencies and disabilities. At the same time, it has enabled the development of the first computer games and applications, mainly for entertainment, and more recently serious games.

In a parallel course with the brain-computer interfaces' advancements and breakthroughs, in the fields of neuroscience and experimental psychology has emerged a new and increasing interest in studying the mechanisms, dynamics and processes of the interaction and synchronisation between multiple subjects and their brain activity. Hasson et al. called in 2012 "for a shift from a single-brain to a multi-brain frame of reference", arguing that "in many cases the neural processes in one brain are coupled to the neural processes in another brain via the transmission of a signal through the environment [...] leading to complex joint behaviors that could not have emerged in isolation." [2].

In this context, after a brief introduction in section 1 to brain-to-brain coupling, we discuss in section 2 interactive works of new media art, computer and serious games that involve the interaction of the brain-activity and hypothetically brain-to-brain coupling between performer/s, spectator/s, and multiple participants/players. And in section 3 we present a new live brain-computer cinema performance with the use of an experimental passive multi-brain BCI system under development. The aim is to explore brain-to-brain coupling between the performer/s and member/s of the audience as means of controlling the audio-visual creative outputs.

1.1   Brain-to-Brain Coupling

Hasson et al. [2] analogised brain-to-brain coupling to a wireless communication system, "in which two brains are coupled via the transmission of a physical signal (light, sound, pressure or chemical compound) through the shared physical environment. [...] The coordination of behavior between the sender and receiver enables specific mechanisms for brain-to-brain coupling unavailable during interactions with the inanimate world."

The authors continue explaining how the exchange of information between two individuals bears similarities to the transmission of information between two areas of a single brain. An example is the coupling and the enhancement of the signal-to-noise ratio of the frequency of the speech with the auditory cortical oscillations that have a similar frequency [2], which can also be extended and further amplified with the presence of visual information and stimuli, like watching the speaker's face and lips. Relevant studies include functional Magnetic Resonance Imaging (fMRI) scanning of both speakers and listeners during natural verbal communication, which have shown that "the speaker's activity is spatially and temporally coupled with the listener's activity". The listener's brain activity on average mirrors the speaker's activity with a delay, but there are also areas that exhibit predictive anticipatory responses and in fact "the greater the anticipatory speaker–listener coupling, the greater the understanding" [3]. Other experiments have shown that performing and observing hand gestures and facial expressions can also result in brain-to-brain coupling [4] and related results have been obtained with experiments that involved facial communication of affect [5]. The majority of these studies investigate brain-to-brain coupling through the use of intersubject correlation (ISC), which is "a measure of how similar subjects' brain activity is over time", and is also considered highly reliable, allowing "the exploration of sensory areas involved in natural viewing of long stimulus segments i.e. >6 min." [6].

The phenomenon and theory of brain-to-brain coupling is not only innovative for the fields of neuroscience and psychology, but the potential applications in the frame of multi-brain interactive works of new media art, computer and serious games is apparent and has already attracted the attention of researchers, artists and developers.

2   From Interacting with Interfaces to Interactive Brains

In this section we will discuss representative examples of interactive works of new media art, computer and serious games, where the brain activity of two or more performers, spectators, participants or players is monitored and processed jointly.

2.1   In Interactive New Media Art

Amongst artists and performers the notion of communicating and establishing a feeling of being connected with each other and the audience is not new, but rather part of their anecdotal experience. However, in recent years with the advancement of neurosciences and the new EEG technology they managed to realise works and projects as a manifestation of their inner subjective experiences. Although to our present knowledge, artists so far have not explicitly addressed brain-to-brain coupling as a concept in their work, they have implemented related ideas, such as coherence and synchronisation between multiple participants or between performer/s and spectator/s.

Mariko Mori's *Wave UFO* (2003) is one of the first examples, an immersive video installation, where computer-generated graphics are not only combined with the "real-time interpretation of three participants' alpha, beta, and theta brain-waves". They are also used as a visualisation of the synchronisation between the alpha-wave activity of each participant's brain hemispheres with a pair of small spheres, the "Coherence Spheres" [7]. When synchronisation is achieved, the "Coherence Spheres" are joining together, and when all three participants reach this state, a circle is created.

More recently, a series of projects, like *Measuring the Magic of Mutual Gaze* (2011), *The Compatibility Racer* (2012) and *The Mutual Wave Machine* (2013), by the Marina Abramovic Institute Science Chamber and the neuroscientist Dr. Suzanne Dikker, explore "moments of synchrony" of the brain-activity between two participants, when they interact by gazing at each other [8]. As Dikker explains by "moments of synchrony" are meant points in time when the two participants present the same predominant brain-activity [9]. In both cases, Mariko Mori's work and the projects by the Marina Abramovic Institute Science Chamber and Dr. Suzanne Dikker, the concept of synchronisation between multiple participants is implemented by focusing in and examining the temporal EEG brain-activity within the range of either one specific frequency band and/or examining a wider spectrum.

In the field of live computer music performances, Eaton, Jin, and Miranda presented in 2014 the piece *The Space Between Us*, where the brainwaves of a singer and a member of the audience are measured and processed in real-time separately or jointly, as an attempt of bringing the "moods of the audience and the performer closer together" [10]. In this case the phenomena investigated, are the levels of valence and arousal levels within the EEG brain-activity [11].

2.2   In Computer and Serious Games

The use of BCIs in computer and serious games is a new trend and as recent as the development of the new low-cost commercial devices. There are different approaches in the implementation of BCIs in games, such as the use of neurofeedback, visually evoked potentials, and motor imagery, while the BCI itself is not always the central game mechanic. In any case though, the majority of the games are designed for the interaction of one player's brain activity. A smaller number, the "multi-brain games" [12], involve the interaction of two or more players' brain-activity, not necessarily at the same time, while they are most commonly designed for multi-brain competition and less often for multi-brain collaboration. However, brain-to-brain coupling seems to be promoted more in conditions of collaboration, than in conditions of competition. A game of this kind, designed for research purposes, is *Mind the Sheep! (MTS!)*, which allows "both BCI and non-BCI play" with the use of an EEG cap, and it is designed for a single-user, but also multi-users either collaborating or competing. The players use BCI/s in order to select and move dogs that help them fence the sheep in, while they can collaborate through visual, vocal and gestural communication [12]. Another similar game is *BrainArena*, a football game for two players with two BCIs. The users "can score goals on the left or right of the screen by simply imaging left or right hand movements". They can play either by competing against each other or by collaborating, in which case their brain activities are combined. The results of the experiments conducted for the evaluation of the performance and the user experience, have interestingly suggested that the multi-user conditions can be "operational, effective, and more engaging" for the players, and even more, some of them showed significantly improved performance comparing to the single-user condition [13]. Observations like these can open a dialogue with behavioural studies, which can further advance the field. For example Bahrami et al. studied collective decision making between different observers. Their results showed that for "two observers of nearly equal sensitivity" collective decision making was more efficient than a single decision making process, "provided that they were given the opportunity to communicate freely, even in the absence of any feedback about decision outcomes." However, for observers with very different sensitivities the collaborative outcome was worse than the single decision making process [14].

Another example of brain-to-brain communication and synchronisation, applied in a computer game, is the first direct brain-to-brain interface (BBI) between two humans, demonstrated by Rao et al. The interface, which is non-invasive, is designed to detect motor imagery in the EEG signals recorded from one participant (the "sender"), which are then transmitted over the internet and delivered to the motor cortex of a second participant (the "receiver") with the use of transcranial magnetic stimulation (TMS). The BBI is used in order for the participants to corporate and achieve a desired goal in a computer game, which was to "defend a city [...] from enemy rockets fired by a pirate ship" with the use of a cannon. More specifically, the "sender" was able to see the game on a computer screen, but could not control the cannon. No input device was provided, but the participant could communicate his intent to fire by imaging right hand movement. Through the recording of his EEG signals a cursor was controlled. When the cursor hit "fire", a signal was transmitted from his computer over the internet, to the computer connected to the TMS machine, which was then sending a pulse to the "receiver". The "receiver" could not see the game, but the stimulation he/she received was causing a quick movement of the right hand, enabling him/her to press a touchpad, in order to fire the cannon. The two participants were remotely located and had no communication with each other, apart from the BBI [15].

The above examples strongly indicate the potential of the use of "multi-brain games" not only for entertainment, but also in the context of applications for educational and health purposes. Indeed, following the trend that has already emerged, the first serious games for single-brain player have been released, and we expect in the near future also the development of the first serious games for multi-users. A relevant announcement was made recently by MyndPlay, which released the game "Focus Pocus", described by the company as an "Interactive attention and brain development training game for children" [16], and is designed for educational purposes as well as a supplementary treatment method for Attention Deficit Hyperactivity Disorder (ADHD). The game can be played by both a single-player, as well as multiple-players.

3   *Enheduanna – A Manifesto of Falling*: A Live Brain-Computer Cinema Performance

Enheduanna – A Manifesto of Falling (2015),[1] directed by Polina Zioga [17], is a new work which falls under the definitions of live brain-computer mixed-media performances, that combine live, mediatized representations and the use of BCIs [1], and

---

[1]   The title and the main theme of the performance are taken from the historical figure of Enheduanna (ca. 2285-2250 B.C.E.), an Akkadian Princess and High Priestess in the Sumerian city of Ur (present-day Iraq), who is regarded as possibly the first known author and poet in the history of human civilisation, regardless of gender.

live cinema, which is "[...] real-time mixing of images and sound for an audience, where [...] the artist's role becomes performative and the audience's role becomes participatory." [18]. The performance, with an approximate duration of 50 minutes, involves the live act of three performers, a live visuals (live video projections) and BCI performer, a live electronics and music performer, an actress, and the participation of at least one member of the audience, with the use of an experimental passive multi-brain EEG-based BCI system we are currently developing at the Digital Design Studio (DDS), Glasgow School of Art.

3.1   The Creative and Cognitive Approach

The performer/s' activity and the participatory role of member/s of the audience are enhanced and characterised by the use of their real-time brain-activity as a physical expansion of the creative process, as an act of co-creating and co-authoring, and as an embodied form of improvisation, which is mapped real-time to the visual (live projections) and/or audio (live electronics) outputs. Additional elements borrowed by the practices of live cinema include the use of non-linear narration and storytelling approach through the fragmentation of the image, the frame and the text, resulting in a greater freedom concerning the manipulation of time and the "start-middle-end" structure.

Therefore the experience and engagement of the audience is multi-dimensional and bears analogies to free viewing for example of films, which is extensively studied in neurocinematics, an interdisciplinary field investigating the effect of films on the spectators' brain activity, searching for similarities in their spatiotemporal responses [19]. In the case of *Enheduanna – A Manifesto of Falling* (2015) live brain-computer cinema performance, our aim is double: the development of a multi-brain EEG-based BCI system, which will enable the use of the brain activity of one performer and at least one member of the audience as a creative tool, but also as a tool for investigating the passive multi-brain interaction between them. We endeavour to find potential evidence of temporal real-time brain-to-brain coupling, which to our knowledge will be the first time under the specific conditions.

3.2   The Passive Multi-brain EEG-Based BCI System

By "passive" BCI we imply that the outputs are derived from "arbitrary brain activity without the purpose of voluntary control", in contrast to "active" BCIs where the outputs are derived from brain activity "consciously controlled by the user", and the "reactive" BCIs who derive their outputs from "brain activity arising in reaction to external stimulation" [20].

The design of the passive multi-brain EEG-based BCI system consists of two main parts and it is based on a model of interactions between the performer/s and the audience in the context of live brain-computer mixed-media performances (figure 1). The model demonstrates the collective participation and co-creation of the mediatized elements of the performance.

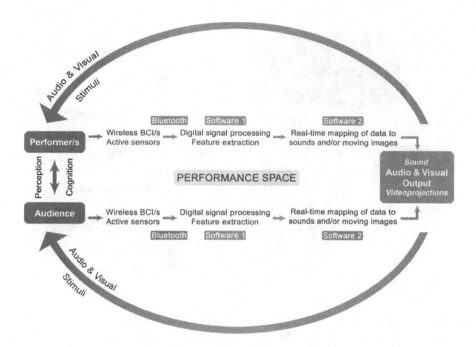

Fig. 1. A model of interactions between the performer/s and the audience in live brain-computer mixed-media performances. Adapted from Zioga et al. [1].

The first part of the system, involves the use of commercial grade EEG-based wireless devices, and more specifically the MyndPlay BrainBandXL EEG Headset, which has two dry sensors with one active located in the prefrontal lobe (Fp1) [21]. The components of the device are presented in figure 2; the headband on which the rest of the components are attached, the unit that transmits via Bluetooth the EEG data to the computer, the USB cable for charging the unit, the two dry sensors attached to a soft material similar to the one used for the headband, and the ear clip with the grounding electrode for the ear lobe.

The first part of the system design involves also the real-time extracting and processing of the raw EEG signals from each participant and device, which are transmitted wirelessly to a computer via Bluetooth, and are collected and processed with OpenViBE software [22] by using algorithms that follow the frequency analysis method. Regarding the processing methodology, the focus is on the oscillatory processes of the performer/s and the member/s of the audience brain activity. The model is dynamic, meaning that the output is depending/changing according to time and it is also causal, meaning that the output depends only on the parameters in specific time and is not able to look/predict into the future [23]. With the use of band-pass filters, the 4-40Hz frequencies, that fall within the spectrum of theta (4-7Hz), alpha (8-13Hz), beta (14-25Hz), and lower gamma (25-40Hz) frequency bands, and are meaningful in the conditions of the performance, are selected. The <4Hz frequency, which corresponds

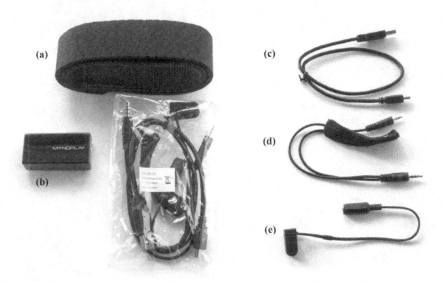

Fig. 2. The components of the MyndPlay BrainBandXL EEG Headset: (a) the headband on which the rest of the components are attached, (b) the unit that transmits via Bluetooth the EEG data to the computer, (c) the USB cable for charging the unit, (d) the two dry sensors attached to a soft material similar to the one used for the headband, and (e) the ear clip with the grounding electrode for the ear lobe.

to the delta band, and is associated with deep sleep, is rejected, in order to suppress low pass noise, electrooculographic (EOG) and electrocardiographic (ECG) artifacts (artifacts deriving from the movements of the eyes and the cardiac muscle respectively). Also the 40Hz and above frequencies are rejected, in order to supress electromyographic (EMG) artifacts from the body muscle movements, high pass and line noise from electrical devices in the proximity of the performer/s and the participating spectator/s. The processing continuous with static and moving average filters in order to compute and output at any given time the power of each selected frequency band and in this way to identify the predominant one. Moreover, the processed EEG data of each participant are being recorded, not only as documentation of the performer/s' and the participating spectator/s' brain-activity, but also in order to be analysed off line after the performance and compare them with related studies conducted in a lab environment.

The second part of the system design is the transfer of the collective processed data to a second software, like Pd-extended and MAX/MSP, in order to map the values of the performer/s and the spectator/s brain-activity, both separately and jointly, to the visual and/or audio creative outputs of the performance. In this way, we attempt to make physically apparent and visualise in a meaningful way the predominant underlying on-going processes and maybe a potentially achieved temporal brain-to-brain coupling.

The performance with the under development system described here is due to be presented in the coming months and the results will be published accordingly.

4   Discussion

The phenomenon of brain-to-brain coupling, the related theories and studies have already set a new horizon in neuroscience and psychology for the understanding of human intersubject communication and interaction. Together with the accelerating advances in biomedical engineering, computer science and the continuous improvement of modern brain-computer interface design, new possibilities are emerging for novel applications. Art and entertainment are undoubtedly at the forefront of imagination and creativity. Today artists, creative practitioners and designers have not only been enabled to use their own brain in their creative practices in the most direct way made so far possible, but they are also given a new opportunity to manifest the real-time brain-activity interaction between the performers, their audience, multiple participants and players. What has already been demonstrated during neuroscientific lab experiments is yet to be proven in the context of interactive works of new media art, computer and serious games. This will also change the map of sharing experiences, co-creating and co-authoring, but it has also great potential for feeding back neuroscience and psychology by proposing novel ways of multi-brain engagement, with potentially educational and health benefits. Of course we are still at the beginning and there are multiple questions arising. What kind of methods need to be developed and what tools to be used in order to investigate brain-to-brain coupling in the context of interactive works of new media art, computer and serious games? Are there specific conditions and cognitive tasks that could be proven more appropriate? What might be the influence of the environment, physical, digital or virtual, where the multi-brain interaction is taking place? What role can the difference in the sensitivity of different subjects play? We hope that the experience and knowledge gained from the live brain-computer cinema performance outlined in this paper will contribute to this discourse, and we expect in the future more answers, questions and new innovative applications to emerge.

Acknowledgements. P.Z. is supported by the Global Excellence Initiative Fund PhD Studentship awarded by the Glasgow School of Art. *Enheduanna – A Manifesto of Falling* live brain-computer cinema performance is due to be presented at the Centre for Contemporary Arts in Glasgow, on the 30th and 31st of July 2015, with the support of NEON Organization's 2014-2015 Grant for Performance Production.

References

1. Zioga, P., Chapman, P., Ma, M., Pollick, F.: A Wireless Future: performance art, interaction and the brain-computer interfaces. In: INTER-FACE: International Conference on Live Interfaces 2014, Lisbon (2014)

2. Hasson, U., Ghazanfar, A.A., Galantucci, B., Garrod, S., Keysers, C.: Brain-to-brain coupling: a mechanism for creating and sharing a social world. Trends in Cognitive Neuroscience 16(2), 114–121 (2012). doi:10.1016/j.tics.2011.12.007

3. Stephens, G.J., Silbert, L., Hasson, U.: Speaker–listener neural coupling underlies successful communication. Proceedings of the National Academy of Sciences of the United States of America 107(32), 14425–14430 (2010)

4. Schippers, M.B., Roebroeck, A., Renken, R., Nanettia, L., Keysers, C.: Mapping the information flow from one brain to another during gestural communication. Proceedings of the National Academy of Sciences of the United States of America 107(20), 9388–9393 (2010)

5. Anders, S., Heinzle, J., Weiskopf, N., Ethofer, T., Haynes, J.-D.: Flow of affective information between communicating brains. Neuroimage 54(1–4), 439–446 (2011)

6. Jola, C., McAleer, P., Grosbras, M.-H., Love, S.A., Morison, G., Pollick, F.E.: Uni- and multisensory brain areas are synchronized across spectators when watching unedited dance recordings. i-Perception 4(4), 265–284 (2013)

7. Mori, M., Bregenz, K., Schneider, E.: Mariko Mori: wave UFO. Verlag der Buchhandlung Walther König, Köln (2003)

8. Dikker, S.: REAL-TIME INTERACTIVE BRAIN INSTALLATIONS (Last Modified September 2014). https://files.nyu.edu/sd1083/public/art.html. (accessed October 19, 2014)

9. Marina Abramovic Institute: Out of the Lab (2014). http://www.immaterial.org/content/2014/6/9/out-of-the-lab. (accessed October 19, 2014)

10. Eaton, J.: The Space Between Us. Vimeo video, 06:35. Posted by "joel eaton" (2015). https://vimeo.com/116013316. (accessed March 04, 2015)

11. Eaton, J., Jin, W., Miranda, E.: The space between us: a live performance with musical score generated via affective correlates measured in EEG of one performer and an audience member. In: NIME 2014 International Conference on New Interfaces for Musical Expression, pp. 593-596. NIME 2014, London (2014)

12. Nijholt, A., Gürkök, H.: Multi-brain games: cooperation and competition. In: Stephanidis, C., Antona, M. (eds.) UAHCI 2013, Part I. LNCS, vol. 8009, pp. 652–661. Springer, Heidelberg (2013)

13. Bonnet, L., Lotte, F., Lecuyer, A.: Two Brains, One Game: Design and Evaluation of a Multi-User BCI Video Game Based on Motor Imagery. IEEE Transactions on Computational Intelligence and AI in games, IEEE Computational Intelligence Society 5(2), 185–198 (2013)

14. Bahrami, B., Olsen, K., Latham, P.E., Roepstorff, A., Rees, G., Frith, C.D.: Optimally interacting minds. Science 329(5995), 1081–1085 (2010)

15. Rao, R.P.N., Stocco, A., Bryan, M., Sarma, D., Youngquist, T.M., Wu, J., Prat, C.: A Direct Brain-to-Brain Interface in Humans. University of Washington Computer Science and Engineering. In: Technical Report No. UW-CSE-14-07-01 (July 2014). http://homes.cs.washington.edu/~rao/brain2brain/UW-CSE-14-07-01.PDF.pdf. (accessed October 22, 2014)

16. MyndPlay: Focus Pocus for Windows (2015). http://myndplay.com/software.php?swid=19. (accessed March 04, 2014)

17. Zioga, P., Katsinavaki, A.: Enheduanna – A Manifesto of Falling. Premiere 30th July 2015. Centre for Contemporary Arts, Glasgow, UK. Performers: Anastassia Katsinavaki, Minas Borboudakis, and Polina Zioga. Director: Polina Zioga (2015)

18. Willis, H.: Real Time Live: Cinema as Performance. AfterImage 37(1), 11–15 (2009)

19. Hasson, U., Landesman, O., Knappmeyer, B., Vallines, I., Rubin, N., Heeger, D.: Neuroci-
    nematics: The Neuroscience of Film. Projections: The Journal for Movies and Mind **2**(1),
    1–26 (2008)
20. Zander T.O., Kothe C, Welke S, Roetting M.: Enhancing human-machine systems with
    secondary input from passive brain-computer interfaces. In: Proceedings of the 4th Inter-
    national BCI Workshop & Training Course, Graz, Austria, 2008. Graz University of Tech-
    nology Publishing House, Graz (2008)
21. MyndPlay: BrainBandXL & MyndPlay Pro Bundle (2015). http://myndplay.com/
    products.php?prod=9. (accessed March 04, 2014)
22. Renard, Y., Lotte, F., Gibert, G., Congedo, M., Maby, E., Delannoy, Bertrand, V. O.,
    Lécuyer, A.: OpenViBE: An Open-Source Software Platform to Design, Test and Use
    Brain-Computer Interfaces in Real and Virtual Environments, Presence: Teleoperators and
    Virtual Environments **19**(1) (2010)
23. Swartz Center of Computational Neuroscience – University of California San Diego: In-
    troduction To Modern Brain-Computer Interface Design Wiki (2012). http://sccn.ucsd.
    edu/wiki/Introduction_To_Modern_Brain-Computer_Interface_Design. (accessed Septem-
    ber 24, 2014)

Literary Play: Locative Game Mechanics and Narrative Techniques for Cultural Heritage

Mads Haahr[(✉)]

School of Computer Science and Statistics, Trinity College Dublin, Dublin, Ireland
mads.haahr@scss.tcd.ie

Abstract. This short work-in-progress paper reports on our ongoing efforts to build a suite of location-based augmented-reality games for a new type of engagement with cultural heritage. Rather than being strongly historical, our games are based on original as well as adapted literary content of particular relevance to the chosen sites. The paper reports on our game mechanics and narrative techniques and discusses the applicability of the approach to other sites and to more historical content.

Keywords: Cultural heritage · Literary adaptation · Augmented reality · Location-based gaming

1 Introduction

The term "locative media" was first used by Karlis Kalnins [13] to describe a "test-category of work" that originated in the now-defunct Locative Media Lab. Many locative media works have been concerned with story experiences, developed either through player engagement with high-activity game mechanics, or using slower, more directly story-driven approaches. In the former category, Blast Theory's *Uncle Roy All Around You* (2003) used a fictional character and the players' quest to find him to explore how game mechanics (e.g., puzzle-solving, time-constrained navigation) could be used to link a virtual gameworld with a real, urban environment. In the latter category, history-focused projects, such as *Geist* [6], *Oakland Cemetery* [4], our own *Media Portrait of the Liberties* [9] and *Riot! 1831* [12] explored how media fragments could be situated in locations that were of historical relevance to the story material, while *REXplorer* [1] and our own *Viking Ghost Hunt* [3] did the same for game activities.

Regardless of approach, situating stories in a relevant physical spaces has a cultural potential that has yet to be widely realised, not only in heritage sites, but also in a broader cultural context, e.g., to capture and re-tell stories of urban and rural spaces. Jason Farman describes this potential as follows:

> What mobile media storytelling projects demonstrate . . . is that someone can be staring at a mobile device and be more deeply connected to the space and to others in that space than other people might perceive.

© Springer International Publishing Switzerland 2015
S. Göbel et al. (Eds.): JCSG 2015, LNCS 9090, pp. 114–119, 2015.
DOI: 10.1007/978-3-319-19126-3_10

Storytelling with mobile media takes the stories of a place and attaches them to that place, offering an almost infinite number of stories that can be layered onto a single site. [5, p.6]

In this short work-in-progress paper, we present a snapshot of our ongoing activities to develop a platform for location-based augmented-reality games for a new form of engagement with cultural heritage. Rather than being strongly *historical*, the efforts are based on original as well as adapted *literary* content of particular relevance to the chosen sites. Using as case studies our award-winning *Bram Stoker's Vampires* (2012) and the H.G. Wells-inspired *The Amazing Transfabulator* (2013), we present the game mechanics and narrative techniques deployed and discuss the applicability of the approach to other sites and to more historical content.

2 Game Mechanics

Both games cast players as paranormal investigators who equipped with paranormal detection devices (smartphones) explore the real world in search for paranormal activity. By collecting and analyzing an increasing body of evidence, players gradually construct the story in their minds and ultimately solve a mystery. In terms of genre, the games fall within the categories of "locally staged treasure hunts" [7, pp.32–34] and "urban adventure games" [7, pp.42–44]. The gameplay is identical in the two games, and each game contains four gameplay modes shown in figure 1, each of which is designed to support particular game mechanics. The play experience consists of a loop containing three tasks—search/exploration, scan/capture and story review—that repeat until the game is finished.

Fig. 1. Gameplay Modes in *Bram Stoker's Vampires*. From top left: Map, Radar, Ghost Viewer and Casebook. Active mode shown with blue glow.

Each game has two modes: *site-specific* in which it is set in a cultural heritage site using curated geographical points for encounters, and *random* in which it stages itself to the player's location. In the former configuration, the game is intended as a visitor experience, and in the latter case as a souvenir—an object that can be taken away and used to invoke memories of the visit.

Search/Exploration The search/exploration mechanic is facilitated by the Map and Radar game modes shown in figure 1. The Map shows the player's location and an outline of the play area, but not the specific locations of paranormal encounters. The Radar shows a traditional "ship's radar" type view of paranormal encounters in the vicinity but no terrain features. The two modes work in tandem: The Map helps coarse-grained player orientation and the Radar encourages players to explore the site in order to get close to the encounters. As the player approaches an encounter, audio layers are built up to increase dramatic tension [10,11]. Leaving out the specific locations of encounters from the Map was a deliberate design choice intended to make navigation more challenging and hence more interesting from a gameplay point of view.

Scan/Capture The scan/capture mechanic is facilitated by the Ghost Viewer game mode shown in figure 1. When a player has gotten close to an encounter, they use the Ghost Viewer to scan (using an augmented-reality camera view) their surroundings for visual evidence of paranormal activity and capture it by taking photos. When a character appears on the screen, an entry sound (typically the voice of the character) is triggered. A successful photo is rewarded with extra visual detail in the character and is entered into the Casebook where it unlocks a short piece of background story about the captured character.

Story Review The last step in the play experience cycle is reviewing the collected evidence. There is no game mechanic associated with this task; the player simply uses the Casebook mode shown in figure 1 to browse the collected evidence and unlocked story snippets. The Casebook serves as a record of the play experience and as a reference to the different characters.

3   Narrative Techniques

Our locative narrative design is heavily inspired by literature, in particular Gothic storytelling [2]. In the following, we discuss how Gothic narrative methods were adapted for the specific use in our games. We group the features under four headings—setting, narrative structure, temporal transgression and spatial transgression—and discuss how the basic elements in the two games were designed to adapt each particular Gothic feature to the medium of the location-based augmented-reality game. The implementation of the story elements uses the narrative architecture from the *Viking Ghost Hunt* project [8].

3.1   Setting

The two games are intended to offer new ways to interact with the cultural heritage associated with a particular site. *Bram Stoker's Vampires* is set in Trinity

College Dublin, Ireland, a 16th century university campus in which the author of *Dracula* was a student. The encounters are placed in areas that the author is known to have frequented and which would have been relevant for his life. When playing the game, the player engages not only with characters from the author's most famous literary work, but also with the space that he inhabited during his formative years.

The Amazing Transfabulator is set in the Victorian Precinct in Oamaru, New Zealand, a town of population 13,650 in which many citizens engage with their Victorian heritage through *steampunk*—a cultural practice involving arts, crafts, festivals and performance in the spirit of fantastical writers such as H.G. Wells and Jules Verne. Our whimsical story of Professor H'rkelheimer and his company of time travellers is in line with the creative cultural practices of the Oamaru historical enthusiasts and their own use of the Victorian Precinct.

From a narrative perspective, we consider the settings for the two games examples of "[h]eavy historical trappings" [2] so popular with Gothic stories. As settings, the College campus and the Victorian Precinct help Gothicize the game's augmented-reality view and the photos collected during play.

3.2   Narrative Structure

Fred Botting describes Gothic stories as "tortuous, fragmented narratives relating mysterious incidents, horrible images and life-threatening pursuits" [2], and the form of *Dracula* is of course deliberately fragmented: diary extracts, medical journal excerpts, personal letters and newspaper clippings. In *Bram Stoker's Vampires*, we retained *structural* fragmentation by dividing the narrative into encounters that players experience in a non-linear fashion and must collate in their minds, similarly to the task performed by a reader of *Dracula*. We further added *spatial* fragmentation by scattering the fragments across the play area. Hence, the act of re-composing the narrative becomes not only an intellectual but also a physical act.

Although *The Amazing Transfabulator* is more whimsical in its flavour, the structural and spatial fragmentation resonates well with its story too: A mad professor's time machine has malfunctioned, leaving its motley crew of Victorian time travellers scattered across the historical quarter in Oamaru. In this case, the act of finding the characters becomes a way to re-establish order (at least temporarily) by restoring the time machine to a functional state.

3.3   Temporal Transgression

Fred Botting writes that "Gothic atmospheres ... have repeatedly signalled the disturbing return of pasts upon presents," and *Dracula* is of course all about the past (Medieval Europe) intruding on the present (Victorian England). In *Bram Stoker's Vampires*, we retained the temporal transgression of Count Dracula upon the Victorian characters, but replaced Dr Van Helsing with the ghost of Bram Stoker. Consequent changes were made in setting and origin of power, as shown in table 1. In addition, we added the present time, facilitating a three-pronged temporal transgression in which the smartphone-carrying player is haunted not only by the vampires, but also by their Victorian author, who is himself haunted by the monsters he created. As time travellers, the characters

Table 1. Temporal Transgression in *Bram Stoker's Vampires*. Transgression happens MA→V, MA→P and V→P

	Middle Ages (MA)	Victorian (V)	Present (P)
Character	Count Dracula	Bram Stoker	Player
Setting	Transylvania	Dublin	Reality
Origin of Power	Occult	Literature	Technology

from *The Amazing Transfabulator* are of course also temporal transgressors, even if accidentally so—like the vampires in Stoker's novel, they are characters from a fictional past, intruding on the present. It becomes the player's task to deal with them, even if the result is temporary.

3.4   Spatial Transgression

Fred Botting writes that Gothic storytelling devices "destabilised the boundaries between psyche and reality, opening up an indeterminate zone in which the differences between fantasy and actuality were no longer secure," and Dracula is an excellent example of such "a fiction with pretensions to ... veracity." To help support the player's suspension of disbelief, we designed our character visuals to be photorealistic and to blend beautifully with the backdrop provided by the settings (figure 2) and also adopted a sophisticated mix of real world and game world audio in order to blur the boundary between fact and fiction [10,11].

Fig. 2. Player Photos from *Bram Stoker's Vampires* (left) and *The Amazing Transfabulator* (right) in site-specific mode

4   Conclusion

This paper has presented locative game mechanics and narrative techniques used to situate original and adapted literary content in cultural heritage sites. Rather than typical historical (e.g., tourist guide type) experiences, the two games are intended to offer a more literary type of cultural experience. While we have yet to conduct user studies, we expect the approach will generalize well to other cultural heritage sites. It is also easy to imagine characters of a more historical nature than those we decided to use for the two games presented here.

Acknowledgments. The author is grateful to the following current and former project contributors: Programming: Roisin Cotton, Katsiaryna Naliuka; Art, Design and UI: Daniel Burke, Tara Carrigy, Neil Delaney, Ant Vaughan; Audio: Natasa Paterson; Story: Regina de Burca. *The Amazing Transfabulator* was developed in collaboration with the steampunk community in Oamaru. *Bram Stoker's Vampires* was commissioned by Science Gallery for their 2012 exhibition GAME. Full credits are included in the respective smartphone apps.

References

1. Ballagas, R., Kuntze, A., Walz, S.P.: Gaming tourism: lessons from evaluating REXplorer, a pervasive game for tourists. In: Indulska, J., Patterson, D.J., Rodden, T., Ott, M. (eds.) Pervasive 2008. LNCS, vol. 5013, pp. 244–261. Springer, Heidelberg (2008)
2. Botting, F.: Gothic. Routledge (1996)
3. Carrigy, T., Naliuka, K., Paterson, N., Haahr, M.: Design and evaluation of player experience of a location-based mobile game. In: Proceedings of the 6th Nordic Conference on Human-Computer Interaction (NordiCHI 2010), pp. 92–101 (2010)
4. Dow, S., Lee, J., Oezbek, C., MacIntyre, B., Bolter, J., Gandy, M.: Exploring spatial narratives and mixed reality experiences in oakland cemetery. In: Proceedings of ACE, pp. 51–60. ACM (2005)
5. Farman, J.: The Mobile Story: Narrative Practices with Locative Technologies. Routledge (2013)
6. Kretschmer, U., Coors, V., Spierling, U., Grasbon, D., Schneider, K., Rojas, I., Malaka, R.: Meeting the spirit of history. In: Proceedings of VAST, pp. 1410–1452 (2001)
7. Montola, M., Stenros, J., Waern, A.: Pervasive Games: Theory and Design. Morgan Kauffman (2009)
8. Naliuka, K., Carrigy, T., Paterson, N., Haahr, M.: A narrative architecture for story-driven location-based mobile games. In: Luo, X., Cao, Y., Yang, B., Liu, J., Ye, F. (eds.) ICWL 2010 Workshops. LNCS, vol. 6537, pp. 11–20. Springer, Heidelberg (2011)
9. Nisi, V., Oakley, I., Haahr, M.: Location-aware multimedia stories: turning spaces into places. In: Proceedings of ARTECH, pp. 72–93 (2008)
10. Paterson, N., Kearney, G., Naliuka, K., Carrigy, T., Haahr, M., Conway, F.: Viking ghost hunt: Creating engaging sound design for location-aware applications. International Journal of Arts and Technology 6(1), 61–82 (2013). inderscience
11. Paterson, N., Naliuka, K., Jensen, S.K., Carrigy, T., Haahr, M., Conway, F.: Design, implementation and evaluation of audio for a location based augmented reality game. In: Proceedings of Fun and Games, pp. 149–156. ACM (2010)
12. Reid, J.: Design for coincidence: incorporating real-world artifacts in location-based games. In: Proceedings of DIMEA, pp. 18–25. ACM (2008)
13. Wilken, R.: Locative media: From specialized preoccupation to mainstream fascination. Convergence 18(3), 243–247 (2012)

Game Design and Development

Casanova: A Simple, High-Performance Language for Game Development

Mohamed Abbadi[1][(✉)], Francesco Di Giacomo[1], Agostino Cortesi[1],
Pieter Spronck[2], Giulia Costantini[3], and Giuseppe Maggiore[3]

[1] Università Ca' Foscari DAIS, Venice, Italy
{mohamed.abbadi,francesco.digiacomo,cortesi}@unive.it
[2] Tilburg University, Tilburg, Netherlands
p.spronck@uvt.nl
[3] Hogeschool Rotterdam, Rotterdam, Netherlands
{costg,maggg}@hr.nl
http://casanova.codeplex.com/

Abstract. Managing the flow of time and the coordination of multiple components in games (and other highly interactive applications) is a challenging task. Therefore game development requires a lot of effort, even for (apparently) simple scenarios. To reduce the cost and effort of game development, we designed a new computer language called "Casanova 2". Using a case study, we demonstrate that Casanova 2 can be used to implement typical game scenario's using functional programming constructs. Our evaluation shows that it has both a high performance and a high usability.

Keywords: Game development · Casanova 2 · Languages · Functional programming

1 Introduction

Computer and video games are a big business, and they have grown to the point that their sales are higher than those of music and movies [5]. For mobile games alone, predicted sales for 2017 exceed 100 billions of dollars [20]. The relevance of games as a social phenomenon is at an all-times high.

In the wake of this widespread adoption of games, their application areas have expanded. They are no longer used exclusively for entertainment. They have found applications in education, training, research, social interaction, and even raising awareness [7,19]. These so-called *serious games* are used in schools, hospitals, industries, and by the military and the government. Researchers use games to simulate environments and evaluate their results. These games do not enjoy the same rich market of entertainment games, but their social impact is nevertheless high [13].

An obstacle to the widespread use of serious games is that they are expensive to build. Since the resources of those who want to use serious games are usually

S. Göbel et al. (Eds.): JCSG 2015, LNCS 9090, pp. 123–134, 2015.
DOI: 10.1007/978-3-319-19126-3_11

quite limited, many serious games (and game-based research projects) fall short of their technological mark or fail altogether. This constitutes a high threshold that may cause innovative projects to be shut down prematurely.

The expenses of building a game are tightly related to the complexity of the structure of the game itself. At its core, a game features a state which describes the game world, plus the game loop that describes how the state changes over time. To avoid duplication of substantial effort in these areas, the game industry often uses ready-made components (also called "engines") [8], for example for graphics and physics, which *encapsulate* functionality in a modular way. As the number of components increases, complex concurrent [6] interactions between the components need to be realized. This yields additional difficulty.

Our main goal in this paper is to reduce the complexity of game code. We introduce *proper abstractions for game development, and build programming tools that implement those abstractions*. These abstractions would help developers in reaching their goals by substantially reducing development efforts, with a special benefit for smaller development teams that work on serious games. Since games are interactive applications, the proposed abstractions should not compromise the performance of the programs.

We begin with a discussion of games and their complexity, introducing a case study. We use our case study to identify issues in the way games are traditionally expressed (Section 2). We propose a tiny, concurrency-oriented, game-centered language (Casanova 2) for describing game logic, and show how the case study is expressed in this language (Section 3). We then evaluate the effectiveness of Casanova 2 for creating games in terms of performance and simplicity (Section 4). Sections 5 and 6 cover future work and conclusions.

2   Technical Challenges in Games Development

In this section we discuss games and their complexity through a case study. We consider a sample which fits within the space constraints of a paper, which at the same time shows the complex interactions that are typical for games.

2.1   Running Example

The running example we use is a patrol moving through checkpoints. The state of the patrol is made up by the position of the patrol P, and its velocity V.

```
P is a 2D Vector V is a 2D Vector Checkpoints is a list of 2D
Vectors
```

The logic of the game is given using a pseudo language:

```
P is integrated by V over dt V points towards the next checkpoint
until
    the checkpoint is reached, then becomes
    zero for ten seconds (the patrol is idle)
```

A game is said to run as a sequence of time slices, called "frames." A typical game runs at 30 to 60 frames per second. The pseudo code above describes the logic of the patrol, which runs every frame. The logic shows a typical dynamic present in any game, which is made up by continuous components (the update of P in our case) and discrete components (the update of V). As a result, P changes every frame, while V only changes upon reaching a checkpoint.

2.2   Common Issues

Dynamics such as the one described above are built in games either with engines or by hand.

Engines. An engine is a library built to offer solutions for specific tasks (such as graphics and physics control) in order to speed up the development process, by promoting code reuse and reducing mistakes. Examples of commonly used engines are: MissionMaker [2] and GameMaker [1]. By hiding complexity inside libraries and editors, developers only need to adapt their design to the engine. While popular, engines tend to have significant issues:

- Engines are often difficult, or even impossible, to expand and to adapt to the needs of the developer using them; this limits developers because some aspects of design might need to be adapted or left out due to of lack of specific support by the engine;
- Engines are often closed libraries. Even though engines are internally optimized, the possibilities for global optimization that take into account the game structure are very limited;
- Expertise is needed to master an engine. Since most (if not all) engines are highly complex to use, a significant effort of the developers is spent on learning the intricacies of the engine.

In general, a good engine offers good performance and a reduced possibility to make mistakes, but at the same time limits developers to the engine features and asks them to master most features before using the full capabilities of the engine.

Hand made implementations. A hand made implementation is used when developers are looking for specific behaviors, want to have more control on the game implementation, or when the support of the underlying platform is poor. Hand made implementations raise important issues to be considered before starting a new project:

- Games tend to be very large applications. As size increases, the number of interactions increases as well, together with the possibility to make mistakes;
- Optimization (when done by hand) adds complexity, because it requires supplementary data structures and may change the implementation of the game interaction. Optimization may also lead to (*i*) implementation issues (for instance some optimization may work only on specific architectures), and (*ii*) maintainability issues (any change in the game design should keep into account its repercussions on the implementation).

We now present an example of hand-made implementation of the patrolling dynamics following the style of [14]:

```
class Patrol:
  enum State:
   MOVING
   STOP

  public P, V, Checkpoints
  private myState, currentCheckpoint, timeLeft

  def loop(dt):
   P = P + V    dt
   if myState == MOVING:
     if P == Checkpoints[currentCheckpoint]:
       myState = STOP
       V = Vector2.Zero
       timeLeft = 10
   elif myState == STOP:
     if timeLeft < 0:
       currentCheckpoint += 1
       currentCheckpoint %= Checkpoints.length
       myState = MOVING
       V = Normalize(
           Checkpoints[currentCheckpoint] - P))
     else
       timeLeft -= dt
```

The `loop` function implements the patrolling behavior. It takes one argument `dt` which represents the delta time elapsed since the last frame. The very first line of the `loop` body implements the position update behavior. The velocity behavior depends on whether the patrol is moving or idle. While moving, we stop the patrol as soon as he reaches the checkpoint, and set the wait timer to 10 seconds. If the patrol is idle and the countdown is elapsed, the next checkpoint is selected. At this point the patrol points toward the new checkpoint and starts moving again.

2.3 Discussion

The patrolling sample illustrates a common division between design and implementation in games. Deceptively simple problem descriptions turn out to require surprisingly articulated implementations. Complexity mainly originates from the explicit definition and management of a series of *spurious variables* that are needed to program the logical flow of the problem but which do not come up in the design. In our case study, the spurious variables are `myState` (together with the definition of the state structure) and `timeLeft`.

A language suited for game development by persons for whom game development is not their main job, has two main requirements:

- *Performance*: games are highly interactive applications which tend to be filled with many dynamic elements; if the language in which they are built does not guarantee high performance, the player experience will suffer;
- *Simplicity*: the language should be easy to understand and easy to express game functionality in; if the language is not simple in these respects, it

requires an amount of training that is not within reach of those who are not game developers by profession.

Below we introduce a game-centered programming language and show how to rebuild the sample above with fewer spurious constructs, in a way that is closer to a higher-level, readable description.

3   Casanova 2

Languages, in general, offer more expressive power than engines, because of the possibility to combine and nest the constructs. A language specifically designed and built with game programming in mind can help with common aspects of game development (such as time, concurrency, and state updates) that regular languages do not encompass. In this regard, we present the language Casanova 2, based on [11], which takes its inspiration from the orchestration model of [15]. We show how Casanova 2 is designed in particular to express the typical dynamics present in games.

3.1   The Basic Idea Behind Casanova 2

An abstraction of a game should be able to represent its main elements, i.e., its state variables and their (discrete and dynamic) interactions. For this purpose, we built an (intentionally) small programming language of which the main features are *state* and *rules*:

(i) The *state* of a game is represented by a hierarchical type definition. Each node of the hierarchy is called an *entity* (besides the root, which is called *world*). Each entity contains a series of fields that represent primitive types, collections, or even references to other entities. Through access to shared data entities we achieve concurrent coordination.

(ii) The logic of each entity is defined as a series of implicitly parallel looping code blocks. Each implicit block, called a *rule*, represents a specific dynamic of the entity. A rule represents a dynamic, which can be continuous (simple and effect-free) or discrete (with side-effect, the most important of which is *wait*).

3.2   Casanova Patrol

We now show how we rewrite the patrol program presented in Section 2 using Casanova 2.

Listing 1.1. Patrol in Casanova 2

```
world Patrol = {
   V : Vector2
   P : Vector2
   Checkpoints : [Vector2]

   rule P = P + V    dt

   rule V =
    for checkpoint in Checkpoints do
       yield ||checkpoint - P||
       wait P = checkpoint
       yield Vector2.Zero
       wait 10<s>
}
```

The first three lines within the definition of Patrol describe the game state, containing three variables: the velocity V, the position P, and a checkpoint list Checkpoints. The next line gives the continuous dynamic, namely the rule P which runs once per frame, i.e., at every frame the position P is integrated by the velocity V over dt (a global value supplied by the system that represents the time difference between the current and the previous frame). The remainder of the definition gives the discrete dynamic, namely the rule V, which represents the movement between checkpoints. The checkpoints are traversed in order, and for each selected checkpoint checkpoint we change the value of the velocity in order to move the patrol towards it (yield checkpoint - P). Then, we wait until the patrol reaches the checkpoint (wait P = checkpoint), and once the checkpoint is reached we stop the patrol, by setting its velocity to 0 (yield Vector2.Zero) for 10 seconds (wait 10<s>). At this point the loop continues and a new checkpoint is selected. We reiterate the list again once we have traversed all the checkpoints.

Note that, in general, a game can be considered a series of entities that run in synchronization in order to achieve a specific goal. In Casanova 2 every entity in the state (as well as every rule in an entity) is in essence an *independent* concurrent program [17]. Coordination between these programs happens through a shared state.

3.3   Syntax

The syntax of the language (here presented in Backus-Naur form [18]) is rather brief. It allows the declaration of entities as simple functional types (records, tuples, lists, or unions). Records may have fields. Rules contain expressions which have the typical shape of functional expressions, augmented with wait, yield, and queries on lists:

Listing 1.2. Casanova 2 syntax

```
<Program> ::=
    <moduleStatement> {<openStatement>}
    <worldDecl> {<entityDecl>}

<moduleStatement> ::= module id <openStatemnt>      ::= open id
<worldDecl>      ::= world id ["(" <formals>")"] =
                     <worldOrEntityDecl>
<entityDecl>     ::= entity id ["(" <formals>")"] =
                     <worldOrEntityDecl>
<worldOrEntityDecl> ::= "{" <entityBlock> "}" <entityBlock>   ::=
{<fieldDecl>} {<ruleDecl>}
                     <create>
<create> ::= Create "(" {<formals>} ") = <expr> <formals>   ::= id
[":" <type>] {"," <formals>} <fieldDecl> ::= id [":" <type>]
<ruleDecl>   ::= rule id {"," id} "=" <expr> <type>        ::= int
|boolean   |float  |Vector2
                 |Vector3 |string |char
                 |list "<" <type> ">" |<generic>
                 |<type> "[" "]" |id
<generic>     ::= " " id <expr> ::= ...( typical expressions : let,
if ,
                 for , while , new, etc.  )
        | wait (<arithExpr> | <boolExpr>)
        | yield | <arithExpr> | <boolExpr>
        | <literal> | <queryExpr> | <seq>
<seq>        ::= <expr> <expr> <arithExpr>  ::= ...//arithmetic
expressions <boolExpr>   ::= ...//boolean expressions <literal>
::= ...//strings , numbers <queryExpr>  ::= ...//query expressions
```

3.4 Semantics

The semantics of Casanova 2 is *rewrite-based* [10], meaning that the current game world is transformed into another one with different values for its fields and different expressions for its rules. Given a game world ω, the world is structured as a tree of entities. Each entity E has some fields $f_1 \ldots f_n$ and some rules $r_1 \ldots r_m$.

```
E = { Field₁ = f₁; ...; Fieldₙ = fₙ;
      Rule₁ = r₁; ...; Ruleₘ = rₘ }
```

Each rule acts on a subset of the fields of the entity by defining their new value after one (or more) ticks of the simulation. For simplicity, in the following we assume that each rule updates all fields simultaneously.

An entity is updated by evaluating, in order, all the rules for the fields:

```
tick(e:E, dt) =
  { Field₁=tick(f₁ᵐ, dt); ...; Fieldₙ=tick(fₙᵐ, dt);
    Rule₁=r₁'; ...; Ruleₘ=rₘ' }
where
  f₁ᵐ, ..., fₙᵐ, rₘ' = step(f₁ᵐ⁻¹, ..., fₙᵐ⁻¹, rₘ)
  .
  .
  f₁¹, ..., fₙ¹, r₁' = step(f₁, ..., fₙ, r₁)
```

We define the step function as a function that recursively evaluates the body of a rule. The function evaluates expressions in sequential order until it encounters either a **wait** or a **yield** statement. It also returns *the remainder of the rule* *body*, so that the rule will effectively be resumed where it left off at the next evaluation of step:

```
step(f₁, ..., fₙ, {let x = y in r'}) =
  step(f₁, ..., fₙ, r'[x:=y])

step(f₁, ..., fₙ, {if x then r' else r''; r'''})
  when (x = true) = step(f₁, ..., fₙ, {r'; r'''})

step(f₁, ..., fₙ, {if x then r' else r''; r'''})
  when (x = false) = step(f₁, ..., fₙ, {r''; r'''})

step(f₁, ..., fₙ, {yield x; r'}) = x, r'

step(f₁, ..., fₙ, {wait n; r'})
  when (n > 0.0) = f₁, ..., fₙ, {wait (n−dt); r'}

step(f₁, ..., fₙ, {wait n; r'})
  when (n = 0.0) = step(f₁, ..., fₙ, r')

step(f₁, ..., fₙ, {for x in y:ys do r'; r''})
  step(f₁, ..., fₙ,
    {r'[x:=y];
      for x in ys do r'; r''})

step(f₁, ..., fₙ, {for x in [] do r'; r''})
  step(f₁, ..., fₙ, r'')
```

3.5 Compiler Description

Specific syntax built around the concept of altering the execution flow of a Casanova program allows the Casanova compiler to translate a Casanova program into an equivalent and high performance low-level program with the same semantics. The result is a high performance program made by a single switch structure, without nesting. A big advantage of this solution is that we may ignore typical software engineering rules, such as readability and code maintainability (as readability and maintainability are only needed for the Casanova specification of the game).

Usually, software engineering implementations are based on a series of nested state machines, but nesting yields a low performance because of the state selection. In contrast, the Casanova compiler produces an inlining of all the nested state machines into a single sound and fast state machine (which code is pretty much unreadable).

4 Evaluation

In this section we present a comparison between Casanova and other programming languages used for game development. The evaluation is based the on two essential aspects mentioned in Section 2: *performance* and *simplicity*. Performance is a fundamental indicator of the feasibility of a programming language that needs to be used in a resource-conscious scenario such as games. Simplicity is important as well, especially in those scenarios where development time and expense constitute a major concern (like for serious and indie game studios).

Table 1. Performance comparison

Language	Time per frame
Casanova	0.07ms
C#	0.12ms
JavaScript	24.07ms
Lua	20.90ms
Python	20.15ms

In particular we observe that, in many cases, programming languages for games offer a difficult either-or choice between simplicity and performance. As we will show, Casanova solves this apparent dichotomy by offering both at the same time.

4.1 Tested Languages

We have chosen four languages which represent various development styles and which are all used in practice for building games. We have mostly focused on those languages which are used for building game logic, and we have shied away from considering languages (such as C++) which are used for building engines or libraries [8], as Casanova is not "competing" with them. Three of the chosen languages are dynamically typed programming languages: Lua, JavaScript, and Python, which have as their main selling points simplicity and immediacy [9]. The fourth chosen language is C# because of its good performance and relative simplicity. One could argue that we are comparing our language, which might appear as a Domain Specific Language (DSL), with General Purpose Languages (GPL's). However, Casanova 2 is actually a GPL, although its main field of application is computer game development.

The "benchmark sample" simulates a game with ten thousands patrols. We made an effort towards implementing the sample by using coroutines and generators [12] whenever available, in order to express the game logic in an idiomatic style for each language. In order to compare the language functionality, we are only running the logic of the game and we do not execute any other component unrelated to it (such as the graphics engine), to produce a fair performance benchmark. The code samples can be found on [3].

4.2 Performance

We have generated tens of thousands of entities in a loop that simulated a hundred thousand frames. This corresponds roughly to half an hour of play time on a reasonably crowded scene. The results are summarized in Table 1.

As we can see from the table, the performance of Casanova 2 is of the same order as C#, and is multiple orders of magnitude faster than that of the scripting languages. In this simple but populated scenario, the limits of Lua, Python, and JavaScript, deriving from the high cost of dynamic lookup, are clearly shown. In

Table 2. Syntax comparison

Language	Syntagms	Lines of code	Total words
Casanova	47	31	104
C#	61	69	269
JavaScript	52	41	257
Lua	47	45	249
Python	50	34	214

addition, all languages use virtual calls to methods, such as those for managing and executing coroutines and generators, which add overhead at the expense of performance. In short, Casanova 2 generates highly optimized rule code which does not require general purpose constructs, such as coroutines in games, that often use virtual methods and dynamic lookups. In a sense, Casanova 2 uses all the static information it can to avoid work at runtime.

We believe that it is worthy of notice how much Casanova in this prototypical implementation offers a performance which is even better than that of a very high quality and mature compiler such as that of C#.

4.3   Ease of Use

Assessing the simplicity of a programming language is a daunting task. Just as much as beauty lies in the eye of the beholder, simplicity in programming languages heavily depends on the programmer preferences, history, and previous knowledge.

For the comparison we have taken the benchmark sample and implemented it with each of the considered languages. In order to assess the complexity of the sources we have:

1. counted the number of lines of each source, thereby assessing the size of the implementation, with the assumption that a bigger sample corresponds to more complexity;
2. counted the number of keywords and operators (syntagms) that come into play for each implementation, with the assumption that a high count corresponds to more required knowledge from the developer.

The results are summarized in Table 2. As we can see, Casanova 2 resulted in significantly less lines of code and syntagms, especially with respect to C# (the only other language with comparable high performance).

4.4   Summary

In conclusion, Casanova 2 has been shown to offer both good performance and simple code at the same time. On the one hand, Casanova 2 is as simple as "easy to use" scripting languages. On the other hand, this simplicity does not

(a) Dyslexia   (b) RTS

Fig. 1. Casanova games

come with the usual associated hit in performance that characterizes these languages. The performance of Casanova is even a bit better than that of C#, a highly optimized commercial language. A series of applications has been built with the language as part of teaching and research projects. One of those is an RTS game (see Figure 1b) that features complex integration with a professional-quality engine, Unity3D [4]. The other notable application is a game for detecting dyslexia in children (see Figure 1a). The game is currently being used as a tool for research and features some articulated animations and state machines. These applications can be found at http://casanova.codeplex.com/.

5   Future Work

The Casanova 2 language is capable of implementing usable and quite complex games. The language, while usable, is currently still in development as it misses a few features. In particular, support for multiplayer games is at this moment lacking. We believe that the existing mechanisms for handling time offered by Casanova 2 could be augmented with relatively little effort in order to greatly simplify the hard task of building multiplayer games. This is part of future work, that we are currently engaging in. We are also doing usability studies using students from various disciplines and backgrounds.

The high level view of the game that the Casanova 2 compiler provides can be exploited in order to improve the programmer experience. This means that we could use tools for code analysis (such as abstract interpretation [16] or type system extensions) in order to better understand the game being built, and to help with correctness analysis, performance analysis, or even optimization.

6   Conclusions

Casanova 2, a language specifically designed for building computer games, may offer a solution for the high development costs of games. The goal of Casanova 2 is to reduce the effort and complexities associated with building games. Casanova

2 manages the game world through entities and rules, and offers constructs (wait and yield) to deal with the run-time dynamics. As shown by the benchmarks in Section 4, we believe that we have taken a significant step towards reaching these goals. In fact, we achieved at the same time very good performance and simplicity, thereby empowering developers with limited resources.

References

1. Gamemaker. http://www.immersiveeducation.eu/index.php/missionmakerm
2. Missionmaker. https://www.yoyogames.com/studio
3. Performance evaluation code comparison. https://casanova.codeplex.com/wikipage?title=CasanovaPerformanceComparison
4. Unity 3d. https://unity3d.com/
5. Essential facts about the computer and video game industry 2011 (2011)
6. Bilas, S.: A data-driven game object system. In: Game Developers Conference Proceedings (2002)
7. Bogost, I.: Persuasive games: The expressive power of videogames. Mit Press (2007)
8. Gregory, J.: Game engine architecture. CRC Press (2009)
9. Gutschmidt, T.: Game Programming with Python, Lua, and Ruby. Premier Press (2004)
10. Klop, J.W., De Vrijer, R.: Term rewriting systems. Centrum voor Wiskunde en Informatica (1990)
11. Maggiore, G., Spanò, A., Orsini, R., Costantini, G., Bugliesi, M., Abbadi, M.: Designing casanova: a language for games. In: van den Herik, H.J., Plaat, A. (eds.) Advances in Computer Games. LNCS, vol. 7168, pp. 320–332. Springer, Heidelberg (2012)
12. Marlin, C.D.: Coroutines: A programming methodology, a language design and an implementation, vol. 95. Springer, Heidelberg (1980)
13. Michael, D.R., Chen, S.L.: Serious games: Games that educate, train, and inform. Muska & Lipman/Premier-Trade (2005)
14. Millington, I., Funge, J.: Artificial intelligence for games. CRC Press (2009)
15. Misra, J., Cook, W.R.: Computation orchestration. Software & Systems Modeling 6(1), 83–110 (2007)
16. Nielson, F., Nielson, H.R., Hankin, C.: Principles of program analysis. Springer, Heidelberg (1999)
17. Schneider, F.B.: On concurrent programming. Springer, Heidelberg (1997)
18. Strings, L.: Backus-naur form. Formal Languages syntax and semantics Backus-Naur Form 2 Strings, Lists, and Tuples composite data types (2010)
19. Susi, T., Johannesson, M., Backlund, P.: Serious games: An overview (2007)
20. Tim, M.: Global games investment review 2014 (2014). http://www.digi-capital.com/reports/

iATTAC: A System for Autonomous Agents and Dynamic Social Interactions – The Architecture

Edgar Cebolledo[✉] and Olga De Troyer

Department of Computer Science, WISE, Vrije Universiteit Brussel, Pleinlaan 2 1050,
Brussels, Belgium
{Ecebolle,Olga.DeTroyer}@vub.ac.be

Abstract. Realistic social interactions are an important aspect for games since it helps to create immersion and engagement. Some games like Façade or Prom Week have an impressive AI engine for this, but it is not an approach that fits all games. In this paper we present iATTAC, a system for realistic autonomous agents and their social interactions. To realize this, the concept of rituals is used to define social interactions, and the agents are given a personality and emotions, as well as a personal agenda and a memory to keep track of previous activities and their success. iATTAC is originally designed to be used for educational games against cyberbullying, but its design is general enough to be usable in other games. We describe the theoretical basis used as well as the architecture of the system.

Keywords: Character · Personality · Agent · Artificial intelligence · Emotions · Mood

1 Introduction

Historically, Role Playing Games (RPG) are the ones with the biggest amount of social interactions; these games contain Non-Player Characters (NPCs, agents, or characters) that interact with the player. Usually, the NPC can fight against the player, provide information, or chat with the player.

In certain situations, in particular for serious games where immersion and engagement are crucial (since some non-gamers can get easily discouraged or bored), it is important that the NPCs show realistic behavior (i.e., they act similar to how a human would behave), and in order to stimulate the player to play the game more than once, the behavior of these NPCs should not be too predictable.

An example of such a serious game is being developed in the Friendly-ATTAC project [1]. The aim is to develop an educational game to tackle cyberbullying (bullying that takes place using electronic technology [2]). Kids who are cyberbullied are more likely to use alcohol and drugs, skip school, have lower self-esteem, among others. There have been projects aiming to help teenagers coping or at least recognizing cyberbullying in social networks [3]. Friendly ATTAC focuses on creating a single player experience with which the player can learn about cyberbullying in a safe virtual environment.

© Springer International Publishing Switzerland 2015
S. Göbel et al. (Eds.): JCSG 2015, LNCS 9090, pp. 135–146, 2015.
DOI: 10.1007/978-3-319-19126-3_12

In the Friendly ATTAC game it must be possible to simulate interactions related to cyberbullying as well as non-bullying ones. In general there are three types of actors in a bullying scenario: the victim, the bully, and the bystander. If we want for instance to have the player play the role of a bystander, we need to have a system that allows NPCs to bully each other, and the player (bystander) must have the option to join in these interactions. We also want the system to adapt to the player's decisions, meaning that the actions have repercussions, so the player can see that helping others is beneficial and bullying or supporting the bully is, in the long term, not.

To deal with such kind of games, we aimed at developing an intelligent dialog system for NPCs that can support the type of advanced interactions described above. The dialog system should satisfy two major requirements. First, the NPCs must be autonomous, i.e. they must act on their own, without the need to script all of their actions. Secondly, we want them to engage in social interactions, to be able to start an interaction with another NPC, or to join an already existing interaction. In addition, the system should be easy to configure, and new NPCs and their behaviors should be easy to specify. The system is called iATTAC; its name referring to the context in which it was developed, the Friendly-ATTAC project.

This paper is structured as follows. First we will describe the state of the art in social interactions in games, then we will explain the basic principles of our system and explain the architecture of our system. Next, the validation of the system is discussed. The paper ends with conclusions and further work.

2   State of the Art and Related Work

We examined several games (not only Serious Games, but also commercial games) and studied their interaction systems. Some games have an advanced interaction system; we will discuss them briefly. We will start with some commercial games and then continue with the games and related work found in the academic community. For the commercial games, full details are not always available. However, it is interesting to consider them as they reflect the state of the art.

2.1   Commercial Games

StoryBricks [4] attempts to create autonomous NPCs that their own goals and non-scripted social interactions. There was an alpha release where it was shown how the NPCs move and react on their own, and they could start interactions on their own. Storybricks also provided a visual editor where adding interactions and goals for NPCs was done with a simple interface. It was intended as a system for easily creating stories for Massive Multiplayer Online (MMO) games.

The adventure, Open world RPG game Skyrim [5] has autonomous agents that pursue their own personal goals, and have their own schedules; when attacked, some can retreat and defend and some are more aggressive and try to fight back. Agents can start interactions with the player and with each other. Skyrim only has scripted conversations, some of them change based on certain actions, but in general they are not adaptive. It also has a subsystem named "Radiant" which can generate random quests, so the player always receives a new quest.

The Sims 3 [6, 7] is a game where the player controls one or more characters, but when the player is not giving input, the characters act on their own. The Sims use a personality model based on personality traits. Each NPC has 5 personality traits out of a list of 80 different ones. The game has a dataset of interactions, expressed in a declarative language. Each interaction can have more than one conditional, for example:

- *If my interlocutor makes a joke, then find it amusing.*
- *If my interlocutor makes a joke, but I have no sense of humor, find it boring*
- *If my interlocutor makes a joke, but I have no sense of humor, but we are good friends, then find it friendly*

When an NPC makes a joke, then the other NPC will execute the right conditional, based on the personal traits. The transactions with more conditions are evaluated first, so if an NPC has no sense of humor, but they are good friends, only the third conditional will be executed. This approach allows the NPCs to respond differently to the same stimulus. While the NPCs are designed so that each one is different and autonomous, there is no focus on dialogues. The Sims game has no dialogues, only symbols to express feelings and emotions.

2.2   Related Work

Façade [8, 9] is an interactive drama game where the player visits a married couple. Such evening meeting quickly turns into a big argument, where the player can takes sides, and each action changes the outcome of the argument. It provides a very dynamic system where the story continues with or without the player's input. The player can listen to the agents' interactions and can interrupt them, the agents also ask for input of the player in real time and react based on this input (or lack of it). The NPCs are autonomous and move based on their own personal goals. In Façade it is not easy to create a new story or to modify the game. First of all, each behavior needs to be written, which is similar to other simulations and games, but in addition of having autonomous characters, Façade also uses a drama manager. The drama manager is continuously monitoring the simulation, and can add or remove behaviors for the NPCs. The game does not indicate when a story beat changes, the story beats can be changed every minute, and chosen from a pool of around 200 beats. Façade took 2 years on authoring alone to have a 20-minute act.

Lies and Seductions [10] is a game in which the player controls a character whose goal is to seduce a rock star [11]. It provides a less dynamic system than Façade; the story of the game also continues with or without the player's input, and the players can see the agents' conversation in real time. Agents can know what the player is talking about if they are close to it and this also affects the game state. The interactions can only be one to one. If an agent is interacting with another, that interaction will be canceled if the player wants to start an interaction with any of the other NPCs. The interactions with the player are not in real time, the player has unlimited time to pick an option for interacting, and besides the main NPC, the player's character can repeat the same dialog over and over with the NPCs. The game uses dialogue trees for each interaction, where some branches are available based on the impression that the NPC has of the player. These impressions are determined by the player's actions on the game.

FearNot! [12] is a serious game about bullying, the player can communicate with the character in the game with free text input, it shares some similarities with iATTAC: it also uses the OCC model [13] for emotions and appraisal, but without a personality model as we do, the characters also have a memory of their actions.

Prom Week [14, 15] is a social simulation game like The Sims, but while The Sims focuses on having characters do all kind of actions like cooking, studying, working, etc., Prom Week completely focuses on social interactions. The game takes place a few days before the Prom night, and each character has different goals (become popular, get a boyfriend, become friends with someone, etc.). The game uses Reiss' personality profile and Berne's serious games (explained in the next chapter) to create believable characters. Although the NPCs can respond to the player based on the personal needs, personality and previous interactions, the NPCs do not start interactions on their own (with a few exceptions), and the game is limited to the player's actions, so the NPCs are not totally autonomous. The game has a large set of interactions and dialogues to make the interactions believable (more than 5000 rules).

Next to the work done in the context of a certain game, there is also work on the creation of believable NPCs. In [16, 17, 18] personality, mood and/or emotions are incorporated. However none of them completely satisfies our requirements (see next section): [16] is very general to be used as it is presented, [17] focuses on creating emotions, while [18] focuses on other aspects such as speech recognition. Therefore we developed iATTAC, which takes features from other models and expands on them.

For a more detailed explanation about dialogues and social behaviors, we refer to [19].

3   iATTAC – Basic Principles

We have two major objectives for our engine. First, the NPCs must be autonomous, i.e., they must act on their own, without the need to script all of their actions. Secondly, we want them to engage in social interactions, to be able to start an interaction with another agent, or to join an already existing interaction. We discuss the principles used to satisfy these requirements in the following two subsections.

3.1   Autonomy

To create NPCs that are autonomous, we decided to use personality models so that our NPCs have their own needs and can satisfy them by doing certain actions. This approach is also used by other games, e.g., The Sims, Prom Week, and StoryBricks.

One of the most recognized personality models is "The Big Five" [20]. This model consists of five personality traits: openness, conscientiousness, extraversion, agreeableness and neuroticism. Each person has a different intensity on each of these traits and that determines his personality. Although this model is widely accepted, it also has received criticism, e.g., Paunonen [21] mentions that there are more than five dimensions of personality.

Another personality model is Reiss' "16 Basic Desires" [22]. This model consists of 16 basic desires that each person has, but with different intensities. So, a person with a high desire for "Eating" is more prone to eat or to pay for gourmet food compared to someone with a low desire for "Eating". Every person has a different intensity for all 16 basic desires, and even if a person's desire intensity is very low, at some point that person will do something to satisfy that desire. Safety is a desire that is important for bullying scenarios, since victims usually do not up stand to the bullies because of fear. So a student with a low desire for safety is less prone to be successfully bullied.

Reiss's personality model is more suitable for our purpose. We could give NPCs different intensity values (target values) for the basic desires and use (some of) these values to drive their behavior. Performing some activities, not performing some activities, or activities performed by other NPCs will change the actual values of a NPC's basic desires. This will trigger the NPC to perform activities that will re-establish the target values of the basic desires. We can think of the 16 basic desires as bars (similar to The Sims) that increase over time; how fast they increase depends on the intensity of that desire. For instance, the actual value for the Eating desire of a NPC with a high desire for Eating will increase faster than for a NPC with a low desire for Eating. Also, when performing a social interaction, we can use the current values of related desires of each participant to predict the outcome of the interaction.

3.2   Social Interactions

Reiss' personality model is used to determine the needs and desires of NPCs. Some of those needs can be satisfied by activities like eating or sleeping, but NPCs also have social needs that can only be satisfied by interacting with other agents. For this, we use Eric Berne's transactional analysis [23] in combination with the "Universal Arbitrary Abstraction" (UAA) approach used in StoryBricks.

Eric Berne analyzed several social interactions and classified them in rituals, procedures, and social games. In them, a social transaction is a series of actions among several roles (each role is composed of one or more persons) with a predefined outcome and each role gets a "benefit" out of it. This benefit can be either positive or negative, and each role gets a different benefit. For example, in a bullying situation, there is usually a Bully, a Victim, and Bystanders. The first action is the bully saying or doing something harmful to the victim, then the bystanders may or may not perform another action. After this, everybody gets a benefit. The bully satisfies his need for Vengeance and Power, the bystanders get similar benefits but in fewer amounts. The victim on the other hand loses some Vengeance and Power, but gains Social Contact and maybe Safety. Using this approach we can structure social interactions in terms of roles, dialogs, and benefits for all parties involved. Berne analyzes several typical social interactions explaining how they are performed and why. This definition of social transactions is very helpful when coding social interactions since it provides information on what the roles expect from the interaction and why they start the social interaction in the first place.

StoryBricks uses the "Universal Arbitrary Abstraction" (UAA) approach to model personality, which is a list of numerical values based on the Big Five, given to behaviors, personality, and even to objects. StoryBricks give every item a UAA, so it is easy for the system to compare them and see how close the items are.

4   iATTAC – Architecture

The architecture of iATTAC is illustrated in Fig. 1. The architecture is based on the following concepts, which are discussed in the following subsections: Personalities, Personal Agenda's, Locations, Rituals, Memories, and Actions.

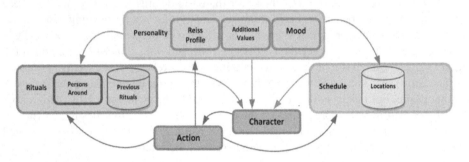

Fig. 1. Each action can modify the mood or add a new appointment or location. Actions are also stored in memory for consultation to decide on future interactions

4.1   Personality

The "personality" model of a NPC is composed of three components: Reiss Profile, Addition Values, and Mood (see the Personality box in Fig. 1).

As already indicated in the previous section, iATTAC uses Reiss' personality model. However, iATTAC is not limited to it as it can also be expanded to include more elements (referred as Additional Values), which may be needed for certain scenarios or game genres, like in SimBully [24]. By adding Additional Values, some rules can be enforced. For example, the "Stand up for yourself" rule in SimBully, which makes NPCs to not stand up to bullying situations, can be added by adding an "standingUp" additional value to all the behaviors that involve standing up to someone (this value could be set to a very high or low value so it would not fit the personality nor needs of any NPC nor action, so those behaviors would not be selected when the NPC updates). Each NPC has its own Reiss personality profile, with values that decrease with time and get changed every time the NPC performs an action, and a personality profile which is stable during the game.

Although the personality model allows us to have NPCs that react differently to each situation, a mood model is also useful since it allows the NPC to show emotions, and also allows to have more believable interactions, since a person can react differently based on the current mood. We use a mood model consisting of 6 emotions: anger, disgust, fear, joy, sadness and surprise [25]. We decided to use this model instead of others like OCC because the 6 emotions model is composed of emotions that can be expressed in facial expressions, so it will be easier to incorporate them into NPCs, i.e., using graphical representations. In principle, NPCs start with no mood at all (although this may be configured differently if we want to have a scenario where a NPC already has a mood at the beginning) and the social interactions can increase or decrease the value of the current needs and mood. Also, each NPC has a decay rate. So, after a while all moods will be back to zero if nothing alters them.

4.2   Location

A location is a place with attributes. Similar to Reiss' profile for NPCs, each location has a Reiss personality profile with Additional Values (called Aura) and a name, which serves as an identifier for the location in schedules. Similar to StoryBricks' UAA, each NPC, location, and behavior has a Reiss' personality profile, which is compared against the NPCs' personalities when a decision needs to be made. Each NPC can have a list of different locations, and even though two NPCs could have the same location in their lists, they may have a different profile for each of them. For example, if a NPC is always bullied in the hallway, then he may start to associate that location with negative social interactions.

4.3   Personal Agenda

Each character also has its own agenda (represented as "Schedule" in Fig. 1), which means that they are given own routines of activities and places (locations) where they regularly go. In the current implementation, each character has weekly activities, from Monday to Sunday. We plan to add support to add or delete activities during the game, so characters can have appointments or more unique agendas.

Like in real life, having an appointment does not mean that the character will attend it, but it will be considered when choosing an action. Furthermore, characters may go to different places during the day if it satisfies a need, even if it is not in their agenda (e.g. going to a cafeteria if the character is hungry).

4.4   Rituals

As already indicated, we used the concept of social interactions from Eric Berne. Although we used the term ritual, we are actually referring to games, rituals, and procedures. There are important conceptual distinctions between them, but for practical purposes, in our engine, we consider them all to be the same.

Rituals are the cores of the social interactions among characters. Rituals contain all information about social interactions: a unique name, frequency, maximum and minimum amount of participants, the type of interaction, the roles, and the ritual structure and steps. Also, some rituals can be used only when a specific ritual is being used, these are called 'counter-rituals'. Rituals are shared among all characters (at least in this version).

Each NPC has a module called "Persons Around", whenever an interaction is happening that allows more participants, this module will ask the NPCs around if they want to join the interaction. Then the NPC will weigh the possible actions and decide if it wants to perform an action. NPCs can decide if they want to participate in a ritual or not, they can also just walk away, or they can use a counter-ritual.

Counter-rituals can also be used by the current NPC in an interaction. For example, if character A is bullying character B, the expected outcome would be for B to feel bad because he was bullied, but if character B does not want to be a victim, then he can play the counter-ritual 'upstanding', where he stands up to character A. At that point, character A can accept the ritual and back off, or if there are more counter-rituals, he may for instance use another stronger type of bullying.

Rituals are not nested, once a ritual is interrupted by a counter-ritual, the social interaction will not go back to it (although it will be saved in memory and can affect future interactions), and the outcome of an interrupted ritual will not be added to any character.

4.5   Memory

Each ritual (finished or interrupted) in which a NPC was involved is stored in the personal memory of the NPC. The stored rituals are used to decide what type of interaction is more probable to be successful for the NPC.

4.6   Actions

Each action can influence the mood of a NPC or add a new appointment or location. It is also stored for determining future interactions. The actions are different for each game, in a First Person Shooter (FPS) for example an action can be to get a health kit or hide behind a box. In a Fighting game it could be to attack or defend, and in a game like The Sims reading a book, using the toilet, and starting a conversation are all actions. The rituals are only one of the many types of different actions.

Each time the engine requires a new action (this is dependent on the game; it could be every few milliseconds on a fast paced game or in a turn based game it would be whenever the turn starts), the NPC searches for the NPCs around him, the possible social interactions he could perform, the activities in his schedule, and the list of possible actions, then it scores all of them, weighting them based on the aura, the current needs, and the success of previous interactions. After weighting all the possibilities, an action is selected. This action is also stored in the NPC's memory for future references.

4.7   Credibility

In order to have believable NPCs, we have followed some of the design patterns for believable NPCs given by [26]:

- Initiative
  "A game component can take an action that is not directly perceived as a consequence of an event".
  In iATTAC, each NPC can decide to act at different times, and each NPC has their own needs and agenda, so they do not only react based on events.
- Awareness of Surroundings
  This refers to *"not only being able to detect player's avatars but all the phenomena in the world which can be affected by player's actions since these can be seen as part of the interaction"*.
  In iATTAC, each time there is an interaction, all the NPCs in the vicinity of the NPCs involved are updated to determine if they will join the interaction of not. Also, each NPC knows who is around them and can decide to interact with them.
- Own Agenda
  "A character can be observed to strive towards personal goals that provides a basis for taking the stance that she has an intentional state".
  In iATTAC, although the NPCs do not have personal goals, they do follow their needs and their own schedule of activities.
- Sense of Self
  "A character can monitor game state values related to that character and based actions on that information"
  In iATTAC, each NPC has a mood that changes with each action (or lack of), and they act based on their own personal needs, which are modified constantly through the use of actions.

There are some patterns given in [26] that are not applicable like "Visual Body Damage" or "Dissectible Bodies". Two others that are not yet covered are "Emotional Attachments" and "Goal-Driven Personal Development". We plan to work on incorporating them in the future.

5   Validation: SimBully

As a first validation, iATTAC was used in SimBully, a bullying simulator to control the NPC's behaviors [18]. SimBully is a simulator where NPCs autonomously move in a 3D environment from one place to another while interacting with each other. At all times the player can see the current time inside the game and the amount of bullying and upstanding per day. The way of interacting with Simbully is by enabling or disabling different social rules and to see how the bullying increases or decreases based on what rules are enabled or disabled. The rules are based on the results of the work of Ferráns and others [27]. The behavior of the NPCs is controlled by iATTAC. iATTAC controls how each NPC moves and interacts in the 3D environment. As explained, each NPC has an agenda and each location has an aura, so the NPCs can decide when to move based on the agenda and current needs. They can also start an interaction at any moment with other NPCs.

The work of Ferráns is adapted in terms or rules on top of iATTAC. Ferráns describes a series of rules that control how and why teenagers react in a school environment, for example, the rule "stand up to your friends" is a rule that indicates that friends are more prone to stand up to a bullying situation if the victim is a friend, but if the friend is the bully, they will support the bullying. These rules are incorporated on top of the weighting used by iATTAC when deciding if a NPC should join an interaction or not. If the rule is activated, then the NPC will join the interaction (on who's side depends on who he is more friends with), skipping iATTAC's weighting. If it is not activated then iATTAC will handle the interaction in the usual way.

6   Conclusions and Future Work

In this paper, we presented iATTAC, an intelligent dialog system that allows NPCs to participate autonomously in social interactions, i.e. they act on their own, without the need to prescript all of their actions, and are able to start an interaction with another NPC or to join an already existing interaction. For this, we have given NPCs a personality based on Reiss' personality model, combined with Ekman's emotions model, a personal agenda, and a memory to keep track of previous activities and their success. Furthermore, we used the concept of rituals to define the NPC's possible social interactions.

Our system is developed in the context of serious games against (cyber)bullying, but we believe that our approach is generic enough to be able to be used in different kind of games. For this reason, we are working on integrating iATTAC in a couple of different (serious) games. In general, most components can be reused but different rituals may be needed for different applications.

One application under development is a social network simulation related to cyber bullying. This requires changes to the rituals since the social rituals in social networks are different from those in face-to-face conversations. In social networks people can reply after days or weeks, and new interactions can occur at different times, which is usually not the case in face-to-face rituals.

Furthermore, we are incorporating iATTAC into an open source implementation of The Settlers of Catan [28]. In this game, we do not have social interactions, but each action in the game (like creating roads or buying cards) has an aura, so iATTAC can be used to compare actions and determine the best move.

References

1. Friendly Attac Project. http://www.friendlyattac.be/en/
2. U.S. Department of Health & Human Services. http://www.stopbullying.gov/cyberbullying/what-is-it/
3. Dinakar, K., Jones, B., Havasi, C., Lieberman, H., Picard, R.W.: Common Sense Reasoning for Detection, Prevention, and Mitigation of Cyberbullying. ACM TiiS **2**(3), 18 (2012)
4. Evans, R.; Short, E.; Bura, S.; Treanor, M. & McCoy, J.: Beyond Eliza: Constructing Socially Engaging AI GDC 2012, San Francisco, CA, USA (2012). http://gdcvault.com/play/1015386/Beyond-Eliza-Constructing-Socially-Engaging. (Accessed 7 July 2012)
5. Skyrim, Bethesda (2011)
6. Sims 3, Electronic Arts (2009)
7. Evans, R.: Representing Personality Traits as Conditionals. Aisb **4**(1), 35–42 (2011)
8. Façade, Procedural Arts (2005)
9. Mateas, M., Stern, A.: Façade: An Experiment in Building a Fully-Realized Interactive Drama: Game Developers Conference 2003, San Jose CA, USA, Game Design track (2003)
10. Lies and Seductions. Petri Lankoski (2009)
11. Lankoski, Petri, Horttana, Tommi: Lies and Seductions. Interactive Storytelling, Lecture Notes in Computer Science **5534**, 44–47 (2008)
12. Vannini, N., et al.: FearNot! a computer-based antibullying-programme designed to foster peer intervention. European journal of psychology of education **26**(1), 21–44 (2011)
13. Ortony, A.; Clore, G.L., Collins, A.: The Cognitive Structure of Emotions. Cambridge University Press (1990)
14. Prom Week, Expressive Intelligence Studio, UC Santa Cruz (2012)
15. McCoy, J., Treanor, M., Samuel, B., Tearse, B., Mateas, M., Wardrip-Fruin, N.: Authoring game-based interactive narrative using social games and comme il Faut. In: Proceedings of the 4th International Conference & Festival of the Electronic Literature Organization: Archive & Innovate (ELO 2010), Providence, Rhode Island, USA (2010)
16. Evans, R., Mark, D., Carlisle, P.: Breaking the Cookie Cutter: Modeling Personality, Mood, and Emotion in Characters. AI Summit GDC 2009, San Francisco, CA, USA (2009)
17. Velasquez, J.D.: Modeling emotions and other motivations in synthetic agents. AAAI 10–15 (1997)
18. Kshirsagar, S.: A multilayer personality model. In: Proceedings of the 2nd international symposium on Smart graphics, ACM, pp 107–115 (2002)
19. Cebolledo Gutierrez, E.O., De Troyer, O.: Dialogue and social behavior of agents in games. The Computer Games Journal 3(1) (2014)
20. Goldberg, L.R.: An alternative "description of personality": the big-five factor structure. Journal of Personal and Social Psychology **59**(6), 1216–1229 (1990)
21. Paunonen, S.V., Jackson, D.N.: What is beyond the big five? plenty! Journal of Personality **68**(5), 821–835 (2000)
22. Reiss, S.: Who am I? the 16 basic desires that motivate our behavior and define our personality. Penguin (2002)
23. Berne, E.: Games People Play: The Psychology of Human Relationships. Penguin (2010)
24. Cebolledo Gutierrez E.O., De Troyer, O.: SimBully: A 'Bullying in Schools' Simulation. In: Barnes, T., Bogost, I. (eds.) Proceedings of the 9th International Conference on the Foundations of Digital Games. Society for the Advancement of the Science of the Digital Games (2014)

25. Ekman, P., Friesen, W.V., Ellsworth, P.: Emotion in the human face: Guidelines for research and an integration of findings. Elsevier (2013)
26. Lankoski, P., Staffan, B: Gameplay Design Patterns for Believable Non-Player Characters. In: Proceedings of the 2007 DiGRA International Conference: Situated Play. (2007)
27. Ferráns, S.D., Selman, R.L., Feigenberg, L.F.: Rules of the Culture and Personal Needs: Witnesses' Decision-Making Processes to Deal with Situations of Bullying in Middle School. Harvard Educational Review **82**(4), 445–470 (2012)
28. Settlers of Catan, Klaus Teuber (1995)

Why Is This So Hard? Insights from the State Space of a Simple Board Game

Mareike Bockholt[✉] and Katharina Anna Zweig

Graph Theory and Complex Network Analysis Group,
Department of Computer Science, TU Kaiserslautern,
Gottlieb-Daimler-Straße 48, 67663 Kaiserslautern, Germany
{mareike.bockholt,zweig}@cs.uni-kl.de

Abstract. Serious Games research has become an active research topic in the recent years. In order to design Serious Games with an appropriate degree of complexity such that the games are neither boring nor frustrating, it is necessary to have a good understanding of the factors that determine the difficulty of a game. The present work is based on the idea that a game's difficulty is reflected in the structure of its underlying state space. Therefore, we propose metrics to capture the structure of a state space and examine if their values correlate with the difficulty of the game. However, we find that only one of the metrics, namely the length of the optimal solution, influences the difficulty of the game. In addition, by focusing on the part of the state space, which is actually explored by human players, we can identify properties that predict the game's difficulty perceived by the players. We thus conclude that it is not the structure of the whole state space that determines the difficulty of a game, but the rather limited part that is explored by human players.

Keywords: Serious games · Human problem solving · Complexity · Rush hour · Network analysis

1 Introduction

Serious Games development has become a growing field in research and industry in the last years. The idea of embedding a purpose, like mental or physical training, into a gaming environment has proven to be a fruitful approach. The core of many Serious Games, especially those concerned with cognitive training, contains a game logic which determines how challenging the game will be for players. In the process of developing Serious Games, it is thus of essential importance to understand what makes a game logic challenging for humans. Otherwise, it would be a matter of chance to design adequately difficult games which are neither too easy – therefore boring for players – nor too hard – and therefore frustrating.

Understanding how humans deal with tasks they are faced with and what they perceive as difficult is of great relevance in the field of *complex problem solving* [1]. Complex problem solving is a broad and active research field [2,3] which

© Springer International Publishing Switzerland 2015
S. Göbel et al. (Eds.): JCSG 2015, LNCS 9090, pp. 147–157, 2015.
DOI: 10.1007/978-3-319-19126-3_13

has produced a wide range of results about how humans solve problems, which heuristics they use, and which properties determine a problem's complexity. The present research focuses on the question which factors determine the difficulty of a problem. There exist several research approaches to identify these factors: Halford et al. [4] propose *relational complexity* as a measure for a problem's difficulty. They introduce the idea of a relation which contains the elements that need to be processed in parallel in order to solve the problem. The dimension of such a relation, hence the number of contained elements, is proposed as a complexity measure. According to Halford et al., humans are only able to process relations of dimension *four* or less, larger relations need to be split and processed serially. Therefore, the number of elements which need to be processed in parallel, can be used as a complexity measure. However, determining the relations and their dimension for a board game, and therefore, determining its difficulty with this method, is not obvious at all.

Kotovsky et al. [5] choose a different approach and show that the difficulty of a problem is strongly dependent on the cover story under which the problem is presented to the player: they presented the players different representations of the problem *Tower of Hanoi* and discovered that the solving performance varies considerably depending on the representation. However, these findings do not explain the *intrinsic* difficulty of a problem, since the *problem* is not varied, but the *representation*. Our focus of interest lies in the difficulty of the problem itself: which kind of structure makes a problem difficult, which one makes it easy – independent of the representation or cover story? In order to address this question, we use the concept and analysis of a *state space* of games as it is defined in the following. As a proof of concept of the proposed method, it is applied to a simple board game with defined states and defined rules of how to change these states for which it is feasible to compute the complete state spaces. Nevertheless, choosing such a simple board game might be of benefit for the development of Serious Games since gaining a general understanding of what is the dominant factor influencing the difficulty of a game, is an important prerequisite for designing appropriately difficult games.

2 Approach

The present work investigates the complexity of a simple board game. Our research is based on the assumption that the structure of the state space of a problem (i.e., of a board game configuration) should reflect the difficulty of the problem. For example, we assume that the size of the state space influences the perceived difficulty of a game, or that the average number of applicable rules per state correlates with the perceived difficulty. A motivation for this assumption can be seen in Figure 1 which shows the state spaces of games with a low and with an advanced degree of difficulty. It is intuitively clear that the structure of the state space should be related to the difficulty of the game. The present work aims to systematically investigate this relationship.

Anderson et al. define problem solving as a "goal-oriented sequence of cognitive operations" that transforms a present state into a desired state [6]. From this definition, the concept of a state space, already proposed by Newell in 1979 [7], arises almost immediately: a state space is a graph $G = (V, E)$, with V the set of all game configurations reachable from the start state by a series of allowed moves, $E \subseteq V \times V$ the set of possible moves. Hence, the state space (two examples are shown in Figure 1) for a fixed game configuration contains one node for each configuration which can reached from the start configuration by moves. The connections between the configurations represent possible moves. In this setting, problem solving consists of the task to find a path through the state space from the start to a goal state, which can be seen as a searching task. The representation as a graph allows us to use ideas from *complex network analysis* [8] to assess the complexity of the structure of the state space.

However, the present work shows that simple metrics to measure the structure of a state space are either not able to capture its structure in sufficient detail, or do not correlate with the problem's difficulty at all. For this purpose, the present paper is organized in two parts: we first introduce several metrics which are based on the structure of the state space and then show that they are – except of one – independent of the problem's perceived complexity. This can be confirmed by an experiment. As a second approach, we focus on the idea that the structure of the whole state space itself is less important than the part that is actually *explored* by a player. The first (qualitative) result is that the solving methods of different players are very similar to each other. Based on this, we focus on the part of the state space that is actually used by the human players. We therefore introduce measures that quantify aspects of the paths used by the participants in an online experiment and show that these measures do correlate with the perceived difficulty of the game. We thus provide evidence that the possible ways to solve a problem are less important than the ones that are normally used to solve it.

3 Analyzing the Structure of a State Space

The board game of interest is called *Rush Hour*.[1] It takes place on a grid of 6×6 fields, representing a parking lot, with one exit (cf. Figure 1). Cars of width 1 and length 2 or 3 are placed on the board vertically or horizontally and can be moved forwards or backwards as long as the needed fields are not occupied by any other car. Cars cannot move sideways and are not allowed to change their row or column, respectively. Given a configuration of cars placed on the grid, the goal is to find a sequence of moves that allows a particular car (the rightmost car in the third row, in Figures 1a and 1c the black one) to be moved from the board through the designated exit. *Rush Hour* is well suited for this research for several reasons: it is easy to understand how to play, yet it is still possible to design arbitrarily complex games as well as very easy ones, i. e. the range of complexity of possible games is broad and diverse. Furthermore, it is not obvious at all what determines the difficulty of a game.

---

[1] The game was invented by Nob Yoshigahara and is distributed by ThinkFun Inc. and HCM Kinzel (Germany).

Figure 1 shows two examples of state spaces. The first one is that of a version of a game which is designed for children, the second one for experienced players. It is obvious that the second network is larger and more complex. This finding was the starting point for devising complexity metrics quantifying the structure of the state space.

In [9], we introduce 17 metrics for Rush Hour start configurations based on the structure of the state space, following the assumption that these network analytic metrics reflect the complexity of solving the game. Out of the 17 defined metrics, only eleven are presented here, since the metrics which are left out are structurally similar to the ones presented here and do not provide any further insights. Detailed information are provided in [9]. The metrics are based on the idea that the perceived difficulty for solving a game could depend on several factors, as exemplified in (i) to (viii) where the metrics are indicated in italic. These factors are

(i)   the size of the state space (number of nodes and edges), since more states may need to be explored (leads to the two metrics *nodes* and *edges*),

(ii) the number of possible moves in every state (leads to the metric *avdg* as the average node degree),

(iii) the minimal number of moves needed to reach the goal state (*lsp* as the length of the solution path),

(iv) the number of correct moves relative to the number of possible moves in every state (*br* as branching complexity), whereas correct moves means all moves which decrease the distance to a goal state,

(v)   the number of possible shortest solution paths (*sp* as the number of shortest paths),

(vi) simple board game properties (*cars* as the number of cars and *fields* as the number of occupied fields on the board),

(vii) the average number of cars which can be freely moved in every state (*mc* as movable cars), since a smaller or larger number of objects which can be chosen as part of the solution way might influence the difficulty, and

(viii) the number of counterintuitive moves required in a solution path (*cm* as the weighted number of needed counterintuitive moves in a solution path and *cmpl* as this number normalized by the solution path length).

Point (viii) is based on findings from research in cognitive psychology which identify heuristics humans apply for solving a task. The most often used heuristic is called *hill-climbing* [10]: in this strategy, the current situation is compared with the desired situation, and the operator which yields a more similar situation to the solution is chosen. In our game, the goal is to unblock the black car and move it forward to the exit. A human playing the game according to the hill-climbing method will try to successively remove the blocking cars out of the way of the black car and to successively move it towards the exit. But there are starting configurations for which the solution requires moving the black car backwards or temporarily blocking the black car by another car. Because these kinds of moves contradict the hill-climbing method, we call these moves *counterintuitive moves* and suppose that a larger number of counterintuitive moves needed in a solution

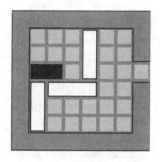

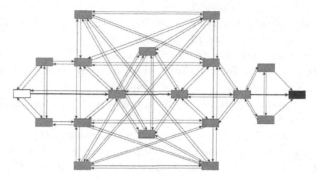

(a) A game configuration designed for children. The black block needs to be removed from the board by moving it through the exit on the right side. The white blocks are cars that can also be moved in their row respectively column. The other cells are unoccupied.

(b) The state space belonging to the board configuration in Figure 1a. Each node represents a board configuration, the edges represent changes of the cars' position. The white node on the left is the the start configuration shown in Figure 1a, the black node is the configuration in which the black car can be moved from the board. The shortest solution path of length four is indicated by bold edges.

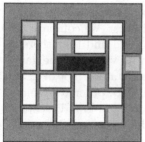

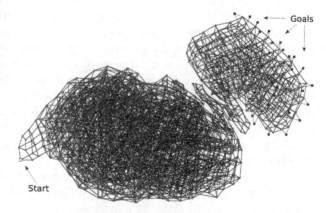

(c) A game configuration of moderate difficulty designed for adults. As in the children's version, the black car needs to be removed from the board through the designated exit.

(d) The corresponding state space to the board configuration shown in Figure 1c. The start node is in the lower left corner, the solution states in the upper right corner.

Fig. 1. Two examples of Rush Hour game configurations and their corresponding state spaces

should increase the difficulty of the game (cm). To reduce the influence of the solution path length, the metric cm is normalized by the length of the shortest solution path ($cmpl$).

In order to test the introduced metrics, an objective measure for the difficulty of a board game is needed. With an objective difficulty measure at hand, one could compare the proposed metrics' values with the true difficulty of the game and check if there is a connection. Though, in general, there is no objective measure for the difficulty of a board game. Therefore, in this article, we use two different sets of difficulty measures to approximate the true difficulty. The first set contains a single measure: the categorization by the manufacturer who classified the games into five categories (beginner (B), intermediate (I), advanced (A), expert (E), and grand master (G)). The second is a set of four measures and is based on online experiments with human players: (i) the perceived difficulty as rated after solving the game, (ii) the participants' average solving time, (iii) the participants' average number of moves, and (iv) the participants' average number of moves normalized by the minimal number of necessary moves. The manufacturer of the Rush Hour game provides five game card sets with start configurations of five different levels of difficulty. Leaving identical configurations and configurations with a slightly different goal aside, 173 start configurations with the manufacturer's rating of complexity are available. The game logic and a breadth first search from every start configuration was implemented in order to create the state spaces and to compute the metrics for every configuration.

We organize the results in two different sections, depending on the set of difficulty measure the metrics' values are compared with: first, we compare the metrics' values with the manufacturer's difficulty rating. We find that there is no correlation for most of the proposed metrics between its value for the game and the game's difficulty rating. The results are visualized in a box plot diagram shown in Figure 2a in which each metric's values are plotted, ordered by manufacturer rating (beginner, intermediate, advanced, expert, and grand master). It can be seen that the only correlation is between the difficulty and the metric lsp which is the length of the solution path. It is a surprising finding that none of the other metrics shows any connection to the difficulty of the problem as categorized by the manufacturer.

As a second set of difficulty measure to compare the metrics with, experimental data is used: we selected 24 games of different difficulty level and conducted a study in which each of the 74 participants played at least six of the selected games. After solving a game, the participants were asked for a difficulty rating. The experiment was conducted as an online study, i.e. the game was browser-based such that the participants could participate at any time and at any place. All moves the players did were logged with timestamps. It was made sure that every participant attempted every game at most once. The majority of the participants indicated that they have not played the game *Rush Hour* before.

From this study, the second set of difficulty measures as described above can be derived. As in the previous analysis, we found that only the solution length

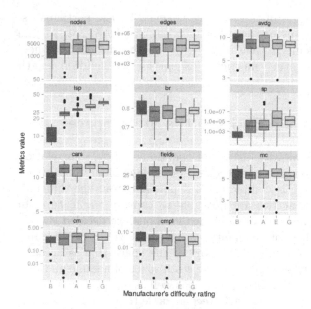

(a) Values of the complexity metrics categorized by the company's difficulty classification (beginner (B), intermediate (I), advanced (A), expert (E), grand master (G)). The scales are logarithmic. Games from the junior edition are excluded from analysis.

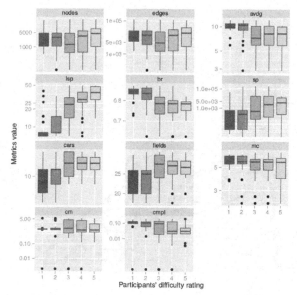

(b) Complexity metrics plotted versus the participants' difficulty rating. The scales are also logarithmic.

Fig. 2. The introduced complexity measures, compared with the manufacturer's difficulty rating and with experimental data

based metric correlated with the difficulty rating assigned by the participants; no correlation was found with any of the other metrics (cf. Figure 2b). All the other participants' based difficulty measures as defined above also do not show any correlation with the state space metrics – except for the solution length based one.

4 Quantifying Navigation Paths in the State Space

Since the proposed state space metrics, except of one, do not show a correlation with any of the difficulty measures, there are two possible explanations: either a game's underlying state space is completely independent from the difficulty of the game, or the proposed metrics are not able to capture the features of the state space which determine the game's difficulty. Thus, we decided to look more closely at how the participants navigated in the state space of the game while solving it, i.e., in the structure of the part of the space that is actually explored by the players. In Figure 3, we show the state space of a game and how the participants navigated through it. Both in this as well as in the visualizations for other games (not shown here), it is clearly recognizable that all of the participants preferred to take almost the same route through the state space although it is not necessarily the shortest one. This qualitative observation supports the assumption that the players are guided by the same heuristics in their solution strategy.

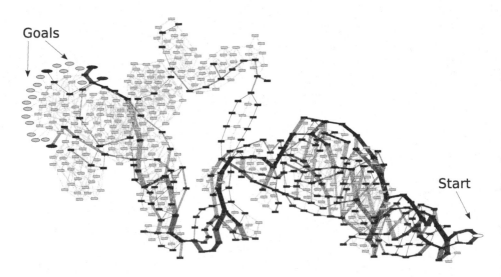

Fig. 3. Visualization of a state space and how the participants navigated through it while playing. The start node is elliptic and white (on the right side), visited nodes are black, not visited nodes are gray. Reached final nodes are black and elliptic, not reached final nodes are gray and elliptic (on the left side). The thickness of the edges shows how many from the 29 players took this transformation.

In order to approach the question of why it is more difficult to find a way through the state space to reach a solution for some versions of the games than for others, we examined the navigation of the participants through the state spaces more closely. The assumption is that participants lose their way while finding a solution, this could give them the impression that the game is harder.

Modeling that a player *gets lost* or is *losing one's way* can be done in several ways. If players struggle with finding a way to a final state, they will surely need more moves than necessary. Therefore, we consider how many moves the players needed in relation to the number of necessary moves. Indeed, a correlation between the perceived difficulty of a game and the number of used moves normalized by the number of moves in the optimal solution can be found as it can also be seen in Figure 4a.

The second approach to quantify a player's loss of orientation is to count the number of times the same state is visited within one trial of solving a game. For each state and player, we define as the *node visitation* the number of times the player visited this node while playing. As a measure for losing orientation while solving the game, the *average node visitation* and *maximum node visitation* are considered, the former being the mean value of all node visitations of all nodes visited, the latter being the maximum value for one player and one game.

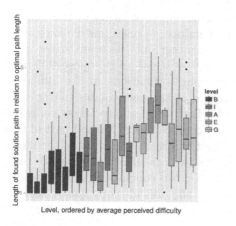

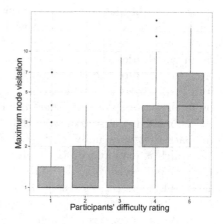

(a) Relative path lengths of the selected games. The x-axis contains each of the 24 games which were played by the participants, the games' ordering on the x-axis is determined by increasing average difficulty rating by the players. The y-axis shows the length of solutions found by the players, normalized by the length of the optimal solution of the respective game.

(b) Maximum node visitation of all players and all games plotted against the participants' rating of the respective game.

Fig. 4. Two different approaches of capturing a player's loss of orientation

Figure 4b shows the *maximum node visitation* for all games and all players, ordered by difficulty rating of the players (the corresponding figure with the *average node visitation* is except of the scale very similar to this one). The figure reveals a significant relation of the node visitations to the difficulty classification of the players. Therefore, the degree of how much a player loses orientation is a good indicator for how difficult he or she will perceive the game. This leads to the conclusion that a problem's complexity does not only depend on objective properties, but there is also a high correlation with the individual performance. Note furthermore that the maximum node visitation takes on surprisingly high values, indicating that getting lost in a huge state space is a general issue in human problem solving. This could also be an important insight for the development of Serious Games since supporting the player not to visit the same state several times, can be realized in a Serious Game and avoid frustration on the players' side.

5   Conclusion and Outlook

The present work shows that although it seems obvious that the state space of a game is expected to reflect the game's difficulty for a human, the most intuitive metrics do not capture the game's difficulty. Only one not surprising metric, the length of the optimal solution path, shows a strong correlation to the game's difficulty. This finding is consistent with the results of Jarušek and Pelánek [11]. Jarušek and Pelánek also assume that the structure of the state space of a problem should determine the difficulty of the problem, and propose different metrics to measure the structure, but find poor correlations to the difficulty as well [12]. However, a qualitative observation of the participants' navigation through the state space confirmed the known fact that humans follow common methods in solving a problem and that this is constrained to a small part of the state space that is actually used by them. By focusing on this part of the state space, which is explored by the human players, we can identify properties that predict the perceived difficulty of the players. We thus conclude that it is not the structure of the whole state space that predicts the difficulty of a game, but the rather limited part that is explored by human players, which is, moreover, less individual than previously thought.

In future work, it might be interesting to consider the structure of reduced state spaces of *Rush Hour* due to the following reasons: in the course of a game, there are situations in which two or more cars need to be moved, but it does not matter in which order these moves are taken. Though, each of the possible move orders induces its own path in the state space while actually representing the same moves. In other situations, it is not of importance for the further game if a car is moved one cell more or less when it blocks the same set of other cars in both situations. Nevertheless, all future game states are multiplied by the number of equivalent move possibilities since every distinct position of a car generates a new state in the state space, even if they represent very similar situations. This is also reason for the large size of the state spaces and might explain why the size of the state spaces does not show any correlation to the difficulty of the game. Therefore, it might be worth shrinking the state spaces in the sense that states with the same meaning as described above are merged into one state. This step should decrease the size of the state spaces enormously and might change the values of our defined metrics. It is imaginable that the size of the reduced state spaces then allows a prediction of the difficulty of the game.

In addition to that, in order to generalize the results to the domain of Serious Games, other games need to be considered. The structure of state spaces might be totally different for other games which might influence the difficulty. For example, not all games generate state spaces in which all moves are reversible: there might be moves which do have a greater influence on the further game course than others since they make the player leave a part of the state space which can not be entered again. Further research needs to show if the presented results can be transferred to different games.

References

1. Frensch, P., Funke, J.: Complex problem solving: The European Perspective. Lawrence Erlbaum Associates, New York (1995)
2. Funke, J.: Problemlösendes Denken (2003)
3. Newell, A., Simon, H.A.: Human Problem Solving. Prentice Hall, Englewood Cliffs (1972)
4. Halford, G.S., Wilson, W.H., Phillips, S.: Processing capacity defined by relational complexity: implications for comparative, developmental, and cognitive psychology. Behavioral & Brain Sciences 21, 803–865 (1998)
5. Kotovsky, K., Hayes, J.R., Simon, H.A.: Why are some problems hard? Evidence from Tower of Hanoi. Cognitive psychology 17, 248–294 (1985)
6. Anderson, J.R.: Cognitive Psychology and its Implications. W. H. Freeman and Co., New York (1980)
7. Newell, A.: Reasoning, problem solving and decision processes: the problem space as a fundamental category (1979)
8. Newman, M.E.: Networks: An Introduction. OUP Oxford (2010)
9. Bockholt, M.: Ein netzwerkanalytischer Ansatz zur Untersuchung der Komplexität des Rush-Hour-Spiels. Bachelor thesis, Heidelberg University, Institute for Computer Science (2013)
10. Anderson, J.R.: Problem solving and learning. American Psychologist 48 (1993)
11. Jarušek, P., Pelánek, R.: What determines difficulty of transport puzzles. In: Proc. of Florida Artificial Intelligence Research Society Conference (FLAIRS 2011), pp. 428–433 (2011)
12. Jarušek, P.: Modeling problem solving times in tutoring systems. Masarykova univerzita, Fakulta informatiky, Disertacnı práce (2013)

Social Network Analysis and Gaming: Survey of the Current State of Art

Wolfgang Eugen Schlauch[(✉)] and Katharina Anna Zweig

Graph Theory and Complex Network Analysis,
Department of Computer Science, University of Kaiserslautern,
Gottlieb-Daimler-Straße 48, 67663 Kaiserslautern, Germany
schlauch@cs.uni-kl.de

Abstract. We report on the current state of the art of social network analysis based on the enormous datasets that exist in massive multiplayer online games and multiplayer online arena games. At least since the rise of World Of Warcraft as a massive multiplayer online game, the online gaming world is slowly becoming a center of attention for game developers and players, but there is still little analysis done on the connections between the players of a game. In this paper, an overview of what can be entailed by such an analysis is given, including a wide range of possible approaches, including classic social network analysis, or how to find a not predefined order of referral between the players. The biggest problem for this new area of research is the dynamic of connections coupled with the enormous amount of data and the unknown relations between players in their real lives and other games. But exactly these connections are crucial for serious game development. Acquiring information about the social structure behind these games can give valuable insights for developers.

Keywords: Massive multiplayer online game · Multiplayer online battlefield arena · Social network analysis

1 Introduction

Despite being on the research agenda for almost 20 years (e.g. [1]), there have not been many in-depth analyses of social network in massive multiplayer online games (MMOG) and even less in multiplayer online battle arena games (MOBA, also known as action real-time strategy, ARTS, or Hero Brawler) that stem from classic one-vs-one games [2]. Social Network Analysis (SNA) is the application of network theory and metrics to data that contains actors and connections between them. The metrics show a great variety, from the number of connections a single actor has to the minimal maximum number of connections one has to use to get from actor A to actor Z to measures of information flow between actors. Which metrics are applied is decided by the researcher and sometimes a major point of discussion.

© Springer International Publishing Switzerland 2015
S. Göbel et al. (Eds.): JCSG 2015, LNCS 9090, pp. 158–169, 2015.
DOI: 10.1007/978-3-319-19126-3_14

Most of the current MMOG research is based on games that are known in a restricted community with a small sample of players, or based on a very small sample of all possible players (< 5000) in very big games [3–6]. Researchers are faced with the masses of players in games like World of Warcraft [7–10] and try to analyze as many of the players as possible. Most of this research is based on methods akin to the ones used in SNA or Organizational Social Network Analysis [11]. There seems to be a silent agreement that the techniques applied are valid for small as well as large networks without any differentiation. In general, the results do support this and reveal that humans stay humans even when they are playing elves, orcs, aliens, or leaders of a military empire. Players trade, interact and attack each other, shun bad guys (i.e. cheaters), and tend to mimic successful playing strategies (depending on their goal), which can be interpreted as a type of learning.

Other gaming activities found in social network analysis literature are actually based on games that can be played in social network platforms, for example "Project Waterloo" [12] or "FarmVille" [13]. Those are also interesting, since they can be based on the competitiveness of actual friends in an online social network, but they are of no concern to us since the social network is not inherent but explicit in the social network platform. Furthermore there exist whole communities for the sole reason of comparison and competition, for example Fitocracy[1], RunKeeper[2], FridgeGraph[3], iDoneThis[4], that allow users not only to achieve goals, but also force them either to exercise, to lie, or to do their tasks, next to their social interaction with other users. This is called gamification. Analyzing those networks might yield information for sociologists, companies, or employers, but it is out of the scope of this paper.

All of the above mentioned different types of games involve not only the game-part, but a social part as well. For this paper we focus on MMOG/MOBA, that usually provide their overwhelmingly large worlds also chatting capabilities, forums, and other forms of interaction. Those games are not designed to offer a social structure, so it is interesting to see how this structure develops and how it changes the behavior of the players. Therefore, the first question is how data is gathered and reduced to networks that can be analyzed. Furthermore, seeing the broad range of sizes networks can have, the analysis itself becomes a hard task. Algorithms that are designed for small networks (< 1000 nodes) can be challenged with large to gigantic networks ($\gg 10^6$ nodes). In the following we will show how data is usually gathered, followed by some of the main facets of analyzing game networks, including group and community analysis, player type analysis and a classic social network analysis. Last but not least we clarify why MMOGs are becoming more important to the field of serious games.

---

[1] fitocracy.com
[2] runkeeper.com
[3] www.fridgegraph.com
[4] idonethis.com

2   Data Gathering

Gathering data from an online game is actually hard. Even though it sounds like a straightforward task, there are different ways to perform this.

An established method is observing a game, getting a clue where many of the players discuss their needs, i.e., finding forums or IRC-chatrooms of players and posting questionnaires there [14,15]. Questionnaires are an established way in social sciences to get information about persons and their relationships to other people. Since questionnaires are answered in a fixed fashion, i.e. multiple-choice, or in a way that the researcher can interpret the answers herself, it is hard to get a complete social network from a questionnaire. Moreover, people tend to answer questionnaires only with their most recent past in mind. Due to this, it can happen that even so they interact daily with another person they forget about this person. Additionally, if an incentive is provided, i.e. there is a price involved, answers can be falsified seeing that people feel obligated to feel positively about the surveyor [16,17]. Besides those effects, the commonly known problems with questionnaires also apply. It is hard to estimate if the sample size is sufficient to retrieve unbiased results, if the questionees are chosen at random or they are biased by the group they belong to, by friendship relations, or some other not necessarily obvious relationship [18].

Another option is crawling websites of the games to retrieve data about games played [19], who joined teams with whom or to get general information about players and their strategics. This method is only applicable to games that log every instance or have a mechanism that allows to get some information. Both of these options are not necessarily complete for the whole game. For MMOG/MOBA usually more than one server exists and logging all games simultaneously onto a single server would be time and (memory-)space consuming. Some researchers log in on a particular server and start scripts that log all players currently on the server [7,20–22]. A very prominent dataset was released by the providers of a game (Everquest II) and much research was done on this game in particular (e.g., [3,9,23]). Besides that, the Pardus dataset, gathered by Szell and Thurner [24] is the most complete dataset known, since the researchers themselves developed and deployed the game. But only few researchers deploy their own servers or even their own game [10,24] but have therefore almost complete data of several years of gaming saved. Other datasets are either subsamples of smaller sizes or not made public available.

More information about issues concerning data gathering can be found in [25].

In the coming section we describe different types of analysis that are performed on game data. Since this is a broad field and includes many different kinds of investigations, only the more prominent facets are mentioned.

3   Analysis

As shown in the last section, there are many ways to gather data on MMOGs. For analyzing, there are many different ways as well. Moreover, is network analysis and graph theory suited for the task of the analysis of several thousands of nodes with possibly millions of edges? In the following we look at different approaches.

3.1   First Steps of Analysis

A paper that was concerned with the analysis of a MMOG was written by Ducheneaut et al. [7]. The game analyzed by the researches, World of Warcraft, existed at this point in time for two years. The researchers did already a rather extensive analysis of their gathered data. They analyzed play time, level-up time, time spend in a level, and performed a comparative study between the time spent playing and the leveling speed. This analysis was based purely on data per player and did not involve any network features. Additionally, they analyzed grouping by playing and grouping in so called guilds, groups of players that work closer together to gather points for their guild. Guilds were identified during their data gathering process by observing team-tags. For grouping by playing they found that the higher the level, the more likely it is to look for groups to fulfill tasks. For guilds they found on average surprisingly small guilds that were, maybe even more surprising, not as tightly knit than thought. Core players of guilds seemed to interact more with their guild and provided the backbone of the guilds. Ducheneaut et al. performed with this analysis a very solid basis analysis. They did not use more involved measures to find their results.

While the first part of the described analysis does not involve SNA, it provides already information about learning and dedication. Especially the leveling speed indicates how well a player understands to use the characters abilities to the best. Analyzing the best players in this regard together with their guild and other co-players can give information about how this knowledge is distributed, how it is copied and how other players adapt this specific style of play to their skill set. To the best of our knowledge this was not done. The serious gaming community can extract form this the learning abilities of players and adapt their games to provide a better experience to players.

While Ducheneaut et al. did look for guilds and their general playing style, the research on guilds can be performed more explicitly, by taking all known members of a guild and analyzing their behavior as is shown in the next section.

3.2   Analysis of Groups

Along the lines of investigation of guilds or other community types in MMOGs, small sized groups are the most common target. Depending on the game, a guild may contain up to 1000 members. The ones under investigation by researchers tend to be smaller or include only the core players. Most of the research concerned with such small groups, in comparison to the amount of players that a game has, touches standard network measures such as density, transitivity, reciprocity, as well as centralities as the in-degree-, out-degree-, and betweenness centrality. Still, even guild-intern networks are, according to Ducheneaut et al. [7], rather sparse. The hypothesis that the density of a guilds communication network correlates to its performance did not hold in an empirical investigation by Lee [26], such that sparsity does not seem to bad to performance, but it still impacts the survival of a guild [27].

For example, Ang [28] analyzed the connections and the type of connection in a small sized group (76 members). Ang looked at the overall connections and furthermore at connections based on asking specifically for help, giving help to open questions, friendly remarks, game chat, real life chat, group management, coordination, task interaction and social interaction. Not very surprisingly some of the networks created by those different views are more sparse than others. Most interesting are the "help"-networks, either asking for or giving help, where one could think to find a relatively higher reciprocity than in other networks. The reciprocity, a measure indicating how often an edge from actor A to actor B is reciprocated by an edge from actor B to actor A [29], was in both below 0.1, supporting the hypothesis of the author that people who ask for help usually do not get asked themselves. Moreover, giving help tends to occur in small closed groups.

Other work investigates the claimed strength of association between guild members and tries to find strong components in the guild [15]. Stensson performed an online survey of a guild of World of Warcraft players, but had a low response rate ($\sim 50\%$). Still, the results show that the longer a player was in a guild and the longer he played, the better embedded he was in the guilds social network.

Another idea that used a multi-layered approach to find clusters or communities was used by Pang and Chen [21]. The researches investigated the activities players could do in their game. These activities are battles with other players, battles as a group against non-player characters (raid), and inner-group activities. Overall, they found that a few key players connect the three possible activities by participating in all of them and being information providers. The researchers discovered that fighting in a group needs a high level of organization, while the other activities do not need as much organization. This is also pointed out by Ducheneaut et al. [27], next to the possibility that a player can have several characters and the more a player is immersed in the game, the more likely it is that next to his main character there is also a second character to level up and a character for trading (and other inner-group activities).

None of the investigations used the network the research was based on as a ground truth and tried to find the communities by a clustering algorithm as the Girvan-Newman algorithm [30,31] or the Louvain-method [32]. This could be fruitful, since the accuracy of the algorithms is said to be rather high. For the guild sizes of up to 1000 members this approach works fine, but for larger networks it might be interesting how well they fare. The use of algorithms could also suggest new groupings, in other words, suggest the change of guild membership for some players.

Overall, grouping is a standard effect of human beings. Still, the development of leading and coordinating functions needed to organize group activities such as raids, to control a group of players, or to manage several accounts seems to be of importance for the more successful groups and players. A better understanding how these skills are developed and transferred throughout connections in a network can be helpful to engage players to play more serious games.

Another facet that was discovered during this research was the difference between the player behavior and how it relates to being part of a guild. Moreover, the more social a player is, the more knowledge of other players and possibly their adventures in the respective world he can have. Such players tend to know how to solve problems or at least know someone who knows how to solve a problem. Thus, an implicit hierarchy may form between core players with a lot of experience and peripheral players, that are in need. How hierarchies emerge in a MMOG is another question considered in the following.

3.3   Establishment of Hierarchies

Another important research item is given by the surprising observance that MMOG and MOBA both develop not necessarily intended hierarchy structures. Most game designs nowadays support the guild/clan/community structure by incorporating it in the game's mechanisms. As an example, World of Warcraft gives special guild reputation points for certain activities. Ducheneaut et al. [7,27], Kirman [4], and Stensson [15] reported that not all members of a guild are equally active and some become more experienced, more interactive with other players, or more helpful during their play experience. Similar effects were also investigated by questionnaires [6]. The researchers were interested in several hypotheses, including if a player is trying to play more often with a successful player, a like-minded player, or a prestigious player. Furthermore, they were interested if a player's performance increases the more often she plays with others. They used Snijders network models [33] to create 106 graphs resembling the real networks to figure out which of their hypotheses are true. They were able to show that some of their hypotheses were plausible explanations for the network structure. Most important among the hypotheses for sociology was that players tend to interact with like-minded players and that transitive closure occurs in game networks as well. This research partly explains the structure and development of a order in a crowd of unordered players. Finding these implicit structures without having information about more than who played with whom was done by Pang and Chen [21]. They gathered data as ground truth and used a label-propagation algorithm to see if it is possible to find players that connect different activities (battle, raid, party) and thus different players. These players were the connecting parts of the investigated group of players. The players that participated in more than one activity can be seen as information provider between the different sets of players. Analysis of time and intensity players invested in the games revealed, that there are three major types which can be called hardcore players, casual players, and peripheral players [4,7]. Especially hardcore players are main pillars of hidden hierarchies, since they build a solid core of a group and can be asked for help quite easily.

A side effect of having a diverse group of players can be clustering of like-minded players, i.e., that guilds form that are devoted to battles but have as good as no social interaction and therefore no hierarchy. Guilds like these usually disband after a short time [27].

We showed that there are many types of analysis possible, but there is actually also "standard" social network analysis done, i.e., a network of the players of a game is taken and several algorithms are run and interpreted afterwards. For this, a complete (sub-)dataset is necessary and was used by Szell and Thurner as shown in the following.

3.4   "Classic" Social Network Analysis

The articles discussed above used none of the more complex measures of graph analysis. They were either based on an analysis of the degree distribution and correlations to the play time, on groups and questionnaires, or on observed behavior in different play modes. We will now show that it is possible to apply more complex measures in this type of research as well, provided that the network is (almost) complete.

The research from Szell and Thurner [10,24] based on the game Pardus is different in several aspects. They developed a game with the purpose of analyzing the players with their consent. They allowed players to befriend one another or be enemies with each other. They measured for a period of 445 days everything a player did, including lifetime (how long a player was active), chatting (how often and how much the player chatted), messaging (how often did the player sent messages), friendships and enmities, as well as the degree sequence to confirm the assumption of preferential attachment. With this data they performed a more classical network analysis based on measures like assortativity, reciprocity and clustering coefficients. Assortativity is a measure of homophily, usually in the sense of either the number of connections or the type of connections. Reciprocity measures how many connections are mutual, while the clustering coefficient compares the number of closed triplets to the number of triplets that are not fully connected. This set of metrics sets them apart from other researchers. The aspect that is most interesting is that it was possible to analyze the development of the network over time with established measures from graph theory, besides the connections the players made to each other. The network provided evidence of network densification as well as triadic closure. Moreover, due to the fact that players could mark each other as an enemy the authors were able to test for evidence of the hypothesis of "the enemy of my enemy is my friend" (and alike balanced complete triads [34,35]). They did not find any evidence to support or deny this theory, so it might be that "the enemy of my enemy is my friend" but it is not necessarily like that. Last but not least they provided similar insights as Blackburn et al. [36]. While Blackburn and colleagues investigated the behavior of honest players against cheaters, Szell and Thurner investigated the behavior of players against private and public enemies. The behavior against private enemies did not influence the overall game-play and resulted in small as well as private wars. Public enemies attacked without differentiation between friend and foe in a destructive role and were thus reported in forums and chats and were marked as enemies by people who were friends with the reporting player; other players who were not friends with the reporting parties still seemed to take those threats earnest and turned hostile against the reported player. Similar behavior was shown by Blackburn et al. [36] in an investigation of players of games from a single company that deployed an anti-cheating system. Players can be marked to have cheated in a game. Known cheaters tend to be dropped as friends, and people who have many cheaters as friends tend to become cheaters themselves.

A complete "classic" network analysis might be too much for serious games per se. But in MMOGs with considerable sizes, an analysis like this can give important information who are key persons in the communication. In games with a purpose that have to be solved by groups communication is key to solve the complete problem in a for all satisfying manner. Independent of the solution, values like the assortativity, i.e., if players tended to talk only to alike players, can help organize a team better. If a serious game is employed to get an overview of the capabilities of a team at work, the usual groupings will try to work out solutions. Silent people might be overseen or shut out, even though their solutions could be of great value. This could be better recognized and, provided the groups are not too large, visualized with the help of a network analysis.

4   Serious Games and MMOG

We showed that there are many different types of analysis that can be done on the social network of a game. The serious game community does investigate MMOG, but usually the games involved are more education based or the analysis more focused on different aspects of the game itself [37,38]. What use do games like World of Warcraft and League of Legends yield to the serious games research?

The aspect of self-regulating hierarchies and communities is an aspect that is not necessarily intended by the game designers, but as shown above it can be observed in many games. In these groups several kind of learning behavior can be observed. First, role-behavior can be observed. In MMOGs this role-behavior can be healer, tank, damage dealer, or other supporting roles. These are usually observed in so called "raids", i.e., group-battles against monsters, but can also be observed in normal game-play. While the role a player adopts is player-dependent, a player still has to learn the full extent and capabilities of the character. Since this is not innate, players can learn this from other players or through testing. Second, correct behavior is not always guaranteed, neither in real life nor in the virtual life. Some communities ban people who misbehave and sow discord. There are cases reported in organizational networks of people who were the bottleneck between two different subgroups of the same network. After intervention, the network was much better connected and the profit increased [11]. This sounds trivial, but is something not looked for in gaming networks. Group behavior is measured in messages and connections. Recently, Lee et al. [26] investigated if the success of a group in a Korean first-person shooter can be based on the structure of communication within the group or the embeddedness within the overall player network. They found, that the internal structure did not help nor hinder the success, while embeddedness was positively related to performance. This implies immediately that there is some kind of learning involved, due to battling with different groups a single group learn new tactics and a more flexible behavior.

To the best of our knowledge, neither of those knowledge flows is recognized as a type of learning in serious games. While these ways of learning are currently related to "killing stats", statistics who "killed" more enemy combattants and objects, the flow of knowledge behind this can actually be of importance for other fields as well. Moreover, based on the social interactions aside from gaming, do groups with a high knowledge flow also share more on other platforms, i.e., do they lend moral support or share insightful hints more easily than the average group?

Another field that could profit from social network analysis is language learning studies. Rankin et al. [39] investigated players of MMOG with English as their second language to see how much they improved their English proficiency skills. Their results indicated that players that interacted with native speakers learned more and understood the vocabulary better. Rankin et al. did not look for social networks developed during the game. Adding this investigative process to the existing work might reveal who taught the most, who showed support and what communities were involved.

Future work in the field of serious games based on MMOGs can involve social network analysis to gather background information. This information can help to identify key persons in the network in regard to learning. Furthermore, better ways to transport knowledge, bottlenecks in a team, or points of interaction with helpful non-player characters for new players might be identified based on the social networks in MMOG.

5   Summary

The topic of social network analysis for online games has been on the research agenda for over 20 years. The large MMOG/MOBA games followed first person shooters like CounterStrike to their success, resulting in communities of hundreds of thousand (e.g. EverQuest, EverQuest II) to several million players (World Of Warcraft, League Of Legends) in some games. Still, these gigantic datasets are not used for complete classic network analysis.

First, there is no system that is capable of computing adequate values for such large numbers of players with respect to algorithms that take $\mathcal{O}(m)$, i.e., are linear in the number of connections, at the best and can be much slower to get communities in a network [40]. More complex measures, like the shortest communication path from actor A to actor Z, can take much longer (up to the cubic of the number of nodes, $\mathcal{O}(n^3)$). Second, numbers alone are not informative about the social structure. They just give a hint that has to investigated to be sure that it is not only based on a forced structure of the network, of the servers, or something not observed. This can be done be comparison to randomized graphs that are in some properties similar, generating these has runtime between $\mathcal{O}(m)$ and $\mathcal{O}(n^3)$. Third, there is no commonly agreed way to analyze a social network. For companies there are established ways to have repetitive questionnaires that can be analyzed to get to the needed information [11].

For the hidden social networks of gamers, there is no established way but several different approaches. First, there are researchers who try to use questionnaires for gamers as well, but they do have the same problem as all questionnaires–not all questionees return their data and the returned data has always a subjective influence. Second, researcher gather parts of the larger social network by gathering play data and analyze that either via the degree sequence or with algorithmic methods. Researchers following the former method tend to propose hypotheses about the network structure, but they can neither be proven nor dis-proven due to the large, unseen part of the network. Only support for their theory can be found. The algorithmic approach results in numbers that have to interpreted in the context of the network, a process that can be biased by the researcher.

Repeating the analysis more often is a promising idea, but the time frame has to be short, since players cannot be expected to play the same game for years. Certain groupings in games do exist only for a month, while others have much longer lifetimes, even in the same game. More importantly, the interactions in an online game are very dynamic and tend to be short. Missing the rise and fall of an influential player can happen very easily [27].

It is also important to note that players of a game can know each other in their offline-lifes as well or due to other games. Established friendships, as well as enmities, may change the behavior in games. For example, an experienced player can help a new player he knows from another game leveling up faster by providing him with tips, items, and other resources.

These indirect effects cannot be observed by analyzing the in-play network alone. Still, the effects are of major importance for a social network analysis, but questionnaires that can capture out-of-game relations between players tend to be answered not by all questionees and the answers capture not necessarily the complete past. All indirect effects that may render a social network analysis inconsequential also apply to serious games that are played in groups, as long as the group has to fulfill a purpose. If the game requires a keen mind and a sound knowledge of a certain subject, a group will always go to the person that showed knowledge in that field beforehand instead of thinking about the problem. With the assistance of social network analysis important persons like this can be identified and the problems posed might be made more approachable for the whole group.

References

1. Parks, M.R., Floyd, K.: Making friends in cyberspace. Journal of Communication **46**(1), 80–97 (1996)
2. Ferrari, S.: From generative to conventional play: Moba and league of legends. DiGRA 2013 (2013)
3. Huffaker, D.A., Wang, J.A., Treem, J.W., Ahmad, M.A., Fullerton, L., Williams, D., Marshall, P.S., Contractor, N.S.: The social behaviors of experts in massive multiplayer online role-playing games. In: CSE (4), pp. 326–331. IEEE Computer Society (2009)

4. Kirman, B., Lawson, S.: Hardcore classification: Identifying play styles in social games using network analysis. In: Natkin, S., Dupire, J. (eds.) ICEC. LNCS, vol. 5709, pp. 246–251. Springer, Heidelberg (2009)
5. Putzke, J., Fischbach, K., Schoder, D.: Power structure and the evolution of social networks in massively multiplayer online games. In: ECIS (2010)
6. Putzke, J., Fischbach, K., Schoder, D., Gloor, P.A.: The evolution of interaction networks in massively multiplayer online games. J. AIS 11(2) (2010)
7. Ducheneaut, N., Yee, N., Nickell, E., Moore, R.J.: Alone together?: exploring the social dynamics of massively multiplayer online games. In: Proceedings of the SIGCHI Conference on Human Factors in Computing Systems, pp. 407–416 (2006)
8. Iosup, A., Lascateu, A., Tapus, N.: Cameo: Enabling social networks for massively multiplayer online games through continuous analytics and cloud computing. In: NETGAMES, pp. 1–6 (2010)
9. Shen, C.: Network patterns and social architecture in massively multiplayer online games: Mapping the social world of everquest ii. SAGE Journals (2014)
10. Szell, M., Thurner, S.: Measuring social dynamics in a massive multiplayer online game. Social Networks 32(4), 313–329 (2010)
11. Cross, R., Parker, A.: The Hidden Power of Social Networks: Understanding how Work Really Gets Done in Organizations. Harvard Business School Press (2004)
12. Kohli, P., Bachrach, Y., Graepel, T., Smyth, G., Armstrong, M., Stillwell, D., Herbrich, R., Kearns, M.: Behavioral game theory on online social networks: Colonel blotto is on facebook (2012)
13. Burroughs, B.: Facebook and farmville: A digital ritual analysis of social gaming and community. In Krzywinska, T. (ed.) Games and Culture. vol. 9, pp. 151–161 (2014)
14. Yee, N.: Motivations for play in online games. Cyberpsy. Behavior, and Soc. Networking 9(6), 772–775 (2006)
15. Stensson, E.: The social structure of massive multiplayer online game communities (2009)
16. Mizes, J.S., Fleece, E.L., Roos, C.: Incentives for increasing return rates: Magnitude levels, response bias, amd format. Public Opinion Quarterly 48(4), 794–800 (1984)
17. Deutskens, E., de Ruyter, K.C., Wetzels, M., Oosterveld, P.: Response rate and response quality of internet-based surveys: An experimental study. Marketing Letters 15(1), 21–36 (2004)
18. Fielding, N.: The SAGE handbook of online research methods. SAGE, July 2008
19. Iosup, A., van de Bovenkamp, R., Shen, S., Jia, A.L., Kuipers, F.A.: Analyzing implicit social networks in multiplayer online games. IEEE Internet Computing 18(3), 36–44 (2014)
20. Kang, S.J., Kim, Y.B., Park, T., Kim, C.H.: Automatic player behavior analysis system using trajectory data in a massive multiplayer online game. Multimedia Tools Appl. 66(3), 383–404 (2013)
21. Pang, S., Chen, C.: Community analysis of social network in mmog. Int. J. Communications Network and System Sciences 3, 133–139 (2010)
22. Zhuang, X., Bharambe, A., Pang, J., Seshan, S.: Player dynamics in massively multiplayer online games (2007)
23. Shim, K.J., Pathak, N., Ahmad, M.A., DeLong, C., Borbora, Z., Mahapatra, A., Srivastava, J.: Analyzing Human Behavior from Multiplayer Online Game Logs: A Knowledge Discovery Approach. IEEE Intelligent Systems 26(1) (2011)
24. Szell, M., Thurner, S.: Social dynamics in a large-scale online game. Advances in Complex Systems 15(6) (2012)

25. Wood, R.T., Griffiths, M.D., Eatough, V.: Online data collection from video game players: Methodological issues. CyberPsychology & Behavior **7**(5), 511–518 (2004)
26. Lee, H.J., Choi, J., Kim, J.W., Park, S.J., Gloor, P.A.: Communication, opponents, and clan performance in online games: A social network approach. Cyberpsy., Behavior, and Soc. Networking **16**(12), 878–883 (2013)
27. Ducheneaut, N., Yee, N., Nickell, E., Moore, R.J.: The life and death of online gaming communities: a look at guilds in world of warcraft. In: Proceedings of the SIGCHI Conference on Human Factors in Computing Systems. CHI 2007, pp. 839–848. ACM, New York, NY, USA (2007)
28. Ang, C.: Interaction networks and patterns of guild community in massively multiplayer online games. Social Network Analysis and Mining **1**(4), 341–353 (2011)
29. Wasserman, S., Faust, K.: Social network analysis: Methods and applications, vol. 8. Cambridge University Press (1994)
30. Newman, M.E.J., Girvan, M.: Mixing patterns and community structure in networks. In: Pastor-Satorras, R., Rubi, M., Diaz-Guilera, A. (eds.) Statistical Mechanics of Complex Networks. Lecture Notes in Physics, vol. 625, pp. 66–87. Springer, Heidelberg (2003)
31. Newman, M.E.J., Girvan, M.: Finding and evaluating community structure in networks. Physical Review E 69(026113) (2004)
32. Blondel, V., Guillaume, J., Lambiotte, R., Mech, E.: Fast unfolding of communities in large networks. J. Stat. Mech, P10008 (2008)
33. Snijders, T.A., van de Bunt, G.G., Steglich, C.E.: Introduction to stochastic actor-based models for network dynamics. Social Networks **32**(1), 44–60 (2010). Dynamics of Social Networks
34. Antal, T., Krapivsky, P.L., Redner, S.: Social balance on networks: The dynamics of friendship and enmity. Physica D: Nonlinear Phenomena **224**(1–2), 130–136 (2006)
35. Heider, F.: Attitudes and cognitive organization. The Journal of Psychology **21**, 107–112 (1946)
36. Blackburn, J., Simha, R., Kourtellis, N., Zuo, X., Ripeanu, M., Skvoretz, J., Iamnitchi, A.: Branded with a scarlet "c": Cheaters in a gaming social network. Proceedings of the 21st International Conference on World Wide Web. WWW 2012, pp. 81–90. ACM, New York, NY, USA (2012)
37. Wendel, V., Hertin, F., Göbel, S., Steinmetz, R.: Collaborative learning by means of multiplayer serious games. In: Luo, X., Spaniol, M., Wang, L., Li, Q., Nejdl, W., Zhang, W. (eds.) Advances in Web-Based Learning - ICWL 2010. LNCS, vol. 6483, pp. 289–298. Springer, Berlin Heidelberg (2010)
38. Wendel, V., Babarinow, M., Hoerl, T., Kolmogorov, S., Göbel, S., Steinmetz, R.: Woodment: Web-based collaborative multiplayer serious game. In: Zhang, X., Zhong, S., Pan, Z., Wong, K., Yun, R. (eds.) Transactions on Edutainment IV. LNCS, vol. 6250, pp. 68–78. Springer, Heidelberg (2010)
39. Rankin, Y., Morrison, D., Shute, M.: Utilizing massively multiplayer online games to foster collaboration and learning. In: 2009 Atlanta Conference on Science and Innovation Policy, pp. 1–10, October 2009
40. Lancichinetti, A., Fortunato, S.: Community detection algorithms: a comparative analysis. Physical review E **80**(5), 056117 (2009)

Poster and Demo Papers

Prevention in Addiction: Using Serious Games to (re)train Cognition in Dutch Adolescents

Wouter J. Boendermaker[✉], Pier J.M. Prins, and Reinout W. Wiers

Developmental Psychology, University of Amsterdam, Amsterdam, The Netherlands
{w.j.boendermaker,p.j.m.prins,r.w.wiers}@uva.nl

Abstract. Excessive use of psychoactive substances during adolescence poses a serious health risk. It can lead to cognitive impairment, as well as addictive problems later in life. Dual process models of addiction suggest that to counter this development, the overdeveloped automatic reactions to drug-related cues should be tempered and cognitive control functions should be strengthened. Recently, several training paradigms have been developed to (re)train these processes. While effective in long time users, most adolescents lack a motivation to train. To motivate them we have developed several serious games that incorporate these evidence-based training paradigms. This paper will present some of them and describe how they work.

Keywords: Serious games · Cognitive training · Cognitive bias modification · Motivation · Adolescents · Substance use

1 Introduction

Adolescents and young adults are known for their experimental and sometimes reckless behavior when it comes to using psychoactive substances. However, especially at that age, misuse of alcohol and drugs can lead to significant problems, such as school dropout [1] and ultimately to later addiction problems. Regular prevention and treatment programs tend to focus on explicit drug education, but only to limited success [2]. An alternative, more implicit approach comes from Dual Process models of addiction (e.g., [3,4]). These propose that the development and maintenance of addiction problems involves an imbalance between two cognitive systems. On the one hand there are several overdeveloped automatic reactions towards the substance, such as biased attention [5] and approach [6] tendencies; on the other hand heavy users tend to have weaker cognitive control abilities, such as working memory [7] and inhibition [8], which then fail to regulate these automatic tendencies. To restore balance, training cognitive control and modifying the biased tendencies (through Cognitive Bias Modification, CBM) have been effective ways to decrease symptoms in long time heavy users [9]. An intrinsic motivation to change problematic behavior may play an important role in these trainings, something younger users often lack, because they do not see their substance use as problematic in the first place [10]. Moreover, the training paradigms used are often long and repetitive and a specific motivation to train

© Springer International Publishing Switzerland 2015
S. Göbel et al. (Eds.): JCSG 2015, LNCS 9090, pp. 173–178, 2015.
DOI: 10.1007/978-3-319-19126-3_15

may also be needed to attain a positive effect. To increase adolescents' motivation to train, one approach is to include game elements in the evidence-based training tasks [11]. Our team has developed several serious games, which will be presented below.

2   Serious Games and Implicit Training

In order to adapt some of the evidence-based implicit training tasks often used for cognitive (re)training, one must consider the delicate nature of these paradigms. Most of them are structured as repeated stimulus-response exercises and tend to be very sensitive to slight structural changes (e.g., changing the display duration of a cue from 500 to 2000 ms may give very different results; [12]). As such, there is a risk that adding game elements to such paradigms may eventually render the task ineffective. Boendermaker, Prins, and Wiers [13] have recently proposed a model that features several different techniques to go about turning a typical CBM task into a serious game (see Figure 1). In this paper we will highlight two of these techniques (Step 2 & 4) and provide examples of some of the games we have developed that fit with these steps.

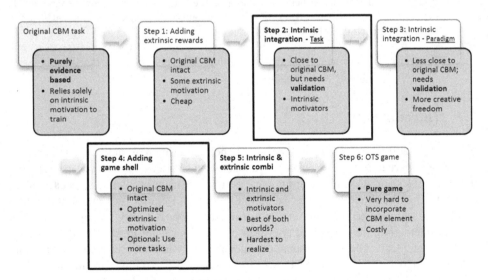

Fig. 1. Gamification model. Six gamification steps from evidence-based paradigm (CBM) to commercial "off the shelf" (OTS) games. Adapted from "Cognitive Bias Modification for Adolescents with Substance Use Problems – Can Serious Games Help?" by W. J. Boendermaker, P. J. M. Prins, and R. W. Wiers, 2015, Journal of Behavior Therapy and Experimental Psychiatry. doi:10.1016/j.jbtep.2015.03.008. Copyright 2015 by Elsevier Ltd. Reprinted with permission.

The first technique (Step 4 in the model) involves adding game elements around the original training task, like a shell, while leaving the task itself relatively unchanged. This has the obvious benefit of minimizing the chance of rendering the training ineffective, but it also leaves the relatively boring task intact, motivating the user primarily by providing points for good task performance (e.g., based on speed and accuracy), which can then be spent afterwards in the game environment. A possible drawback to this approach is that while potentially motivating as a whole, the fun part remains separated from the training task. Such motivators are sometimes called extrinsic and are viewed as inferior to intrinsic motivators. An example of this type of serious game training is the CityBuilder game [14], featured in Figure 2. In this game, players can train different cognitive aspects, such as working memory and attention. The original training task is presented on top of the game, as shown in the right figure (task instructions are in Dutch). In doing so they receive points for speed and accuracy, which can later be spent buying a variety of objects to build a custom city. The game also includes social features, as well as daily achievements. One advantage of this game type is that it can incorporate several different training tasks.

Fig. 2. Shell game. Game screen on the left; Embedded training task on overlaying the game screen on the right.

Another technique is to make changes to the original training task itself, increasing the motivation to train through the use of intrinsic motivators, making it more fun to perform the task itself (Step 2 in the model). As some key elements of the paradigm may get lost in this process, these games will have to be revalidated. An example of this type of serious game training can be seen in Figure 3.

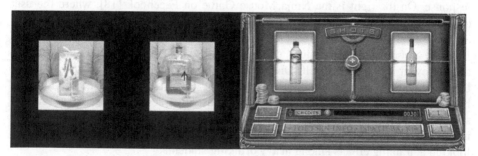

Fig. 3. Attentional Bias. Original task on the left; Game version on the right.

On the left we see a regular Visual Probe Task (originally developed by [15]), used in attentional bias modification. In this task, an alcohol-soda pair of pictures appears simultaneously on screen. After 500 ms a small arrow becomes visible on either one of the pictures (only the soda during training). The user is instructed to quickly respond to the direction of the arrow (up or down). The bias is measured be comparing average reaction times on trials (stimulus-response pairs) where the arrow appears on the side of the alcohol picture, compared to when it appears on the side of the soda picture. The idea is that if there is an attentional bias towards the alcoholic beverages, this will be reflected by slower reaction times. On the right side of Figure 3 is the Shots Game [16], where this mechanism is embedded in a slot machine-like game. The game features fancy graphics and animations, as well as an elaborate reward system with the intention to make the training task itself more motivating. To use the machine, i.e., to spin the wheels, participants need to spend a coin. When the wheels are done spinning, a small arrow appears on either side, and if the response is correct, the player can earn up to 3 new coins, based on the speed of the response.

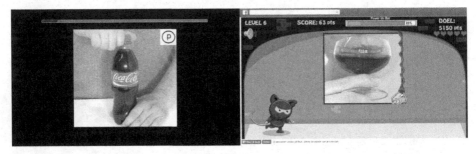

Fig. 4. Response Matching. Original task on the left; Game version on the right.

Figure 4 shows another example where game elements have been integrated directly into the task paradigm. The left image shows a typical Go/Nogo Task [17], where an unrelated cue (a letter P or F) appears on the image to indicate whether or not the user should press a response key. Interestingly, the content of the pictures is irrelevant to the task's instructions. However, by repeatedly pairing the no-go cue with pictures of alcohol, participants can be trained to associate alcohol stimuli with withholding a response. On the right is the Ninja Mouse Game on Facebook [18], where the user controls a Mouse character running through a tunnel, grabbing pieces of cheese and avoiding cats. The cheese and cats are similar to the P and F cues in the original task. Both are accompanied by 'posters' of alcohol and soda beverages in the tunnel, which are irrelevant to the game itself. One notable difference with the original task is that the game features a lateral scrolling movement of the pictures, while the original task has static pictures. Hence, validation of the adjusted paradigm is necessary. First results using pilot versions of these games indicate that participants are indeed more motivated to use them, compared to the original tasks. Currently ongoing research is looking at training effects among heavy drinking students.

3   Conclusion and Future Work

Typically, the measurement of these biases takes about 80 trials, whereas retraining can take up 600-2000 trials. As such, one needs significant motivation to sustain a certain level of performance on these tasks. While these game versions show promise in terms of motivating adolescents to train, it should be noted that this may not be enough to get regular, heavy drinking youth to spend the necessary hours on these trainings. A basic motivation to change their habits may be indispensable in order to actually achieve real behavioral changes. As serious games are inevitably a combination of some game elements and something serious, their level of fun often lies somewhere in between the regular task (boring) and the commercial games they are familiar with (mostly fun). As such, if they lack a motivation to change their problematic behavior, then their motivation to train may quickly decline and the training may be ineffective. We are currently setting up new research in which we assess both types of motivation in order to see the effects they may have on training efficacy.

Acknowledgements. This research was supported by National Initiative Brain & Cognition Grant 433-11-1510 of the Dutch National Science Foundation, awarded to the second and third author, as well as a VICI grant (453-08-001), awarded to the third author, both from the Dutch National Science Foundation, N.W.O.

The authors wish to thank Elisabeth Enthoven, Antonios Georgiadis, Sylvia van Schie and Ans de Nijs for their invaluable work on the development of these games.

References

1. Singleton, R.A.: Collegiate alcohol consumption and academic performance. Journal of Studies on Alcohol and Drugs **68**(4), 548–555 (2007)
2. Werch, C.E., Owen, D.M.: Iatrogenic effects of alcohol and drug prevention programs. Journal of Studies on Alcohol **63**, 581–590 (2002)
3. Deutsch, R., Strack, F.: Reflective and impulsive determinants of addictive behaviors. In: Wiers, R.W., Stacy, A.W. (eds.) *Handbook of implicit cognition and addiction*, pp. 45–57. Sage, Thousand Oaks, CA (2006)
4. Wiers, R.W., Bartholow, B.D., van den Wildenberg, E., Thush, C., Engels, R.C.M.E., Sher, K.J., Grenard, J., Ames, S.L., Stacy, A.W.: Automatic and controlled processes and the development of addictive behaviors in adolescents: a review and a model. Pharmacology, Biochemistry, and Behavior **86**(2), 263–283 (2007). doi:10.1016/j.pbb.2006.09.021
5. Field, M., Duka, T., Eastwood, B., Child, R., Santarcangelo, M., Gayton, M.: Experimental manipulation of attentional biases in heavy drinkers: do the effects generalise? Psychopharmacology **192**, 593–608 (2007)
6. Wiers, R.W., Rinck, M., Dictus, M., Van den Wildenberg, E.: Relatively strong automatic appetitive action-tendencies in male carriers of the OPRM1 G-allele. Genes Brain & Behavior **8**, 101–106 (2009)
7. Grenard, J.L., Ames, S.L., Wiers, R.W., Thush, C., Sussman, S., Stacy, A.W.: Working memory moderates the predictive effects of drug-related associations on substance use. Psychology of Addictive Behaviors **22**, 426–432 (2008)

8. Houben, K., Wiers, R.W.: Response inhibition moderates the relationship between implicit associations and drinking behavior. Alcoholism: Clinical and Experimental Research **33**, 626–633 (2009)
9. Wiers, R.W., Gladwin, T.E., Hofmann, W., Salemink, E., Ridderinkhof, K.R.: Cognitive bias modification and cognitive control training in addiction and related psychopathology: Mechanisms, clinical perspectives, and ways forward. Clinical Psychological Science **1**(2), 192–212 (2013). doi:10.1177/2167702612466547
10. Johnston, L.D., O'malley, P.M., Bachman, J.G., Schulenberg, J.E.: Monitoring the Future: National Survey Results on Drug Use, 1975-2012. Volume I: Secondary School Students. NIH Publication No. 10-7584. National Institute on Drug Abuse (NIDA) (2012)
11. Gladwin, T.E., Figner, B., Crone, E.A., Wiers, R.W.: Addiction, adolescence, and the integration of control and motivation. Developmental Cognitive Neuroscience **1**(4), 364–376 (2011). doi:10.1016/j.dcn.2011.06.008
12. Field, M., Mogg, K., Mann, B., Bennett, G.A., Bradley, B.P.: Attentional biases in abstinent alcoholics and their association with craving. Psychology of Addictive Behaviors **27**(1), 71–80 (2013). doi:10.1037/a0029626
13. Boendermaker, W.J., Prins, P.J.M., Wiers, R.W.: Cognitive Bias Modification for Adolescents with Substance Use Problems – Can Serious Games Help?. Journal of Behavior Therapy and Experimental Psychiatry. doi:10.1016/j.jbtep.2015.03.008 (2015)
14. Boendermaker, W.J., Prins, P.J.M., Wiers, R.W.: Documentation of the CityBuilder game. Theoretical background and parameters. University of Amsterdam, Amsterdam, the Netherlands (2013)
15. MacLeod, C., Mathews, A., Tata, P.: Attentional bias in emotional disorders. Journal of Abnormal Psychology **95**, 15–20 (1986)
16. van Schie, S., Boendermaker, W.J.: Measuring attentional bias towards alcohol in adolescents using motivating game elements. University of Amsterdam, Amsterdam, the Netherlands (2014). (Unpublished master's thesis)
17. van Deursen, D.S., Salemink, E., Smit, F., Kramer, J., Wiers, R.W.: Web-based cognitive bias modification for problem drinkers: protocol of a randomized controlled trial with a 2 × 2 × 2 factorial design. BMC Public Health **13**, 674 (2013)
18. de Nijs, A., N., S., Boendermaker, W.J.: Using a Facebook game to train alcohol inhibition. University of Amsterdam, Amsterdam, the Netherlands (2014). (Unpublished master's thesis)

"How to Fail Your Research Degree"
A Serious Game for Research Students in Higher Education

Daisy Abbott[(✉)]

Digital Design Studio, Glasgow School of Art, Pacific Quay, Glasgow G51 1EA, UK
d.abbott@gsa.ac.uk

Abstract. This work in progress game was created to deliver knowledge and understanding of research processes and techniques, within the context of a postgraduate training programme at Glasgow School of Art. Development was in relation to the concepts of encouraging creativity and risk-taking within a safe game environment and of learning by (potentially) failing. Game characteristics and intended learning outcomes were defined, leading to game mechanics and text that emphasise player agency, working within a time limit, and humour. Initial small-scale evaluation shows that the game is highly successful at delivering the intended learning outcomes and is a memorable and enjoyable complement to the existing course curriculum.

Keywords: Serious games · Games for learning · Research skills · Higher education

1 Introduction

Like many institutions, the Glasgow School of Art (GSA) provides a programme of core research skills; training aimed at postgraduate and PhD students with a specific focus on developing the knowledge and techniques required to do a research degree. The programme encompasses (amongst other things) good academic writing, best practice in research, and processes for managing a research project and incorporates the expertise of the academic researchers who teach on these courses, the direct value of which is emphasised by the Teaching and Learning Research Programme [1] (pp.14-15) and is equally applicable more generally at all levels of education [2]. Whilst developing and improving an existing course within this programme (delivered by GSA's Digital Design Studio, which also offers a Master's degree in Serious Games) consideration was given to how how this widely applicable training could be delivered in a more interactive way (and to a larger cohort of students) in the form of a serious game.

2 Academic Context

The value of play to learning has been recognised and interrogated for centuries [3]. Furthermore, various commentators on higher educational policy have noted the

S. Göbel et al. (Eds.): JCSG 2015, LNCS 9090, pp. 179–185, 2015.
DOI: 10.1007/978-3-319-19126-3_16

movement of pedagogical rhetoric away from inspiration and enjoyment of learning towards a growing obsession with metrics (especially those that can be directly tied to economic activity) [4]. The purpose of teaching research skills is to enable students to critically and rigorously discover, analyse and interpret, but to also encourage the motivation to do so (hence the importance of emotional effects such as inspiration and enjoyment), leading to both deep understanding and robust lifelong learners. Within this local and wider context, therefore, the creation of a serious game for teaching research skills was highly appropriate.

A common concept in niche play activities such as live roleplaying, and latterly in the registers of critical debate and leadership/self-help [5,6], is that of "winning by losing". That is, that the outcome of the game is centred around enjoying the process of the game rather than focussing on the result, and that a "loss" can actually be more enjoyable and/or useful than a "win". With just a little terminological tweaking, the same concept underpins the educational philosophy and pedagogical discipline of "learning by failing", particularly noticeable in early years learning and training artificial intelligence [7, for useful applications to wider pedagogy]. Again, these concepts focus on engagement with the activity itself, not measuring the outcomes. It is also particularly pertinent in the context of training research students to not only acknowledge but embrace the notion that an element of risk-taking is required to produce original and innovative work [8] (p. 303). The concept of the serious game was to fully embrace the motivating factors (of which enjoyment is just one) that embed these critical skills into the students' ongoing practice, to include the ideas of risk-taking and learning by failing, as well as encouraging creativity, imagination, and problem solving – and to do this in a sufficiently structured and 'safe' playful environment [8] by reinstating fun play as a means to establish knowing [3] (p.18). Therefore, a primary driver for the serious game How to Fail Your Research Degree was to embed this learning strategy directly into the course to complement the existing more traditional and didactic methods currently used (primarily lecture-based with some discussion and tutorial sessions). This builds on the much more well-established educational practice of learning by doing, i.e. being directly involved and invested in the outcomes of the educational activity.

3   Game Design

3.1   Supporting Learning

Game design began by defining the general game characteristics needed (based on the general academic context outlined above as well as the local context of the research skills programme at GSA). This was followed by clearly delineating learning outcomes for the game based on the existing curriculum for a single course within the overall programme.

3.2   Game Characteristics

The game characteristics were defined so that the game would:

— Be based on the curriculum for the Research Methodology and Scientific Writing taught module in Core Research Skills at the Glasgow School of Art.
— Be deliberately abstracted, simplified, and made light-hearted. It is not intended to be a simulation of doing research!
— Be simple in terms of game rules, focussing on the learning outcomes, not the skill of gameplay itself.
— Be playable in groups but also support individual play. The game will not be (directly) competitive or co-operative, however playing together with other people will reinforce the learning outcomes and the fun social aspect.
— Be playable within a fairly short time (e.g. under 30 minutes) to allow for play and discussion within a lesson/tutorial context.
— Enable and provide references for discussion and analysis after a play session.
— Include the principles of student-centred learning by being: fun and light-hearted; memorable; directly relevant to students' situations; and of practical use in reinforcing the learning outcomes of the course.

3.3   Intended Learning Outcomes for the Game

To support learning outcomes of the research methods training course, the game should:

— Highlight various risks of research projects and suggest their impact on projects
— Reinforce dependencies between tasks at different stages of research
— Directly reinforce the interrelations of different risks with the activities taken to negate or ameliorate them
— Replicate the time-critical nature of short research projects

3.4   Review of Existing Games

A review reveals only one serious game that exists for broadly similar goals. The Continuing/Higher Education in Research Methods Using Games project "aims to develop a game to support students as they develop an understanding of research methods and statistics" [9] and has produced digital mini-games focussed on a particular topic (diet) and aimed primarily at social science and nursing students. The intention of *How to Fail Your Research Degree* was to be non-subject specific (i.e. research methods is the subject) and playable in a group tutorial context, therefore the solo, digital mode of play was not appropriate. Several games exist in the field of project management, none of which featured the game mechanics that would support the learning outcomes defined. Several were luck-based and use a snakes-and-ladders model[1] which is not a good fit for the non-linear, iterative, and thoughtful process of doing research. The circular model of a serious board game like CURATE[2] is

---

[1] Project   Risk   http://www.purplepawn.com/2009/08/project-management-training-board-games/; Virgin Blue http://www.torstenkoerting.com/2010/01/13/how-to-celebrate-project-closure-with-a-unique-board-game/

[2] http://www.digcur-education.org/eng/Resources/CURATE-Game

somewhat more appropriate, however did not support the idea of active, self-determined building of a research framework which supports the production of results. Other games focussed on the research process were either fictional(!) and/or discipline-specific[3] or little more than infographics aimed at a much lower educational level.[4]

3.5   Game Mechanics

In response to the defined characteristics and intended learning outcomes for the game, mechanics were designed to emphasise the player's control and agency over building up their research framework, whilst including elements of luck in drawing cards representing different risks and events.

Players use Activity cards to construct a research framework in four stages: PLAN; RESEARCH CONTEXT; RESEARCH & ANALYSIS; and WRITEUP. The PLAN stage acts as a setup and practice phase where exactly 8 cards are laid out side-by-side. The three remaining stages each have two phases. First, there is a timed phase (the Activity phase) where players frantically build up their activity for that phase by turning over face-down Activity cards and fitting them into their project framework. It is important to work fast to get enough research done so that players can build on it in subsequent rounds. This is followed by an Events phase where players draw Events cards at random and resolve the impact of the event on their research.

With the exception of the PLAN stage, Activity cards are played within a 2 minute time limit, drawing and placing cards as many cards as the player can. This timed element is intended to be frenetic, demonstrating the passing of real time in which to perform research and also adding an emotional/adrenalin element to the game. To represent the thoughtful research process and enable player agency, each Activity card has arrows (or blank edges) that must match the cards around it. Players must play all cards from each stage in one horizontal layer, but is otherwise free to place a card whereever it is legal to be played. An example framework showing valid and invalid plays is shown in Fig. 1.

After each timed Activity phase, players take turns to draw three Events cards from the Events deck, read each out to the other players and then apply them to the research framework. Events can have disastrous (or occasionally helpful) effects on the research. Effects typically take the form of removing existing Activity cards (representing for example, data that cannot be used because it was not collected in an ethical manner) or 'blocking out' spaces in future Activity layers, making them unplayable and therefore making future rounds more difficult (representing for example, not doing enough reading for a literature review). Events can typically be negated or ameliorated by activities the player has successfully completed. For instance, a computer failure is entirely negated if the player has played the 'Research data management (RDM) Strategy' card in her PLAN activity framework and a

---

[3]   Research Lab: http://bigbangtheory.wikia.com/wiki/Research_Lab; Sharkworld https://store.itpreneurs.com/en/sharkworld-a-project-management-game

[4]   E.g. How to Do research: http://classroom-aid.com/2013/04/05/how-to-do-research-game/

'Procrastinate' event can be ameliorated by having played a 'Milestones' Activity card. The tone of the cards and rules is lighthearted, making it clear that the research is an abstraction and exaggeration of real research, whilst having activities and events that are directly relevant to students.

The purpose of the game is to join as many Thesis cards (Activity cards with a solid black line at the top) as possible together in the WRITEUP phase (and to have the longest line of conjoined cards survive the final events phase). Fig. 1 shows an example framework with three conjoined Thesis cards, marked in red. The length of the longest line of joined Thesis cards demonstrates the success and robustness of the research project.

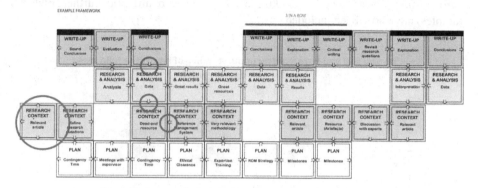

Fig. 1. Example gameplay showing illegally placed cards (circled) and conjoined Thesis cards

4   Preliminary Evaluation

How to Fail Your Research Degree is a work in progress. The game was tested informally and an initial set of improvements were made, largely to make the card layout more visually understandable and to tweak explanations within the rules document. Some feedback suggested making placing Activity cards more difficult (by reducing the numbers of joining arrows). This suggestion was rejected due to the context of a game that is likely to be played only once or twice by a general cohort of students, the majority of which will not be experienced board gamers. Whilst placing the cards will quickly be recognised as too easy by experienced gamers, the worst potential outcome of the game is if a student does not manage to place enough cards in a single phase and is therefore knocked out before the end. This outcome would be neither emotionally nor educationally rewarding and it was decided to reduce the chances of this as much as possible, without compromising the need to actively think about where each card is placed. After intial refinement, the game was played in the final tutorial of the research methods course (2014 cohort). A short questionnaire tested the Intended Learning Outcomes (defined in 3.3 above) and gathered freetext responses about lessons learned and the experience of playing the game.

As Fig. 2 shows, the game was extremely successful in communicating the types and impacts of risks during research, as well as the interdependencies between early and later activities. It was also moderately successful at emulating the time-critical nature of short-term research projects. Freetext comments highlighted the major lessons learned or reinforced from the game, all of which align with the intended learning outcomes of the course. The game satisfies all learning outcomes specified and both formal and informal feedback shows that it was a funny, memorable experience for the students and relevant to their lives. Measured against the design criteria (specified in 3.2) the only area in which the game fails is in the length of time needed to play (it takes about 45 minutes to explain and then play the game with 4 players) and arguably, the clarity of the rules document itself – although the students found the rules easy to understand once explained verbally. Further refinements to improve rules clarity (e.g. the addition of a game board and further pictorial examples) have now been included.

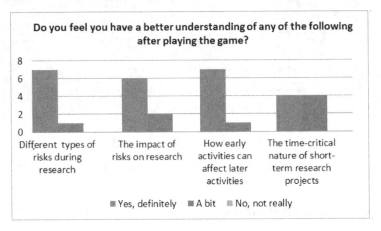

Fig. 2. Chart showing responses to game learning outcomes

5   Conclusions and Next Steps

How to Fail Your Research Degree has produced largely positive initial results in terms of both learning about research methods and player experience. The major next step is to continue incremental improvements based on ongoing feedback and to corroborate initial results with a larger scale evaluation. The game is still a little too reliant on luck in the initial PLAN stage (which deliberately strongly influences how well the fictional research project stands up to the disasters that befall it). Therefore, optional rules are being considered which allow students to 'purchase' a limited number of missing elements (e.g. a data management strategy card). This would give players more control in creating a strong research framework. Through future use, the game will also allow a semi-structured longitudinal comparison of the understanding students have of the course material. Played once at the beginning of the course and once at the end, the abstractions provided by the game will allow students to recognise and reflect upon the techniques and processes they have learned before they put them into practice in their research degrees. Additionally, a structured game environment lends itself easily to adaptations that could allow tutors to explore issues such as equality and diversity. Games allow the explicit foregrounding of "unfair rules" in a safe and uncomplicated environment which functions as a useful abstraction to discussing these issues as they play out in real life [10]. The game could be used in this way in any research-centred training.

Not least, this game brings back the fun into what risks being a rather dry subject if delivered in a didactic format. Games can, and do, have a place in making our learning environments effective and inspirational places.

References

1. Teaching and Learning Research Programme: Effective learning and teaching in UK higher education: A Commentary by the Teaching and Learning Research Programme. Teaching and Learning Research Programme, London, UK (2009). http://www.tlrp.org/pub/documents/UKHEfinal.pdf
2. General Teaching Council for Scotland: The Standards for Registration: mandatory requirements for Registration with the General Teaching Council for Scotland (2012). http://www.gtcs.org.uk/web/Files/the-standards/standards-for-registration-1212.pdf
3. Games, A., Squire, K.D.: Searching for the fun in learning: A historical perspective on the evolution of educational video games. In: Tobias, S., Fletcher, J.D. (eds.) Computer Games and Instruction, pp. 7–46. Information Age Publishing, Charlotte NC (2011)
4. Phipps, A., Saunders, L.: The sound of violets: the ethnographic potency of poetry. Ethnography and Education 4(3), 357–387 (2009). http://www.tandfonline.com/doi/full/10.1080/17457820903170168#.U-ywHcVdWgY
5. Dignus Muneris, Do you have the courage to win by losing? (2014). http://dignusmuneris.co.uk/contracting-for-coaching/
6. Statton, J.: How you can win by losing (2012). http://www.jeremystatton.com/win-by-losing
7. Beaumont, C.: Beyond e-learning: can intelligent agents really support learners? In: Campbell, A., Norton, L. (eds.) Learning, Teaching and Assessing in Higher Education: Developing Reflective Practice. Learning Matters Ltd., Trowbridge (2007)
8. Fry, H., Ketteridge, S., Marshall, S.: A Handbook for Teaching and Learning in Higher Education: Enhancing Academic Practice, 3rd edn. Routledge, Abingdon (2003)
9. Continuing/Higher Education in Research Methods Using Games (CHERMUG) (2013). http://www.chermug.eu/
10. Mukhopadhyay, C.: Starpower: Experiencing a Stratified Society (2014). http://www.sjsu.edu/people/carol.mukhopadhyay/race/Starpower%20Activity%202014.pdf

LiverDefense: An Educational Tower Defense Game as an Evaluation Platform

Julia Brich[✉], Julian Frommel, Katja Rogers, Adrian Brückner,
Martin Weidhaas, Tamara Dorn, Sarah Mirabile, Valentin Riemer,
Claudia Schrader, and Michael Weber

Ulm University, Ulm, Germany
{julia.brich,julian.frommel,katja.rogers,adrian.brueckner,martin.weidhaas,
tamara.dorn,sarah.mirabile,valentin.riemer,claudia.schrader,
michael.weber}@uni-ulm.de
http://www.uni-ulm.de/in/

Abstract. This paper presents LiverDefense, an educational tower defense game illustrating the basic functions of the human liver. LiverDefense can be adapted with regard to its degree of difficulty via XML input files. Thus, researchers without programming skills can customize the game easily according to their needs. As such, it was tested in a user study to explore the effect of perceived control settings on players' affective states, and learning outcomes.

Keywords: Serious games · Education · Evaluation platform · Tower defense

1 Introduction and Related Work

Serious games [1] are games where entertainment is not the primary focus [10]; instead, the human drive to play is exploited to convey knowledge or train skills [7]. Interactive media and video games are especially suited to engage contemporary students who tend to find traditional media boring and crave active involvement in the learning process [9,11]. Avery et al. found Tower Defense (TD) games a suitable testbed for research [2]. This genre is made appealing by its easy-to-understand mechanics as well as its challenging and addictive nature [2,3]. The genre's principle is as follows: Players are given an object to defend (e.g. a castle) and have to withstand an onslaught of enemies by placing defensive units (towers) along a given path. For more details, Avery et al. provide a comprehensive analysis of the genre [2]. Bassilious et al. [3] developed *Power Defense* to teach numeracy skills needed by diabetes patients. They employ the metaphor of an unstable power plant (i.e., the body's blood sugar level) that needs supplemental energy (incoming food) and incidental cool downs (insulin) to maintain an optimal power level. To avoid power failure or blowup, players need to calculate the right amounts of coolant and energy particles allowed into the plant. Clements et al. [5] developed a game to let players experience the

© Springer International Publishing Switzerland 2015
S. Göbel et al. (Eds.): JCSG 2015, LNCS 9090, pp. 186–190, 2015.
DOI: 10.1007/978-3-319-19126-3_17

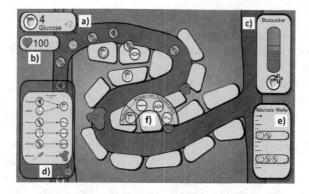

Fig. 1. Screenshot of the LiverDefense player interface (in German)

behaviour of the human immune system. They chose a TD game since they found its mechanics most suitable to illustrate the underlying biological processes. To prevent infection, players could utilize immune system cells in order to defend against pathogens in the blood stream. Clements et al. used a cartoon-like, 2D approach to support a fanciful atmosphere while retaining biological accuracy as much as possible.

Both Bassilious et al. [3] and Clements et al. [5] used TD games successfully in a medical-biological context. We saw similarities between the liver's metabolism (neutralize harmful or waste materials) and TD games (neutralize assaulting enemies) and decided to employ the same approach. Our intention was to teach the basic functions of the human liver via TD gameplay. However, we did not want to create just another serious game. We intend our game to be a useful research tool in the field of serious games. Due to the inherent multidisciplinarity of the field, tools ideally should not require researchers to be proficient programmers to make the changes they need. In this spirit, we introduce LiverDefense, a serious game of the TD genre, which can serve as an easy-to-use evaluation platform for psychological studies. The game and its customisable features are explained in the following.

2   The Game

LiverDefense aims to convey basic human liver functionalities to players with little or no previous knowledge in this area. With regard to Clements et al. [5], we chose a cartoon-like 2D look. The player interface (see Fig. 1) was kept simple to keep the player's focus on the advancing waves of enemies. Players learn how waste materials such as ammonia, alcohol, and pharmaceuticals are metabolised by corresponding enzymes within the liver cells [8,13], with a focus on a single, exemplary bloodstream. Following traditional TD games, each liver cell bordering on the bloodstream can be specialised to deal with a specific material. Alternatively, liver cells can be assigned to manufacture glucose. Glucose functions as the game's currency (see Fig.1, a); with it, the player can specialize liver cells via a build menu (Fig.1, f) and manage the blood sugar level (Fig.1, c) by keeping it within acceptable bounds. To defend against bacteria, Kupffer cells can be built. The underlying biological processes are illustrated in a simplified manner to reduce the cognitive impact and enhance playability. In contrast to actual liver cells, game cells can each be specialized for one liver function only, for example *glucose hepatocyte*. Kupffer cells do not cover the entire wall of the bloodstream; instead, they can be built at 3 distinct positions in the middle of the stream. The player starts out with 100 health points (Fig.1, b). Each time an enemy particle reaches the end of the depicted bloodstream, points are lost according to the damage potential of the particle. Blood sugar mismanagement also costs the player points. The goal is to survive as many enemy waves as possible before being reduced to 0 health points. An introductory tutorial teaches players the basic liver functions and associated game elements, e.g. "an alcohol dehydrogenase hepatocyt metabolizes alcohol particles". Information can later be retrieved via mouse-overs on the various elements and is shown in the info box (Fig.1, d). A preview for incoming enemy waves is also included (Fig.1, e).

While looking into player-centered game design, Charles and Black found that the difficulty of a game influences its perceived entertainment value [4] and provides an interesting starting point for future research on game adaptability, as well as motivational and emotional impact. Van Lankveld et al. [14] researched the affective impact of various difficulty settings based on Rauterberg's incongruity theory [12]. In contrast to their approach of automatically adapting the game's difficulty to provide a constant positive incongruity for growing player skill, we propose a tool where difficulty can be adjusted manually to induce affective states as needed for psychological studies. LiverDefense allows for the adjustment of difficulty via various parameters, independent of the program code. Basic conditions such as the initial glucose balance, time between antagonistic elements and waves, as well as wave composition are specified via easily-changed XML files. Several game elements have additional attributes that can be modified as well. For each new study, the experimenter can thus adjust the difficulty of the game anew and on various levels. Furthermore, customised 7-point Likert scale questionnaires can be specified in XML. Their display can be interwoven into the gameplay, potentially after every wave of enemies. Due to layout constraints, one questionnaire frame is currently limited to displaying 5 items.

LiverDefense has been successfully used as evaluation tool in a psychological study with 121 participants. The study in general was aimed at exploring the effect of varying perceived control over the game on affective states and learning outcome. Among other things, perceived control [6] was measured in the form of one item (*"I have control over what is currently happening in the game."*, translated from German) on the employed 7-point Likert scale questionnaire, where 0 embodied "not at all" and 6 stood for "absolutely". Preliminary analysis shows that the three employed game settings *easy*, *normal* and *hard* were indeed perceived as varying in difficulty. The means and standard deviations for perceived control among the three groups were as follows: 5.22 (*SD 1.41*) for the easy setting with low difficulty, 4.36 (*SD 1.17*) for the normal setting with medium difficulty, and 4.02 (*SD 1.25*) for the hard setting with high difficulty. Participants felt less in control the harder the game setting was.

3 Conclusion

LiverDefense is a useful tool for the evaluation of serious games that employ the TD paradigm. It includes various enemy particles and additional factors such as the blood sugar level to supply a challenging experience. Game difficulty can be manually adjusted via XML files in order to create various study settings. Likert-scale questionnaires can easily be edited and substituted via XML as well. We have shown the successful use of LiverDefense in a psychological study, which indicated among other things that the chosen difficulty settings were perceived as intended. LiverDefense can be adapted by non-programmers to fit their needs.

Acknowledgments. This work was funded by the Carl Zeiss Foundation and the German Federal Ministry of Education and Research (FKZ: 16OH21032).

References

1. Abt, C.C.: Serious games. University Press of America (1987)
2. Avery, P., Togelius, J., Alistar, E., Van Leeuwen, R.P.: Computational intelligence and tower defence games. In: 2011 IEEE Congress on Evolutionary Computation (CEC), pp. 1084–1091. IEEE (2011)
3. Bassilious, E., DeChamplain, A., McCabe, I., Stephan, M., Kapralos, B., Mahmud, F., Dubrowski, A.: Power defense: a video game for improving diabetes numeracy. In: 2011 IEEE International Games Innovation Conference (IGIC), pp. 124–125. IEEE (2011)
4. Charles, D., Black, M.: Dynamic player modeling: a framework for player-centered digital games. In: Proc. of the International Conference on Computer Games: Artificial Intelligence, Design and Education, pp. 29–35 (2004)
5. Clements, P., Pesner, J., Shepherd, J.: The teaching of immunology using educational: gaming paradigms. In: Proceedings of the 47th Annual Southeast Regional Conference, p. 21. ACM (2009)
6. Grodal, T.: Video games and the pleasures of control. Media entertainment: The psychology of its appeal, pp. 197–213 (2000)
7. Li, M.C., Tsai, C.C.: Game-based learning in science education: a review of relevant research. Journal of Science Education and Technology **22**(6), 877–898 (2013)
8. Liehr, H.: Leber, Galle, Bauchspeicheldrüse: Wirksame Hilfe bei Beschwerden (German). Trias (2002)
9. Mangold, K.: Educating a new generation: Teaching baby boomer faculty about millennial students. Nurse Educator **32**(1), 21–23 (2007)
10. Michael, D.R., Chen, S.L.: Serious games: Games that educate, train, and inform. Muska & Lipman/Premier-Trade (2005)
11. Prensky, M.: Computer games and learning: Digital game-based learning. Handbook of computer game studies **18**, 97–122 (2005)

12. Rauterberg, M.: About a framework for information and information processing of learning systems. In: ISCO, pp. 54–69 (1995)
13. Riemann, J.F., Fischbach, W., Galle, P., Mössner, J.: Gastroenterologie in Klinik und Praxis (German). Thieme (2007)
14. van Lankveld, G., Spronck, P., van den Herik, H.J., Rauterberg, M.: Incongruity-based adaptive game balancing. In: van den Herik, H.J., Spronck, P. (eds.) ACG 2009. LNCS, vol. 6048, pp. 208–220. Springer, Heidelberg (2010)

Combining the Virtual and Physical Interaction Environment

Stephen Hibbert[(⊠)]

School of Art Design and Architecture, University of Huddersfield, Huddersfield, UK
s.p.hibbert@hud.ac.uk

Abstract. Mark Weiser famously proclaimed a possible future in his 1991 paper 'A computer for the 21st century' [1] in which he discusses a world filled with connected devices able to "weave themselves into the fabric of everyday life until they are indistinguishable from it"[1]

1 Introduction: What Does the Future Look Like?

Mark Weiser famously proclaimed a possible future in his 1991 paper 'A computer for the 21st century' [1] in which he discusses a world filled with connected devices able to "weave themselves into the fabric of everyday life until they are indistinguishable from it"[1].

We now stand at point in history where ubiquitous computing (ubicomp) can be said to be closer to a reality than ever before. However the definition ubicomp and the proximate future continue to be redefined and evolve as technology and society adapt to new technological paradigm shifts. For example one could argue that the continuing efforts to define and standardize the 'Internet of Things' (IoT) appears to be fast becoming the current media-term for Weiser's original vision.

Alongside these developments a new era of portable, wearable devices harnessing continuing advancements in mobile technology and sensor refinement, promise to revolutionize how we might interact with the wider digitally connected world. These have now evolved to a point where a potentially viable 'invisible' computing experience can be integrated into truly mobile multifunction devices.

This paper serves as the introductory part in an investigation into both the metaphysical and cybernetic considerations that influence the potential design of a graphic user interface, which the author has entitled the 'Xuni Augmented Reality' interface. By combining the use of a number of devices including a VR headset, a depth sensing camera, alongside a smartphone 'hub', it is envisaged that an individual user wearing these devices might be able to operate a mobile, highly responsive and practical 'mixed reality' user interface [2], [3].

2 Method

2.1 Investigation

The hybrid augmented reality system investigation, which the author has entitled 'Xuni AR' (Xuni), makes use various devices in concert, functioning together to operate a

© Springer International Publishing Switzerland 2015
S. Göbel et al. (Eds.): JCSG 2015, LNCS 9090, pp. 191–194, 2015.
DOI: 10.1007/978-3-319-19126-3_18

theoretical interface through 'a symphony of interaction between multiple smart mobile devices.' [4]. The purpose of the experiments was to:

— Investigate the likelihood of generating real-time environment data to be used within a Xuni AR interface using a depth sensor.
— Investigate the potential to rapidly integrate low-density meshes into a 3D graphics engine and HMD (Head Mounted Display) related enviornment.

Compatibility Test One – Processing for Kinect Software. Given the lower level language access Processing for Kinect provides, a greater amount of control over individual Kinect sensor functionality could be implemented. If the Kinect continues to be used the Processing integration may be extended in future testing, if Unity® software proves to be unsuitable for use in this project over the longer term.

Compatibility Test Two – Skanect Software. 'Skanect' environment capture software was used to create a three dimensional mesh of a physical environment. By capturing depth and point information using the Kinect sensor a high-density 50,000-point mesh was calculated. Skanect is compatible with a portable depth sensor, the 'Structure Sensor', which allows for much higher fidelity and near-real-time dense-mesh generation and analysis, also seen in the Microsoft Kinect Fusion application.

Compatibility Test Three - Virtual-Reality-Glasses Testing. As AR glasses were unavailable, a VR device was used. The Oculus Rift DK2 display integrates numerous sensors including a Gyroscope, Accelerometer and Magnetometer calculating momentum and rotation tracking. Oculus Rift also has the provision for an additional input on the HMD itself which could convert the VR HMD into a 'video see-through' AR device. A low-density replica environment of the Creative Arts Building (CAB), University of Huddersfield was integrated into a Unity3D scene file to simulate a real world location using resolution parameters gathered from the earlier Skanect testing.

Summary of Investigation phase. The Oculus Rift experiments indicate the viability of efficiently combining with the Kinect Sensor depth based data experiments. It can be surmised therefore that designing an interface framework, which assumes the use of a depth aware AR environment could be efficiently generated.

2.2   Visualization

This section discusses the considerations for Augmented Reality interface design; the requirement for design research related to Human Computer Interaction (HCI), User Interface design (UI), User Experience Design (UXD) and gesture recognition; and documenting the process of creating a pre-rendered visualization.

The possibility exists, given the additional sensor arrangement included with many commercial depth sensors including the Kinect tested here, that the CG interface might be able to use color data gathered from the physical space to influence the color, lighting and texture of the CG objects. In attempting to visualize how the Xuni AR system might look, an short animation based on findings taken in the invention phase alongside references to other AR and user interface designs was created.

Table 1. Gestures referenced from 'User-defined gestures for augmented reality' [5]

	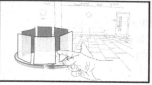	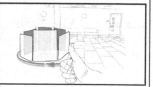
Fig. 1. Browsing: Next (using all 4 fingers)	**Fig. 2.** Browsing: Next Item (Index finger)	**Fig. 3.** Editing – Accept: Thumb Up

Gesture Recognition. The design for the Xuni AR system incorporates the use of a pair of 'smart-armbands' to detect and automate control of content displayed on the AR HMD. The armbands integrate a collection of battery operated electromyographic (EMG) sensors in conjunction with other built-in orientation based sensors [6]. They use these sensors to accurately read changes in arm muscle tension, orientation and acceleration. The armbands detect of all this data and match this to a pre-defined set of gestures using specially designed algorithms to filter out random noise. These pre-defined gestures could be amended or added to using developer created API's. Incorporating these factors into the design of the Xuni AR system would allow for measured responsive motion feedback through the AR HMD display.

Gesture recognition taxonomy was implemented referencing the work of HitLabNZ, University of Christchurch, NZ. Their study 'User-defined gestures for augmented reality' [5] records extensive blind testing of various hand poses or 'tasks' that might be implemented within an AR related interface. Using this information three distinct tasks were implemented in the Xuni system animation shown in Table 1.

Resulting Interface for Xuni AR. The animation demonstrating a basic Xuni AR interface combines the Xuni system features with the various conventions from the research gathered and illustrates how such an interface might look from a users point

Fig. 4. 'Browsing: Next' computer graphic simulation.	**Fig. 5.** 'Edit: Accept' computer graphic simulation.

of view. To replicate depth-based data, three-dimensional point data was gathered by use of video motion tracking software. This generated a virtual camera that calculated its position relative to other scene objects in virtual volume of space. The resulting reference points were then exported to Cinema4D scene file to be time matched with the animated CG interface objects.

Summary of Visualization Phase. As this project continues AR interface research and design will continue to inform and amend the prototype draft shown here, with real-time graphic techniques employed to replicate some of the features shown.

3   Discussion and Conclusions

The compatibility testing and basic implementation of this Xuni AR service indicate that such a system should be viable given the correct combination of inputs. However the amalgamation of these devices requires careful thought into the means by which they can be fully harnessed to exploit their individual characteristics in search of a truly immersive and productive whole. Alongside the many technical hurdles that need to be overcome in getting the a Xuni styled interface to work properly, challenges still remain in terms of common gestural interface taxonomy and user experience design. The device needs to not just work, it needs to 'disappear' if it is to be truly effective in its operational goals. With this in mind, further analysis into the metaphysical embodiment of a mixed reality interface and its requirement for representational user interaction is now required.

These will inform future research into mixed reality user experience.

References

1. Weiser, M.: The computer for the 21st century. Sci. Am. **265**(3) (1991)
2. Haller, M., Billinghurst, M., Thomas, B.H.: Emerging Technologies of Augmented Reality. IGI Global, Hershey Pa; London (2007)
3. Milgram, P., Kishino, F.: A Taxonomy of Mixed Reality Visual Displays. IEICE TRANSACTIONS on Information and Systems **E77-D**(12), 1321–1329 (1994). The Institute of Electronics, Information and Communication Engineers
4. Chen, X., Grossman, T.: Duet: exploring joint interactions on a smart phone and a smart watch. In: Proc. 32nd Conf. Hum. Factors Comput. Syst., CHI 2014, pp. 159–168 (2014)
5. Piumsomboon, T., Clark, A., Billinghurst, M., Cockburn, A.: User-Defined Gestures for Augmented Reality. In: Kotzé, P., Marsden, G., Lindgaard, G., Wesson, J., Winckler, M. (eds.) INTERACT 2013, Part II. LNCS, vol. 8118, pp. 282–299. Springer, Heidelberg (2013)
6. Attenberger, A., Buchenrieder, K., Human-Computer Interaction. Advanced Interaction Modalities and Techniques, vol. 8511. Springer International Publishing, Cham (2014)

Author Index

Printed in the United States
By Bookmasters